D1191147

DRIVING VALUE USING ACTIVITY-BASED BUDGETING

Wiley Cost Management Series

Activity Accounting: An Activity-Based Costing Approach by James A. Brimson

Activity-Based Costing: Making it Work for Small and Mid-Sized Companies, Second Edition by Douglas T. Hicks

Activity-Based Management: Arthur Andersen's Global Lessons from the ABM Battlefield, Second Edition edited by R. Steven Player and Roberto Lacerda

Activity-Based Management for Service Industries, Government Entities, and Nonprofit Organizations by James A. Brimson and John Antos

Activity-Based Management in Daily Operations by John Miller

Driving Value Using Activity-Based Budgeting by James A. Brimson and John Antos

Journal of International and Strategic Cost Management edited by Barry Brinker

DRIVING VALUE USING ACTIVITY-BASED BUDGETING

**James A. Brimson
John Antos**

with contributions by
Jay Collins

JOHN WILEY & SONS, INC.

New York • Chichester • Weinheim • Brisbane • Singapore • Toronto

Library of Congress Cataloging-in-Publication Data:

Brimson, James A., 1947–
    Driving value using activity-based budgeting / James A. Brimson,
  John Antos.
      p.   cm.
  Includes bibliographical references and index.
  ISBN 0-471-08631-2 (cloth : alk. paper)
    1. Activity-based costing. 2. Managerial accounting. 3. Cost
  accounting I. Antos, John. II. Title.
  HF5686.C8B6743   1998
  658.15'4—dc21   98-28231
                                              CIP

CONTENTS

PART 1   OVERVIEW

PART 2   ACTIVITY-BASED BUDGETING PRINCIPLES

PART 3   METHODOLOGY

ACKNOWLEDGMENTS

No book is solely the effort of its authors. The authors would like to give credit to the many consulting clients and seminar attendees who have given us new insights. We would also like to thank Rose Kernan, who converted our seminar presentation and notes into the draft that became the basis for this book. This information will continue to be used in our seminars. We would like to thank Sam Kusuma for all his efforts in customizing the software to support our case study and Steve Peacock who teaches ABB with us for the American Management Association.

Jim Brimson would like to thank those special people—his wife, Sheryl, and his children, Jimmy, Katy, Heath, Heather, and Carter, and parents, Peggy and William Kiernam—for all their love and support.

John Antos would like to thank all the great people at the American Management Association; Jim Antul, CFO, Experion; Keith Arbuckle, President, Home Care of Carolinas; Mark Colburn, Controller, Allmerica; Tom Freeman, Cost Management Systems Director, CAM-I; Brad Gillespie, Dana Commercial Credit (Malcolm Baldrige winner); Bill Golomski, past President, American Society of Quality; Howard Katz, ABM Director, General Services Administration; Kate Morrison, CFO, March of Dimes; Gerard Nierenberg, President, Negotiation Institute; Galen Barnes, President, and Bob Oakley, CFO, Nationwide Insurance; Fred Williams, JC Penney Direct Marketing; Mike Roberts, VP, Mevatec; Phil Rooney, Vice Chairman, Service Master; Elizabeth Russell, CFO, Delta Dental; Wayne Simpson, Director of ABM, City of Indianapolis; John Torrens, Treasurer, Wausau Insurance; John Wallerstedt, Treasurer, Sallie Mae; Cherry Whiting, President, Personal Home Care; Pete Wilke, President, Hammond Group; Joe Yob, Senior VP, Novus (Discover Card); Ron Zech, Chairman of GATX, and all the people of the Value Creation Group throughout the world. John thanks those special people—his wife, Lana, and his children, Emily and Austin—for their support and inspiration.

Jay Collins would like to thank those who helped make this book possible—his wife, Patty, and his children, Alyssa and Mitchell.

The authors would like to thank the support of Arthur Andersen, especially Paige Dawson and Mitch Max, for their work on the ABB seminar, Paige Dawson for coordinating our publication efforts, Randolf Holst and Rene Kiehn for their research assistance, Robin Baumgartner for keeping all our lives on track.

PREFACE

If you ever struggled to live within a personal budget, you know the role budgeting can play in achieving your desired outcomes. If you overspend in one area, you are forced to cut back elsewhere. Life is comprised of many tradeoffs. The planning and budgeting process merely recognizes this process and allows you to understand the tradeoffs of different options. The tools and techniques you use to perform this process determine how well you can see these options and the future they provide for you.

Likewise, business organizations have many options from which to select. They use the planning and budgeting process to provide a vision of the expected outcomes of their decisions. The tools currently used to achieve this vision are woefully lacking in many ways. They reflect an abstract financial reality but often fail to provide the managers with the clarity needed to shape and change their direction. In today's world of leaner, flatter operations, many managers have begun to question the value of their existing planning and budgeting processes.

A few disgruntled managers, financial as well as operational, have begun to suggest elimination of the budgeting process altogether. Yet, is this the proper response? It would imply shifting to no future vision planning. We feel the future is an activity-based budgeting approach based on feature costing.

Most financial executives have heard of the term *the new finance*. It describes the multitude of changes occurring within existing financial management techniques. Improvements in computer systems are enabling those changes by dramatically reducing the time needed to process transactions and prepare financial information. This creates exciting new possibilities for finance professionals, but it also can be viewed as a severe threat.

Increasing automation can be easily viewed as an opportunity to shrink the size of the finance department. Instead it represents an opportunity to do more value-adding activities that there is not enough time to perform such as activity-based budgeting.

Since 1986, when the modern age of activity-based costing (ABC) was launched by the Consortium of Advanced Manufacturing–International (CAM–I), there has been a steady rise in the uses of activity-based information—from product costing to customer costing to channel costing. Activity-based costing has grown in uses. In 1991, the terms were broadened to refer to activity-based management (ABM), which focuses on cost reduction and operational uses of the information. These include understanding operational cost drivers, linkage to other improvement methods, and the variety of ways companies achieve activity-based savings.

This book will help you continue the expansion by focusing activity-based information on making the budget process more meaningful. Traditional budgeting techniques that obscure cause-and-effect relationships must give way to an activity-based budgeting approach.

In addition to improving the budgeting process, this book will also help improve your existing ABC implementations through the use of feature costing. As ABC usage has continued to expand into deeper understanding of operations, it has often become very complex and difficult to run on an ongoing basis.

The concept of feature costing is the next evolution beyond ABC. Using feature costing allows one to understand similarities of root causes of problems, thus to better understand the complexity of products and services in much greater detail. It does so in a way that greatly lowers the cost of maintaining an ongoing system.

This approach can be used within your organization at an enterprise-wide level. It can easily be applied on a divisional, departmental, or individual work group basis. We urge you to try it in your organization, at any level, as quickly as possible.

Activity-based budgeting and feature costing are new and in many respects revolutionary. This book represents our attempt to accelerate their development by articulating them in these chapters. Included are numerous examples and case studies embedded in the text. Our intent is to help illustrate these points in a concrete manner. As with any learning, working through the examples will help you more fully understand how to apply these concepts in your organization.

We encourage you to experiment, share your learnings, and call us with your comments, questions, and feedback. That is how this field moves forward. We can be reached at the following phone numbers:

John Antos, President	Value Creation Group, Inc.	(972) 980-7404
Jim Brimson, President	Innovative Process Management	(817) 275-6677
Jay Collins	Arthur Andersen	(813) 222-4692

For those of you who call, we will share our continued learning and developments as this field evolves.

We look forward to your feedback.

Part 1

OVERVIEW

1

DRIVING VALUE: THE OBJECTIVE OF BUDGETING AND FEATURE COSTING

This chapter will:

- Review how value is created and why organizations are emphasizing it.
- Explain how traditional planning and budgeting often leads to destruction of value.
- Discuss how activity-based budgeting (ABB) and feature costing are being used as effective approaches in creating value.

CREATING VALUE IS THE "GOAL"

Companies that understand the need to create value are challenged with how to measure it. For commercial enterprises, value has traditionally been determined by financial measures, such as profit, price to earnings, cash flows, and return on equity. More recently, shareholder value measures such as economic value-added and market value-added have gained prominence as measures for determining the value created by an organization. Regardless of the financial measure used, its purpose is to provide shareholders with an *external view* of the organization's financial performance.

For noncommercial entities such as government agencies and not-for-profit companies, a similar value equation exists; however, measures are focused both internally and externally. In these applications, value is based on the full cost of achieving the outcomes of the organization such as the cost of constructing a highway or the cost of executing a social program. The return is the measured benefit to society in comparison to the cost. Generating the same benefits at a lower total cost enhances value, as does generating greater benefits at the same cost.

In addition to financial measures of value, both commercial and noncommercial entities create intangible value. This is often captured in the form of intellectual capital, such as process knowledge and innovation capacity. It can also take the form of relationship value; such as with customer relationships, evidenced by brand loyalty; or employee satisfaction, measured by employee retention. Although current accounting systems have difficulty measuring this value, most financial and operational people agree that it is critical to understanding the value created by an enterprise.

For purposes of this book, the focus will be on tangible value creation that can be expressed in financial terms. The discussion will cover ways to create value as well as why so many organizations are focusing on value creation.

HOW IS VALUE CREATED?

Value is created when customers of the organization are willing to use their products or services. To create value for a customer requires an organization to translate its vision into a strategy with definable objectives. Objectives, which create value, are:

- Acquire or grow market share (A)
- Improve sales growth rate (B)
- Increase profit margins (C)
- Reduce expenses (D)
- Reduce cash taxes (E)
- Increase asset productivity (F)
- Reduce cost of capital (G)

See Exhibit 1.1 for an example of this equation.

Acquire or Grow Market Share

Growing the business profitably over time creates value. A wide range of strategies are employed by companies to grow the business, anywhere from introducing new products and services to forging alliances or acquiring competitors. Companies that fail to hold market share have more funds to reinvest with customers. Achieving this creates stability, thus reducing the risks to key stakeholders. A company with stable and consistent returns will

Sales   **(A and B)**

<u>**–Cost of goods**</u>
=Profit margin   **(C)**
–Expenses   **(D)**
<u>**–Cash taxes**</u>   **(E)**
=Cash operating return
<u>**–Capital charges**</u>**=[Net assets (F) x Cost of capital (G)]**
=Value created ⟶

Time

Exhibit 1.1   How value is created.

have a higher perceived value than one with more volatile returns even if the more volatile company has a higher average return. This is because stability reduces the risk-adjusted cost of capital.

Improve Sales Growth Rate

Another way to create value is by growing sales or revenue. Companies can increase their sales growth by offering new or continuously improved products and services to customers. Go-to-market strategies are an essential component to increasing revenue for a company. Some of these approaches might include direct sales for complex or high-dollar products and services or value-added distribution for commodity-type products. The sales strategy translates into a product build strategy, such as build-to-order, configure-to-order, or build-to-ship. Marketing and product management play key roles in deciding how to increase the top line.

Increase Profit Margins

Increasing profit margins is an important way of growing value. One common misconception is that if you increase revenue, you thereby increase profits. Companies too often find that this does not happen in every case. Value creation requires companies to increase profits while increasing revenue. Volume-related increases can improve margins by decreasing unused capacity and spreading fixed costs over a greater number of products. However, many companies find that volume increases often result in greater fixed costs when capacity and bottlenecks are not properly managed. To address this, companies must understand their customer requirements, set product targets, and structure world class activities to use the minimum necessary capacity.

Reduce Expenses

Reducing expenses is an obvious approach to create value. Expenses include cost of goods sold (material, labor, and overhead); selling, general and administrative; and research and development (R&D) expenses. Although a reduction in any of these expenses can have an immediate positive impact, great care must be exercised to avoid damaging a company's long-term capability to compete. For example, dramatically reducing all R&D expenses will reduce costs, but it could potentially affect future revenues if the life-blood of the company is rapid product introduction.

Reduce Cash Taxes

The last income statement–related factor for creating value focuses on reducing cash taxes. It is important to have the lowest legal effective tax rate because money paid to the government is not available for growing the company. Managers must understand the tax implications of their decisions, which in turn affect the level of cash flow and profits.

Increase Asset Productivity

Many companies overlook efficient use of assets as a way to increase value. A variety of techniques increase the turnover of working capital (the combination of cash, accounts receivables, inventory, and prepaids, less the amounts of current liabilities). The goal is to reduce working capital to free up money for reinvestment or return to stockholders. Companies must manage activities that affect working capital levels to have the correct capacity when needed. Companies must also manage intellectual assets (also known as knowledge capital). For many organizations, intellectual assets such as patents, trademarks, customer and supplier relationships, industry knowledge, a trained workforce, and knowledge of the business are far more valuable in many cases than their fixed assets.

Asset productivity optimizes the assets needed by the company, hence lowering the capital needed to generate a higher rate of return, and thereby creating greater value.

Reduce Cost of Capital

A final leverage point in value creation is reducing the cost of capital, which can be achieved by adjusting the company's financial leverage and by improving the predictability of reported earnings. Because equity financing is long term and thus riskier to the investor than debt financing, it carries a higher rate of capital cost. By shifting to a higher ratio of debt financing, companies can achieve a lower cost of capital. However, care must be taken to ensure that current debt maturities can always be met. Acquiring lower interest rates can also reduce the cost of capital. In addition to finding lower interest rates, companies must examine the total cost of debt. This includes capital tied up in compensating balances, holding accounts, and other non-productive uses.

WHY COMPANIES ARE EMPHASIZING VALUE CREATION

Value creation is seen as being the number one priority for managers today. Value creation appears to be the universal theme of various improvement methods, such as total quality management (TQM), activity-based cost management, just-in-time (JIT), re-engineering, time compression management, and so forth. Managers have come to realize that improvements on individual performance measures must be translated into adding value to the entire organization, not just an individual department. Progress in a single area does not ensure long-term success; therefore, improvement must be sustainable, optimizing the entire company.

In recent years, the focus on value creation has been fueled by greater emphasis on more encompassing value measurements, such as economic value-added. Although not new, enablers such as activity-based costing (ABC), total quality (TQM), more powerful database and analysis tools, and greater distributed processing have allowed companies to implement these measures to a far greater degree than previously thought possible.

Single-focus improvement methods have often failed to fully optimize value creation over the long term. For example, re-engineering efforts often yield immediate cost reductions that appear to increase value. Yet, these approaches can rarely be sustained. At some point, companies must focus on growth.

The stock market has already realized companies cannot succeed by reducing costs alone. Some believe that the stock market gives three times greater weight to companies that increase profit by sales growth versus those who increase profit by expense reduction. Although expense reduction will temporarily boost profits, those savings must eventually be focused on growing the company. Said another way, an organization cannot shrink its way to greatness; it must find more effective ways to grow profitably.

Organizations need to explore multiple venues of growth and capitalize on those avenues that make the most sense. First, growth opportunities should be developed from emerging markets. These may be due in part to geographic expansion, or they may originate through new sales channels such as the Internet, direct mail, or new buying groups.

Second, companies should encourage growth by effectively redefining the marketplace. Many companies are finding that their customers want a complete bundled solution of both products and services. Customers seek more efficient buying from fewer suppliers. Organizations must understand how their activities as a group allow them to address these needs. What activities will give them a competitive advantage? What are the core competencies (i.e., those activities that are strategic to the business), and how well does the company perform them? By structuring and managing related activities, organizations can better understand their competitive positions.

Third, organizations should grow through introducing new products and services. Organizations must understand their customers' needs as well as the gaps and benchmarks in meeting those needs. By the time the competition catches up, leading companies have already developed the next-generation product or service. In fact, some organizations intentionally obsolete products to drive new product introduction.

Finally, today's companies derive value from learning and knowledge management rather than from bricks and mortar. One school of thought advocates that the only competitive advantage is to learn faster and share knowledge more effectively than the competition. Growth opportunities will come to those who effectively manage knowledge.

To stay competitive, organizations must be consistently vigilant in their quest to keep pace with new products/services, tools, and organizational structures. However, in keeping pace, companies must grow profitably while simultaneously improving quality and customer service as well as managing costs.

TRADITIONAL PLANNING AND BUDGETING OFTEN LEADS TO DESTRUCTION OF VALUE

Traditional planning and budgeting often does not create value (or at best only marginal). Traditional methods attempt to allocate a company's resources to departments for expense objectives, based on forecasted sales targets. The problem is that traditional planning and budgeting focuses on resources rather than activities, which are central to value creation. The traditional approach results in a number of problems with trying to budget resources by departments:

- It focuses on resources that are inputs to a process rather than outputs or customer requirements.
- It focuses on functional departments rather than the interdependencies between departments, suppliers, and customers.
- Budget amounts are often the results of looking at past periods and merely projecting some linear relationship to the future.
- It buries waste and inefficiencies rather than identifying the root causes and sources of variation needed for continuous improvement.
- It does not consider workload relationships on a formal basis.
- Often, it does not look at the cost and benefit tradeoffs of different service levels.
- It tends to be viewed by the operational people as an accounting exercise resulting in a lack of operational commitment.
- It tends to be evaluated more on an aggregated basis rather than on a more specific, actionable basis.
- It does not explicitly connect business strategy to employee actions.

As a result, traditional budgets are stated only in financial terms. They present abstract relationships to the underlying operational processes, which must be evaluated against them. The planning assumptions integral to their creation may be included as support documentation (or in many cases omitted) and not embedded within the budget process.

Traditional budgets often become nothing more than static pictures rooted in a set of assumptions. As the year progresses, actual events often are radically different from those assumptions. However, unless restated, traditional budgets do not adjust for change. For instance, new products introduced can increase the number of customer service calls. If the rate of increase exceeds the budget assumptions, the budget constrains management's response to customer needs. Likewise, if demand does not occur as fast as the budget anticipated, the reverse happens. Rather than constraining spending, the budget encourages overspending. In both cases, the assumptions made in the prior period have more influence than in the current activity.

Like many existing financial tools, traditional budgeting falls short in its ability to aid in value creation. Primarily serving only the financial community, traditional budgeting is often a time-consuming process that is largely ignored by operational managers. At its worst, traditional budgeting has managers looking in the wrong places for the wrong things.

With this background, it is easy to understand why many companies have contemplated abandoning the traditional budgeting process. However, the need to create value still remains. This requires organizations to set performance targets and identify actions to achieve the targets. Once those actions are implemented, there is a need to monitor the execution. Therefore, to drive value creation, companies are implementing ABB.

NEW APPROACHES TO BUDGETING AND PLANNING THAT CREATE VALUE

Fundamentally, ABB focuses on understanding activities and their relationship to achieving strategic goals. Used with ABB, feature costing seeks to identify process variation caused by unique requirements or conditions (features) of individual products or services. This knowledge of "features" enables an organization to understand and minimize variation, resulting in more predictable, controllable costs.

By combining ABB and feature costing, organizations can create a value-driven plan. The ABB component of the plan translates the business strategy into the activities necessary to implement that strategy. The focus is on the activities and workload of the organization rather than just resources. The feature costing component relates the capabilities against expected workload. Features analysis provides a feedback loop on how closely an organization's capabilities match its strategic goals.

Activity-based budgets are more actionable and understandable than resource-based budgets (see Exhibit 1.2). The example shows how a budget manager from a major insurance company sought to make the budget more useful and meaningful to management. However, it is difficult for a budget composed of resources (i.e., salaries, supplies, rent) to provide adequate insight to management. How can they look at resources and make intelligent decisions? It is easier for everyone to react to an activity-based budget because it is based on the work people perform.

It is true that a well-run organization would be asking some of these workload questions anyway. However, presenting a formal activity-based budget makes this process easier and stimulates many more questions and alternatives. It not only helps managers to understand where the money is being spent, but it also helps them to understand what work they expect to perform. With this information, management can decide the best use of the organization's dollars and what the investment will produce.

Traditional Budget

Expense Category	Budget $
Salaries	$500,000
Benefits	$150,000
Rent	$40,000
Supplies	$60,000
PC	$50,000
Travel	$30,000
Consulting	$70,000
Telephone	$30,0000
	$930,000

Activity Budget

Activity Description	Cost per Output	Usage of Output	Activity Cost
Process mail	$0.25	20,000	$ 5,000
Initial review	$17.50	20,000	$350,000
Professional review	$50	1,000	$ 50,000
Adjuster review	$30	2,000	$ 60,000
Create EOB	$9.00	20,000	$180,000
Create check	$6.00	12,000	$ 72,000
Answer questions	$4.20	10,000	$ 42,000
Litigate claims	$300	500	$150,000
Manage department			$ 21,000
			$930,000

Exhibit 1.2   Comparing an activity budget with a traditional budget.

Value-Driven Planning Using ABB and Feature Costing

Value-driven planning using ABB *enables every employee to create value for the organization. This is achieved through planning and managing expected activities and business processes to meet the forecasted workload and strategic goals. Value-driven planning allows the organization to understand causes of variation so the variation can be controlled.*

Value-driven planning focuses on *expected activities* and *business processes* as a basis for deriving the needed resources. Business processes and activities, not cost elements, are the important areas of focus in creating value.

The key to any successful plan or budget is to assign financial and operational accountability toward achieving the organization's vision and strategies. The value-driven planning process links operational work with the financial process. Therefore, it is the tracking and managing of operational performance that is paramount to achieving the financial results.

BENEFITS OF USING ABB WITH FEATURE COSTING

Switching to ABB with feature costing helps resolve many of the problems associated with traditional costing. ABB and feature costing:

- Places responsibility and accountability on employees to manage their activities to achieve their performance targets
- Presents a more realistic view of workloads including the impact of service levels
- Yields insights into causes of variation that are actionable
- Provides an ability to understand how products/services create demand (or pull) for specific activities that in turn drive the requirement of resources
- Embeds a process view, which more explicitly illustrates departmental interdependencies
- Creates the ability to monitor and control at a more actionable level
- Provides visibility into managing excess and/or insufficient capacity

The remainder of this book will address the process of implementing ABB with feature costing. It is organized into three parts: an overview, ABB principles, and methodology, which includes an illustrated case study and company examples.

In addition to this first chapter on what drives value, the overview consists of Chapter 2, which reviews the problems typically encountered with traditional budgeting and sets the stage for moving to ABB, and Chapter 3, which discusses linking strategy and the budgeting process.

Part Two sets the foundation for ABB by articulating its key principles. Chapter 4 provides the framework for translating strategies into a process and activity framework. Chapter 5 discusses forecasting demand revenue, volume, and workload. Chapter 6 contains a discussion of the impact of capacity. The concept and usage of feature costing is presented in Chapter 7.

Part Three presents the methodology for implementing ABB. This begins with Chapter 8 on creating an activity budget. Chapter 9 discusses reviewing and finalizing the activity budgets. Using the information is the focus of Chapter 10. It is followed by a review of gap analysis and planning guidelines in Chapter 11 and performance reporting and analysis in Chapter 12. This section concludes with a discussion of organization-wide improvements in Chapter 13.

Chapter 14 provides a summary and focuses on getting started. Appendix A discusses target-setting techniques which includes how to incorporate customer surveys, core competencies, benchmarking, house of activities, and reverse engineering into the budgeting process. Appendix B presents some specific company examples. The book also includes a glossary of terms.

2

COMPANIES MIGRATING FROM TRADITIONAL BUDGETING TO ACTIVITY-BASED BUDGETING AND FEATURE COSTING

This chapter will:

- Review the pitfalls of traditional budgeting.
- Explore the advantages of using activity-based budgeting (ABB) and feature costing to drive value.

TRADITIONAL BUDGETING: WHY IT FAILS MOST ORGANIZATIONS

This chapter will review how most organizations budget and report, as well as highlight the problems associated with the traditional way of budgeting. Armed with this information, you will be able to communicate the advantages of a value-driven planning process using ABB and feature costing.

WHAT IS TRADITIONAL BUDGETING?

Traditional budget and income statements simply show revenue and expense categories such as cost of goods sold, salaries, rent, supplies, depreciation, income taxes, and so forth. This approach matches the reporting typically provided by most departments. These reports are a summary of the resources that have to be acquired and the revenues from items sold (see Exhibits 2.1 and 2.2).

(000s)	Actual	Budget	Variance
Revenue	$26,000	$28,000	−$2,000
Cost of goods sold	22,500	22,150	−350
Gross margin	3,500	5,850	−2,350
Operating expenses			
Sales	1,000	900	−100
Distribution	700	600	−100
Finance	700	700	
Information systems	600	500	−100
Human resources	200	150	−50
TOTAL	3,200	2,850	−350
INCOME	$300	$3,000	−$2,700

Exhibit 2.1   Manufacturing income statement.

(000s)	Actual	Budget	Variance
Sales	$26,000	$28,000	−$2,000
Direct costs	22,500	22,150	−350
(e.g., jet fuel, interest, claims)			
Salaries/Benefits	1,000	900	−100
Travel	700	600	−100
Supplies	700	700	
Depreciation	600	500	−100
Telecommunications	200	150	−50
TOTAL	3,200	2,850	−350
INCOME	$300	$3,000	−$2,700

Exhibit 2.2   Service organization income statement.

In monthly evaluations, companies simply take the actual performance for a time period and compare it to the budgeted numbers to derive a variance. Most managers believe this particular approach to planning and budgeting is not very useful for numerous reasons.

A common problem is that these reports are stated in strictly financial terms. This is not the way operating people typically think. As such, these reports require translation into operating terms before they can become actionable.

Often, the focus of budgeting revolves around how to spread resources rather than how to create value. The focus of budgeting should be on creating value by driving the deployment of the organization's strategy. Important questions must be answered, including:

- Do we have the proper type of assets and capacity to meet our strategic goals and customer needs?
- Are we building intellectual capital and sharing knowledge throughout the organization?
- How should the organization be structured?

Unfortunately, organizations often expend the most effort on where to put the resources rather than how to create value with those resources.

PITFALLS OF TRADITIONAL BUDGETING

The traditional budgeting process has a number of pitfalls. In many cases, traditional budgeting:

- Does not support value creation
- Is a spreadsheet exercise applying an arbitrary percentage to prior period actuals
- Focuses on inputs rather than outputs
- Does not identify and understand product and customer features that cause variation
- Does not support continuous improvements
- Focuses on cost centers rather than on business process improvement
- Does not control cost during growth
- Promotes budget gamesmanship
- Does not consider activity workload
- Does not provide business process financial statements
- Does not identify levels of service
- Does not identify waste

- Does not connect budgeting to economic value and strategy
- Does not focus on unused capacity, but only fixed and variable costs

Driving value using ABB and feature costing provides the necessary information to increase productivity and support continuous improvement. It also provides the tools needed to achieve excellence.

Traditional Budgeting Does Not Support Value Creation

Traditional budgeting is missing actionable information as well as focus on customer requirements. Where is the usable information needed to create value? Basically, traditional budgeting provides little insight. It focuses on inputs (i.e., resources to be consumed) rather than outputs (e.g., services provided, customer needs met, products produced).

Traditional budgets allocate costs rather than assign them to activities. An organization must understand what impact its budgeting process has on the way decisions are made. This book emphasizes that the key to value-driven planning using ABB and feature costing is to better understand:

- What drives value
- Sources of variation
- Costs

A *Fortune* 100 executive once stated that, given the same information, most employees make the same decision. The purpose of value-driven planning using ABB and feature costing is to give managers and employees the right information about activities, business processes, features, and workload, at the right time, so that everyone makes the right decisions.

The Typical Budget Process Is a Spreadsheet Exercise

For many organizations, a typical budgeting process starts with senior executives announcing general guidelines for the upcoming budget. The marketing department forecasts that sales will be up 10 percent. Then, most managers simply increase their budget by this same 10 percent. This is generally how they set up their new budget. The question is: On what informative foundation is each of these decisions based? Marketing forecasts? Old expenses and inefficiencies? How has workload changed in each department? What is being done to improve the activities and business processes? How can anyone budget for the upcoming year based on last year's information?

Most organizations budget in ineffective ways in the world of spread-sheets. In Column A, managers put last year's expense numbers. In Column B, they create a formula that takes last year's numbers in Column A and multiplies last year's expenses by the forecasted increase in sales. As one might expect, the next step is to invoke the copy function for all remaining categories.

The traditional budgeting practice of adding percentage increases to last year's expenses based on forecasted revenues is not practical or logical. One should ask:

- What does this spreadsheet budgeting process do for management?
- What usable information are they gleaning from these numbers?
- How do these new budgets affect the internal workings of the organizations?
- Are the forecasts correct? What if they are not?

What would happen if this pattern continued each year? Budgets go up, but revenues and sales go down. What would happen? Losses!

Traditional Budgeting Focuses on Inputs Rather Than on Outputs

The typical budget is prepared in financial terms rather than operational terms. For example, a call center manager does not think in terms of rent, supplies, and personal computers. Instead, the call center manager thinks in terms of workload (i.e., number of phone calls), variation (i.e., how calls vary during the day, week, month), and staffing to meet the projected workload and variation.

Similarly, think of a basketball player. Do basketball fans care about how often the athlete runs around the gym, does pushups, or runs the stairs? No, basketball fans ultimately care about the output or baskets made. Likewise, managers should begin with a focus on the output, which is payroll checks prepared, contracts negotiated, and performance reviews completed. Knowing the output expected is critical to evaluating how many resources are needed to perform the activities necessary to produce them.

Traditional Budgeting Does Not Identify nor Explain Product and Customer Features That Cause Variation

Without information on how products cause variation, an organization will not understand what actions to take. As a result, managers may focus improvement efforts in the wrong area or expend time solving the wrong problem. It is critical to understand product features.

For example, an organization that manufactures jeans might find that using white material requires equipment to be cleaned during a product run so as not to pick up any oil, whereas blue or black material does not require this extra step. If the mix of white and nonwhite material changes during the year, this will change the cost of manufacturing.

Traditional budgeting does not identify customer features that cause variation. For example, some customers may accept delivery only during certain times of the day. Attempts at delivery outside of specified times are usually rejected, causing a second delivery and/or a penalty. Customers who charge the vendor for poor quality or who order at the last minute are examples of additional sources of customer variation. Each of these customer features increases the cost of doing business. Unless an organization understands how customer features affect its cost structure, costs can get out of control.

Traditional Budgeting Process Does Not Support Continuous Improvements

As discussed previously, budgeting is often a spreadsheet exercise with inefficiencies from prior years built into the current year's budget. Often, a formal program does not exist to build continuous improvement into the budget.

The existing resource base and performance level is the typical starting point for traditional budgeting. Embedding continuous improvement first requires a definition of what existing performances are. What services or products are produced by each part of the business? At what service level are they being produced? Embedding continuous improvement requires measures of quality, timeliness, customer satisfaction, and other attributes as well as cost.

Some assume that continuous improvement is measured only by cost reduction. This can lead to inappropriate cost reductions that hurt the organization.

For example, if a call center is working at best-in-class standards, to cut expenses by some arbitrary percentage may be destructive. If a company overcuts in customer service areas, it may face unhappy customers. Likewise, a company could properly choose to increase funding in areas such as research and development (R&D) or marketing to achieve strategic objectives.

Continuous improvement efforts are not limited to the private sector.

Government agencies must learn to improve as well, as they are not immune to the requirements of an ever-changing world. For example, the competition continues to increase between the U.S. Postal Service and FedEx. Many federal government organizations are completing A-76 studies to review internal processes and determine whether the federal government should outsource key business processes and services.

A recent newspaper article stated that the Navy motto was to do more with fewer resources. With the tremendous downsizing in the military, everyone is being asked to improve their operations. The challenge to continuously improve is present in all sectors—both public and private.

Some organizations are forcing continuous improvement by setting cost-reduction goals for their budgeted expenses annually. If the budget has been reduced, organization members are forced to identify better, faster, and more cost-effective ways to produce the same product or service. Example 2-1 illustrates this point.

Example 2-1: Continuous Improvements Can Be Affordable

Bill, a typesetter, has built his business based on his reputation for quick delivery, accuracy, quality, and his ability to keep up with the latest software and hardware products for quality page layout. His clients could request projects assembled using a variety of software packages and hardware platforms.

Each year, in order to stay current with all possible software and hardware changes, Bill found himself upgrading his current computer systems and software packages as well as purchasing new ones. The cost of "keeping current" was killing his profits, not to mention the time it took to train his employees on each new program. The financial resources did not exist to keep up with all the changes, but without current skills, he would lose customers. He had to find a way to make the improvements, yet not spend more.

Steve, a computer consultant, advised Bill to buy one program offered by a major computer manufacturer that could read and convert a file from any platform to whatever software program he chose. This conversion allowed him to work with an even greater variety of packages. With this software, Bill saved money on equipment, software, and employee training. He improved his production process while reducing his retooling and retraining expenses. He found a way to make improvements while saving money in the long term. Continuous improvement can mean additional profits.

Traditional Budgeting Focus: Cost Centers versus Business Process Improvement

Traditional budgets focus on individual cost centers, which comprise departments, divisions, and subsidiaries. Cross-functional business processes are often ignored. For example, most organizations would have difficulty identifying the total cost to create the budget, acquire a new customer, develop a new product/service, or hire and train a new employee. They could tell you the cost of the budgeting department or the cost of the training department, but, in most cases, they could not tell you the total cost of creating the budget, including all the people who are involved with preparing, consolidating, and reviewing the budget. Likewise, they could tell you the cost of the human resource department, the cost of the security department, and the cost of the training department. However, they would be hard pressed to tell you the cost of hiring, training, and obtaining security approval for a new employee.

Because most organizations do not focus on cross-functional processes, they find it difficult to continually improve these business processes. Instead, from time to time, they employ re-engineering techniques to improve a specific process.

Traditional Budgeting Does Not Control Costs during Growth

Although growth can cover mismanagement of costs, eventually growth stops or slows down. Review some of the top companies over the last 20 years to see what happens when growth stops or slows and the company does not keep focused on controlling its costs. Organizations must control costs so they can reinvest those available resources to continually grow and create value, as shown in Example 2-2.

Example 2-2: Controlling Costs during Growth Is Essential

Many corporations lack foresight during growth periods. Many of these corporations, once the market share leaders in their markets, were considered dependable blue-chip corporations. Companies such as General Motors, IBM, and AT&T took growth for granted. They opened numerous facilities and hired thousands of workers without hesitation. The market was considered theirs, no questions asked. Other, more agile businesses came along and toppled them. No one predicted the growth of these small businesses and what it could do to the market share of these established leaders; needless to say, the outcome has become clear. The former leaders were forced to downsize.

Organizations must begin controlling costs when times are good rather than after an earnings slowdown. They must reinvest those savings to drive value and create additional growth. The healthcare industry provides a good example. With Medicare being completely revised, costs are being reduced by 10 percent per year. Without a proper understanding of costs, healthcare providers will incur losses in revenues and, more importantly, profitability.

Traditional Budgeting Process Promotes Gamesmanship

During the planning and budgeting cycle, many middle managers create a plan and assemble a budget. The managers have some general understanding of organizational objectives as well as general planning and budgeting guidelines (such as the general direction of the organization and what average salary increases to give their employees); however, many times, they are unaware of the big picture. They submit their plans and budgets based on what they know and what they can predict from their limited knowledge of the organizational goals. For the most part, their plans and budget requests return from senior management who say expense budgets are too high and revenue budgets are too low.

Next, the negotiation stage begins. The managers who are better negotiators are often able to negotiate that their department's needs are of top priority. They convince senior management that with the requested budget, their department will help achieve the organizational objectives. Each manager, in turn, vies for the prime position in the race to acquire funds.

Sometimes, the winning manager is one who pads the budget the most, so when management cuts the budget, they will, in reality, be cut the least. In fact, some managers estimate how much their budget will be cut and then pad their budgets by an amount equal to that. In effect, the budgeting process becomes a game of guessing how much the manager expects to be cut by each level of review and then inflating his estimates so that the net result is something that can be comfortably met.

Traditional Budgeting Does Not Consider Activity Workload

Traditional planning, budgeting, and reporting does not identify activity workload. It does not show how many payroll checks will be issued or how many purchase orders will be written to get the job done. Typically, workload is not a formal part of the process, nor is it a formal part of the monthly reports. Effective managers will consider the workload in preparing their department or cost center budget; however, it is not a formal part of the budget process for most organizations. Example 2-3 illustrates this point with a simple example of a mismanaged workload budget.

Example 2-3: Overtime Quickly Increases Costs and Reduces Profit

The law offices of McMillan and Carson employ 25 people. With the holiday season rapidly approaching, the senior partner decided to present each of the employees with a beautiful, personalized basket of gourmet foods. He contracted with Robin Littlefield of the Gift Basket Shoppe to create the baskets and deliver them to each employee before Christmas for $50 per basket. He thought Christmas Eve, the last working day before the holiday, would be an appropriate delivery date, but did not specify the date in the contract.

Robin employed only two additional helpers during the busy holiday season. She was confident that they could create and deliver the 25 baskets by Christmas Eve. Robin had budgeted $2,000 in December (the same as every other month) to pay her helpers. On December 15, the senior partner phoned and asked that the baskets be delivered the following day so the employees could take them home following the firm's annual Christmas party. To make the delivery of the baskets, Robin paid her helpers double time to work through the night. Suddenly, Robin's profit margin on her gourmet baskets was dramatically reduced due to the increased cost of help. Robin's mistake is that she did not properly plan for an increase in workload. If she had properly budgeted for the increase in workload, she could have anticipated the increased costs of her Christmas baskets, factored the overtime into her cost structure, or possibly found alternate ways of providing the service with minimal additional costs.

Traditional Budgets Do Not Use Business Process Financial Statements

Very few organizations have begun to explore business process financial statements. Even fewer organizations are actually reporting by business processes, which are networks of interdependent activities linked by the outputs they create. The activities are related because a specified event initiates the first activity in the process, which then triggers subsequent activities (see Examples 2-4 and 2-5).

Example 2-4: A Salesperson's Business Processes and Activities

The activity of preparing a proposal may be distinct from the activity of pricing the product/service, yet both are part of the sales and marketing function. A salesperson might perform a myriad of activities, including soliciting customers, traveling to customer sites, preparing proposals, presenting proposals, and negotiating/signing contracts. These activities are all part of the business process of "acquiring customers."

There are other activities the salesperson might be involved in such as handling customer complaints. This activity is probably not part of the business process of acquiring customers but part of the business process of "managing customers." Likewise, if salespeople are involved with customer focus groups for new ideas, this activity would be part of the "develop new products" business process.

All of the expenses of marketing and sales would be in the marketing and sales department. However, when discussing business processes, the activities of a business process are often in a variety of functions. Addressing all the activities helps to avoid problems created by handoffs between functions. Most traditional budgets do not budget at this business process level. Therefore, traditional budgets do not provide the necessary understanding of interdependencies between activities and departments.

Example 2-5: How Major Corporations Are Using the Business Process Financial Statement

Companies such as Levi Strauss and Union Pacific have begun to explore the business process financial statement to focus on business process improvement. In one facility of Union Pacific, six major business processes have been defined. Process managers who report to the president have been identified. Traditional support areas such as accounting and human resources were set up as support teams to these major business processes.

Levi Strauss has also identified a number of major business processes. People are being removed from traditional department roles and assigned to business process teams. For example, the accounts payable contact may no longer report to the controller's department. The activity of paying invoices still exists, but the person performing that activity is now part of the procurement business process and is physically located with people who perform related activities for the procurement process. These people include purchasing, receiving, and receiving inspection, as well as accounts payable. In this environment, accounts payable may have only dotted-line responsibility to the controller. By reporting to the business process manager of procurement, employees are more motivated and better able to understand the various interdependencies among activities.

The concept of business process applies to government as well as the private sector. The Internal Revenue Service has identified six major business processes. It is organizing workers around these six major business processes, which are customer focused.

Traditional Budgeting Does Not Consider Service Levels

Employees provide a service to external customers when they deliver a product, respond to a customer request, or provide maintenance for a customer's product. A service is provided to internal customers (i.e., other departments, divisions) when the organization issues paychecks (e.g., weekly or monthly) or when they prepare, analyze, and distribute the organization's management accounting statements. Traditional budgets do not account for the service levels delivered by employees in performing their activities. Traditional budgets also fail to identify how the employees' activities create value.

Service levels are closely related to workload. For example, in understanding the frequency of paying employees, one could say the number of employees is the workload, and the frequency of payment accuracy of amounts paid and timeliness are the service-level components. Even if the number of employees remains the same, changing the service level (i.e., frequency at which employees are paid) will affect the budget of the payroll department. Likewise, hiring or laying off employees will also affect the payroll department activity costs because more new employee setups or special handling of final paychecks is required. Therefore, another important dimension to be considered in the budgeting process is service level.

Traditional Budgets Do Not Identify Waste

For most organizations, the traditional budgeting process hides rather than identifies waste. Some organizations create a cost-of-quality statement or a cost-of-nonconformance statement. These statements tend to identify partial aspects of waste, but do not account for waste totally or consistently. They often look at traditional prevention costs, appraisal/inspection costs, and internal and external failure costs. These statements are visually produced monthly, quarterly, or annually depending on the organization. The amount of nonvalue cost captured varies from organization to organization. An activity-based budget can identify waste and non–value-added items for management to clearly and quickly review. Then everyone can work to reduce or eliminate this nonvalued waste.

Traditional Budgeting Does Not Connect
the Strategy to the Budget

Most people believe that senior management is responsible for strategy in the organization. Additionally, they believe employees who have front-line responsibility for the organization's main activities do not have responsibility for strategy. Many employees believe strategy is something senior management touts in the annual report or a memo—a formality rather than an action plan.

Value-driven planning using ABB and feature costing holds every department and every employee accountable for creating value by

- Clearly identifying the organization's strategic and financial goals
- Connecting the budget to economic value
- Creating an atmosphere of employee empowerment
- Defining workloads
- Insisting on continuous improvements
- Defining the business processes required to meet these objectives
- Using features to understand the source of product variation
- Using customer characteristics to understand how customers create variation

Traditional Budgeting Does Not
Focus on Unused Capacity

Traditional budgeting focuses on fixed and variable costs, which leads to theoretical debates about what costs are fixed and what costs are variable. Some people believe that only raw material and some supplies are variable. Others think that all expenses are variable, which they are in the long run. Some managers think that employees' wages are fixed, whereas others argue that employees' wages are variable.

Traditional budgets rarely connect to the strategy of their organization. A simple exercise can prove this point. Pull out your traditional budget for the year. If you examine it, does it tell you anything about the strategy of your organization? Rarely is this information found. The financial language of traditional budgets omits any discussion of core competency or key actions that must be achieved to deploy the overall strategy. This does not alarm most organizations.

Once costs are identified as fixed, the prevailing attitude is that there is not much an employee can do about a fixed expense, because it is fixed.

Instead, budgeting should focus on used and unused capacity which is more actionable. Once managers identify capacity as unused, they can identify ways to sell it, consolidate it, lease it, and/or save it for future growth. Understanding unused capacity is far more actionable than viewing costs as fixed and variable.

THE ADVANTAGE OF USING ABB AND FEATURE COSTING TO DRIVE VALUE

Value-driven planning using ABB and features can provide a clear view to the path toward driving value. As organizations attempt to drive value, they must review the factors that will enable them to achieve the goal. In the following discussion, the principles of driving value focus on improving the organization.

Achieving Excellence by Eliminating Waste

An organization should focus on eliminating waste (non–value-added activities) to drive value. The organization needs a budgeting and reporting system that will identify and highlight the amount of waste in the organization.

Many people wish to argue about whether waste can be totally eliminated; however, this discussion is best left to philosophers because it misses the critical point that every organization can improve its profitability by making waste visible. Only then can action plans be created to reduce these costs. The marketplace and/or organizational strategy dictates the amount of waste that must be eliminated.

A common technique for making waste visible to the organization is to use attribute flags on those activities. This flagging allows management to group and summarize the amount of non–value-added activity costs in a given process, department, or function. This allows improvement teams to focus on why the non–value-added costs are incurred and what can be done to eliminate them.

Many companies choose to provide additional levels rather than the simple value-added versus non–value-added designations. Examples of other attributes used to create visibility include:

- High, medium and low value-added
- Value-added, non–value-added, and business sustaining
- Mission critical and non–mission critical
- Primary and secondary

These attribute flags reinforce the goal to provide visibility for improvement, not criticism of workers. Often, the process is broken, not the worker.

Every employee should understand how to reduce and eliminate waste. Management may have a reasonable plan to eliminate waste; but if the plan is not communicated to employees, with emphasis on how such a plan could benefit all members of the organization, even the best-laid plan will not be realized.

Achieving Excellence by Reducing Workload

Driving value requires determining ways to reduce workload without reducing output quality. This can be accomplished by adjusting service levels or by decreasing the units of output. For example, an organization might reduce the number of schedules produced in each closing process, or it might reduce the number of closings each year, which produces financial statements. Likewise, an organization might reduce the number of budgets it creates each year. Instead of creating a 5-year strategic budget, an annual operating budget, and a midyear update to the annual budget, it might discontinue the midyear budget, thus saving both the employees' time and the costs involved with preparing and distributing another budget. Or it might reduce the budget requirements or improve the process so that less effort is required for budgeting.

The key to successfully reducing workload is to obtain a deep understanding of customer-required outputs. This is more than just knowing what the customers (both internal and external) desire. It also means understanding the need for the output and how it is expected to be used.

CHANGE IN PHILOSOPHY TO USED AND UNUSED CAPACITY IS REQUIRED TO CREATE VALUE

To create value in today's market, an organization must change its philosophy from variable and fixed-cost budgeting to one of value-driven budgeting. Part of the problem with fixed and variable costing is the term *fixed*. If someone identifies an expense as fixed, the belief appears that nothing can be done about the expense; the definition of fixed implies that the expense cannot be changed.

Instead of pondering on something that cannot be changed, management should focus on used and unused capacity. Example 2-6 illustrates this point in relation to capacity.

Example 2-6: Fixed Costing Costs MuchoPlastic Mucho Money

MuchoPlastic, Inc., a company that issues credit cards, can emboss 1,000 cards per shift. Thus, during three shifts, it can emboss 3,000 cards. Assume that the fixed costs are $3,000 to produce 3,000 cards, or $1 per card for the three shifts. Currently, the company is working only two shifts. If the company is working only two shifts, it will produce only 2,000 cards. Under traditional accounting, management would have taken the $3,000 and spread it across the 2,000 cards made on the two shifts to derive a fixed cost of $1.50 per card.

Assume volume went down to 1,000 cards the following year. Accounting would take $3,000 of fixed costs and divide it by 1,000 cards to derive a $3.00 cost per card. Imagine the strange looks operating managers would have on their faces when told that their unit cost has changed from $1.50 to $3. Accounting would explain this change by telling managers that they need to take the total fixed cost and divide it by the expected volume to derive a cost per unit. This may seem like a clear explanation to an accountant. However, this explanation does not make sense to an operating person. All the operating or marketing person knows is that the cost of embossing cards increased from $1.50 per card to $3 per card.

ORGANIZATIONS MUST DEFINE THE PRACTICAL AND EXCESS CAPACITIES

When pursuing excellence, an organization must look at its practical capacity. Practical capacity takes into account normal preventative maintenance, upgrades, holidays, and so forth. In Example 2-6, MuchoPlastic's practical capacity is based on a three-shift, 5-day workweek. Other organizations might use a three-shift, 7-day workweek, if that makes sense. However, this example assumes a 5-day workweek; therefore, practical capacity for a 5-day, three-shift operation is 3,000 embossed cards, so the $3,000 would be spread across 3,000 cards. This approach results in a cost of $1 per card ($3,000 divided by 3,000 cards), as shown in Example 2-6.

If the company is producing only 2,000 cards at $1 per card, this results in only a $2,000 cost. The company is actually spending $3,000, so what will it do with the other $1,000 of cost—the difference between the $2,000 just calculated and $3,000 of actual fixed costs? The $1,000 should go into an account titled "excess capacity." What happens when the company starts producing 2,400 cards? It multiplies 2,400 cards by $1 per card to derive a cost of $2,400. Its excess capacity is $600 ($3,000 of actual fixed costs minus $2,400). Thus, the company is not using $600 of capacity to its advantage.

Those who were taught to look at fixed and variable costs can quickly see that measuring utilized and underutilized capacity is a more consistent way of reviewing costs. In most cases, the organization does not need to consider costs as fixed or variable. In this case, MuchoPlastic must realize it is using only a portion of its potential (it is working only two shifts). If it were working at full capacity (i.e., three shifts producing 3,000 cards), then it could spread its costs over those 3,000 cards.

When an organization makes excess capacity visible, management can easily recognize the problem and therefore make a more informed decision as to what to do about this excess capacity. Can they:

- Sell it?
- Lease or rent it?
- Consolidate operations from other locations?
- Use the time or space for other purposes?

Some accountants will worry about how to account for unused capacity. The more important question, however, is how to manage capacity? Once those questions are resolved, accounting can determine an effective way to assign the costs of unused capacity.

Using Practical and Excess Capacity to Help Plan Expansions

Fast-growing organizations sometimes increase their volume by 30 to 100 percent a year. Such organizations then must consider expanding. They will need to hire more staff and buy more office space, equipment, and computers. These organizations still need to consider practical and excess capacity to help them with planning expansion. They need to understand that as they buy additional capacity, only a part of that capacity will be used immediately. Therefore, they need to understand how total costs, excess capacity, and practical capacity costs vary as they expand.

In today's world of creating value, the following questions should be asked before expansion is considered:

- Does that activity have to be done?
- Is the customer willing to pay for it?
- Do we create value for the customer by performing that activity or could some other organization perform it better and cheaper?
- How can our current capacity be used?
- What assumptions about capacity should we question?

VALUE DEPENDS ON SUPPLY-CHAIN SYNCHRONIZATION

Value requires the organization to synchronize and coordinate activities within its own structure, as discussed in Example 2-7. However, this process also needs to include the organization's customers and external suppliers within this coordination. This supply-chain synchronization—of supplier to organization to customer—is a key to adding value. Activity-based budgeting enables organizations to coordinate work among internal departments as well as customers and vendors.

Example 2-7: Eliminating the Walls between Departments

Xerox and General Electric (GE) are two companies that have been nationally recognized for eliminating some of the walls between departments/cost centers. General Electric talks about "boundarylessness," stressing the importance of eliminating boundaries between management layers as well as between the company and its suppliers and customers. Theoretically, a janitor in a GE plant should be able to call the chairman of GE when a reason exists.

At some of the leading auto companies, an assembly-line worker can request a meeting with the vice president of research and development (R&D). The purpose of the meeting might be to offer suggestions on how to improve a product or notify R&D of problems with a car's design. Previously, organizations had "adversarial relationships" with suppliers; whoever gave them the lowest price received the business. Now, organizations are partnering with suppliers, thus consolidating their vendor base. For example, a *Wall Street Journal* article explained how companies such as Xerox, Motorola, Ford, and Texas Instruments have reduced the number of vendors significantly. Wal-Mart has spent considerable time including its suppliers as part of its planning process. Like a marriage, they are committing to work with each other.

As part of this partnership process, some vendors have physically located in the same building as their customers. The vendors may have visibility to the organization's production planning systems, for example. Some companies allow the vendor to even order on behalf of the organization. Other vendors are heavily involved in product design and promotion. Some companies using electronic data interchange (EDI) have the customer's production personnel interface directly with the vendor's scheduling personnel. This procedure bypasses the customer's purchasing agent and the vendor's sales and order-taking departments. The historically adversarial relationship between vendor and customer has transformed to a win–win combination, dramatically reducing lead times and costs.

The vendor rechannels resources from selling and marketing into activities that are more valued by the customer. One such example is assigning resources to activities such as improving product and service design. Because the vendor has a guaranteed customer, it can plan more effectively, ensuring a steady rate of operations and a steady cash flow.

Achieving Excellence Means Managing Causes, Not Effects

A main component of value creation requires the organization to control the process rather than the result. Focusing on after-the-fact results is too late. The organization must determine how to control activities and business processes while they are happening rather than, based on the results, after they have occurred. By controlling activities, action can be taken on a timely basis, reducing the cost associated with rework or scrap.

In quality terms, people discuss results using **cause-and-effect diagrams,** also called **fishbone diagrams** or **Ishikawa diagrams** (named for the person who is given credit for inventing them). With cause-and-effect diagrams, key words are used to stimulate thought concerning what causes a certain effect (e.g., a monthly report is producing incorrect results) (see Exhibit 2.3).

On the right-hand side of the diagram under Effects, the organization enters "incorrect results on reports." Then, to the left-hand side of the diagram, the organization enters major cause boxes. The words in these boxes are often referred to as the **four *M*s**: manpower, machine, materials, and methods. Under this analysis tool, an organization would ask:

1. Manpower:
   - Could this be a person issue?
   - Could the wrong person be in the job?
   - Is it the wrong working environment?
   - Could the person have insufficient training?
2. Machine:
   - Is something wrong with the computer hardware that produced these reports?
   - Is something wrong with the software that produced these reports?
3. Materials:
   - Does cheap computer paper result in rerunning reports that are torn or jammed?
4. Methods:
   - Are there cutoff issues that need to be addressed?
   - Are the handoffs between departments well defined?
   - Is too much time spent in producing the report and not enough time in analysis?
   - Are insignificant changes being made that cause delay?

This is one of the tools that helps an organization identify and eliminate root causes rather than focusing on effects.

- Construct cause-and-effect diagram (also called fishbone or Ishikawa diagrams)
  - Place problem statement in circle on right
  - Place 4 major cause in boxes on left with arrows pointing to main line
  - Place subsequent cause as branches off major causes

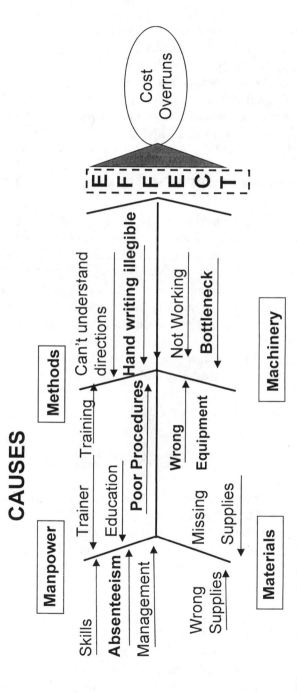

Exhibit 2.3 Cause-and-effect diagrams.

EXCELLENCE REQUIRES CUSTOMER FEEDBACK

Excellence requires that the organization include the customer in the decision-making process. Survey results indicate that more organizations are
getting the customers involved with determining the following:
- What products and services are desired
- When they want these products and services
- Under what delivery conditions are products and services wanted
  (quality, time, and price)

MISTAKES ARE FOR LEARNING, NOT FOR BLAMING

"What have you done for me today?" is a common phrase used by both
internal and external customers. Therefore, organizations need to empower
people to continually satisfy the customer's needs. The president of Wal-Mart
believes that one of Wal-Mart's great strengths is empowerment of its employees. Not only must the organization talk about empowerment, but also
the employees must actually feel empowered for the program to work. If they
make a mistake in trying to satisfy their internal and external customers, the
employees must not be criticized. Instead, they must be made to feel that even
if they make a mistake, they will be asked to learn from that mistake to avoid
it in the future. Also, they will be asked to think about what could have been
done to avoid that mistake in the first place. These exercises are meant to be
learning exercises rather than disciplinary actions.

FOCUSING ON FEATURES

Features are those specific tasks or extra steps that affect the cost of an
activity. The following discussion of a blue jeans manufacturing company
will help clarify the concept of feature use. Blue jeans style XYZ comes with
either a zipper or buttons down the middle of the pants. The equipment
necessary to sew on zippers is different from the equipment needed to sew on
buttons. The company could structure the sewing of zippers or buttons as two
activities that would increase the complexity of the activity-based budgeting,
or the organization could simply define a single activity called "manufacture
blue jeans style XYZ."

    When it comes time to create the budget, the company can weigh the
output volume by the difference in time and/or resources for sewing zippers
versus sewing buttons. By using a weighting of volumes rather than creating

and tracing two different activities, the organization can simplify the budgeting model. (For more explanation of this technique, see Chapter 7.)

APPLYING THESE PRINCIPLES TO ABB

ABB highlights what changes should be made in an organization. This approach helps to remove the fear of making problems more visible. It is interesting to note that in Japanese companies, managers are encouraged to bring problems to meetings to get ideas from their fellow managers. In other countries, including the United States, more often than not, the culture frowns on bringing problems to a meeting, because some may believe that it shows that the manager cannot solve his or her own problems. The latter approach is seen as not necessarily the most effective way to solve problems.

Everyone in an organization needs to focus on how they create value. However, just telling employees to think about creating value is insufficient unless the organization provides the necessary tools to create value. This book illustrates how ABB and features help everyone to better understand their activities and business processes and how they create value.

In order to make any organization successful, both employees and management must strive to create value. Value-driven planning and budgeting highlights the need for everyone to create value and provide specific techniques to achieve value creation.

3

LINKING STRATEGY AND THE BUDGETING PROCESS

This chapter will:

- Define ways of aligning an organization's budget with strategy.
- Outline specific guidelines to achieve this goal.

ALIGNING ORGANIZATIONAL STRATEGY

Traditional budgets often fail to link an organization's strategy and its budgeting process. Therefore, most managers are unclear when asked if their operating budgets support the strategy. To go further, most employees do not know if their activities are aligned to support the organization's strategy. Without a "clear view" of how strategy and goals relate to both budgets and activities, a major disconnection exists. This disconnection typically results in inefficiencies and higher costs.

DEFINING ORGANIZATIONAL GOALS AND STRATEGIES

Driving value starts with senior management's defining organizational goals and strategies. Through a series of steps, it allows for those strategies to be easily translated to the business processes, activities, and features.

There are a number of books and articles available on the subject of strategic management and the techniques to develop a strategic plan. Thus, this book will not provide a detailed discussion of those techniques; rather, it will assume that a strategic plan exists and has been documented. Discussion will center on how to incorporate organizational goals and strategic plans into the budgeting process. Examples of organizational goals include the following:

- Increasing cash flow, market share, economic value, and market price
- Providing safe neighborhoods
- Lowering tax rates (e.g., government)
- Finding the cure for certain diseases (e.g., American Cancer Society)

A wide variety of strategies might be employed to achieve organizational goals, such as:

- Faster learning
- Greater knowledge sharing
- Global presence
- One-stop shopping
- Wider or more narrow product/service lines
- Greater penetration into current customer base
- Highest customer satisfaction
- Lowest price
- Best customer service
- Best engineering of new products/services for customers
- Widest distribution
- Best-trained sales force
- Increased funding for research and development

Senior management's role is to provide strategic direction and to set performance targets based on the strategic goals. These performance targets may be for sales, number of new services and/or markets, cycle time, cost, quality, or customer service levels.

The process manager works with various people who perform the activities in order to achieve or exceed those targets. The process manager, and those who perform the work, must translate strategic objectives and performance targets to business process and activity-level targets if they expect to achieve overall performance targets. As such, process and department managers must ensure service requirements are a reflection of customer needs.

TRANSLATING CUSTOMER REQUIREMENTS TO TARGETS

The strategy-setting process starts with an analysis of customer requirements and knowledge of the market and the competition, as well as the value proposition to be delivered. Then, strategic objectives must be set. The marketplace determines the selling price. The organization either must redefine the marketplace to create greater value and hopefully additional profit, or it must clearly understand what price the market is willing to pay for a specific product or service.

Once the market price is determined, the organization can calculate how much cost is allowable to achieve a desired profit margin. In some industries, this is called the *profit planning process,* which results in targeted cost. In other industries, this is referred to as an *allowable cost*. These targets are then translated into activity-level targets for each activity (see Exhibit 3.1).

Strategic objectives must be translated into tangible and measurable actions that improve an organization's business performance. Increasingly, strategic goals include guidelines on improving intangible measures such as customer satisfaction and employee morale. Some leading companies are becoming more sophisticated in understanding the interrelationships between these intangible areas and the financial results. *Harvard Business*

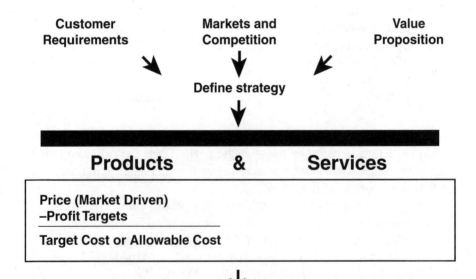

Exhibit 3.1   Target costing.

Review[1] profiled Sears' statistical linkage of how increased employee satisfaction results in higher customer satisfaction, which in turn leads to higher sales.

Translation of strategic objectives and goals is linked to the budgeting process through use of budget planning guidelines. Under activity-based budgeting (ABB), these guidelines are applied to the activity level understanding of the organization rather than just the resource level.

Budget planning guidelines typically include the following elements:

- Financial elements
  - Changes in expected market size
  - Sales growth and market share assumptions
  - Assumptions on market pricing
  - Timing and impact of new product introductions
  - Changes in wage rates
  - Changes in supplier costs
  - Capital investment plans
  - Inflation and interest cost assumptions
  - Tax rate changes
- Operational elements
  - Impact of new processes
  - Changes to activities
  - Assumptions on employee productivity
- Strategic elements
  - Sourcing assumptions
  - Products/service mix assumptions

SET REALISTIC GOALS BEFORE DETERMINING AN ORGANIZATIONAL STRATEGY

Management must be realistic when setting performance targets. No strategy will be successful if a goal is believed to be unattainable. Management must understand the market and then, using the organization's strengths, set achievable targets. EZ Money Bank is used in Example 3-1 for illustrative purposes.

Example 3-1: Hitting EZ Money Bank's Strategic Goals

EZ Money's loan department has set aggressive goals for new auto loans, standard mortgages, and large mortgages called jumbo mortgages. The organization could use the following simple steps to articulate its strategic goals:

Step	EZ Money Bank Example
Define mission statement	To have largest auto loan, standard mortgage, and jumbo mortgage market share in the city while achieving a return on assets of 1 percent
Define strategy	• Provide high customer satisfaction • Create bottom-line shareholder value
Establish critical success factors (CSFs)	• Quick loan application processing • Low interest rates • Asset management
Establish product/service line targets	• Increase market share of secured auto loans by 7 share points, standard mortgages by 6 share points, and jumbo mortgages by 5 share points • Discontinue unsecured consumer loans
Establish performance targets	• Evaluate all loans within 24 hours • Decrease loan costs by 8 percent • Reduce loan errors from 4 percent to 1 percent • Increase percentage of loan phone inquiries converting into applications from 30 to 40 percent • Create shareholder value of $50 million

EZ Money Bank wants to have the largest consumer loan market share in the city for auto loans and mortgages. It wants to achieve a return on assets of 1 percent, a good percentage in the banking industry. Its strategy for achieving these goals is to provide high customer satisfaction and better asset management.

Critical success factors are determined: quick loan application processing, low interest rates, and efficient asset management. These can be stated as service/product line targets. Once established, the targets should increase market share for new auto loans by 7 percent; new standard mortgages by 6 percent; and new jumbo mortgages by 5 percent. In addition, EZ Money decides to discontinue its unsecured consumer loan business.

To achieve these market shares and product/service line targets, EZ Money plans to evaluate all loans within 24 hours, which will provide applicants with faster responses. This response is subject to normal processing of a valid auto or home title and a good survey.

To become more competitive and still make its return on assets goals, EZ Money will need to decrease loan application costs by 8 percent. As part of reducing costs, it has set a target to reduce loan errors from 4 percent to 1 percent.

Finally, EZ Money wants to increase the loans issued ratio from phone inquiries from 25 percent to 33 percent. EZ Money originally decided that this performance measure should be phone calls converted into applications. However, this practice might encourage applications that might not be creditworthy. Therefore, they would achieve the performance goal but, in turn, hinder the financial goal of 1 percent return on asset.

Aligning performance measures with corporate strategy, such as reducing errors, along with 24 hours to evaluate a loan, was critical to provide high customer satisfaction. The company set performance measures for converting phone inquiries into loans and for decreasing costs by 8 percent to achieve the mission. The cost reductions would allow EZ Money to keep rates competitive so it could grow market share. At the same time, the cost reduction would help increase the company's profit margins.

Exhibit 3.2 highlights EZ Money's process, which has an established cost-reduction target for all five activities. The total reduction of $64 is an 8 percent reduction from last year's total bill of activity costs.

Travel could be reduced $1,000 by better scheduling trips to applicants. Initially, management opted to make fewer trips to applicants and ask the applicants to visit the bank. However, the corresponding strategy of customer service resulted instead in management's scheduling applicants better or taking applications over the phone. They would even accept credit card payments for the application fee.

With applications scanned into the computer, the reduction in the activity of "filing" would save $2,000 for part-time employees' wages and benefits. By setting planning guides and very specific targets for each activity and process, EZ Money can reduce costs and improve efficiency—two pluses on the way to its goal of obtaining higher market share.

The company followed a process, which included reviewing the mission statement; defining strategy; and establishing critical success factors, product and service line targets, and performance targets for cost, time, and quality.

Performance targets can be set for the business process as a whole as well as for each activity. As mentioned earlier, a goal must be attainable in the eyes of the people performing the activities. In this example, EZ Money had to concentrate on cornering the market in its city. The company's performance measures clearly related to the mission and strategy.

Activity Description	Cost/ Output	Units of Output	Service Cost	Target Activity Reduction	Target Cost/ Output
Take application	$100	1	$100	5%	$ 5	$ 95
Order reports	50	3	150	10%	15	135
Review loans	200	1	200	7%	14	186
Complete paperwork	100	1	100	30%	30	70
Disburse funds	250	1	250			250
TOTALS			$800	8%	$64	$736

Exhibit 3.2 Bill of activities for "Review standard mortgage applications" and "Disperse funds" business processes.

DEFINING PLANNING GUIDELINES

Once attainable targets have been set, management can define the necessary planning guidelines to reach those goals. For example, an organization could identify activity/business process–level projects with the goal of continuous improvement. The budgeted workload would be divided into three categories for each activity or business process:

- Mandatory
- Discretionary
- Available if the customer is willing to pay for it

This split helps EZ Money decide what activities to eliminate. For example, EZ Money might decide it is mandatory to be open from 9 A.M. to 5 P.M., Monday through Friday, and from 10 A.M. to 2 P.M. on Saturday. Management believes it is discretionary to be open evenings during the week and longer on Saturdays. They believe that the customer is not willing to pay for those extra hours. Therefore, the bank determined to set its hours based on just the mandatory requirement. Example 3-2 revisits EZ Money Bank to explain.

Example 3-2: Defining EZ Money's Planning Guidelines

Example 3-1 identified EZ Money's goal to have the largest auto loan and mortgage market share in the city while achieving a return on assets of 1 percent. Its stated critical success factors were quick loan application processing and low interest rates. Its product/service line targets were to grow auto loans by 8 percent, standard mortgages by 7 percent, and jumbo mortgages by 6 percent, while discontinuing unsecured loans.

Exhibit 3.3 shows EZ Money's planning guidelines broken down into current performance, target goals, and the percentage change needed to achieve those target goals. Under the heading of critical success factors, EZ Money's planning guidelines show management seeks a 7 point growth in market share—an increase from 15 percent to 22 percent.

To achieve the proposed increase in market share, it will have to approve loans more quickly. Thus, loan processing, which currently averages 48 hours, should be reduced to 24 hours. From this list of planning guidelines, a budget could be developed for each activity involved with consumer loan sales in EZ Money's loan department.

An activity-based budget such as the one shown in Exhibit 3.4 could be created for each business process, and then actual performance could be

Mission Statement
Manage largest consumer loan market share while achieving a return on assets of 1%

Today	Target	Change
15%	22%	+7%
48 hours	24 hours	−24 hours

Critical Success Factors
Market share
Low fees
Quick loan application processing

Assumptions
- Information technology usage will be accelerated
- Deploy teams for all consumer loans
- New competition from out of state
- Inflation factor—4%
- Productivity increase—8%

Exhibit 3.3 Management defines planning guidelines.

Amounts in thousands	Value	Non-Value Added ($000s)	Total
Projected Revenue	**$26,000**	**$**	**$26,000**
<u>**Minus Target Profit**</u>			<u>**−1,000**</u>
Target Cost/Allowables			**$25,000**
Interest Expense	15,000	3,200	18,200
Acquire Consumer Loans	**800**	**400**	**1,200**
Process Loans	1,300	500	1,800
Provide Customer Service	700	300	1,000
Invest Capital Process	400	100	500
Procure Capital	500	400	900
Create New Services Process	100	100	200
Provide Resources: Financial	300	200	500
Provide Resources: IT Systems	300	300	600
Provide Resources: People	200	100	300
Infrastructure: CEO, Charity, PR	<u>450</u>	<u>50</u>	<u>500</u>
TOTAL COSTS	**$20,050**	**$5,650**	**$25,700**
(Over) Target Cost Gap			−$700

Exhibit 3.4 Activity-based budget—EZ Money Bank.

measured against the budget. (This is just a sample of how such a budget could be developed. Not every activity has been included in the business processes "review mortgage loan applications" and "disburse funds.")

Example 3-2 provides a simplified version of planning guidelines for the sample banking institution. We only touched on the business processes "review mortgage loan applications" and "disburse funds." The same planning guidelines should be used for every activity within each department. Also, remember setting realistic and attainable planning goals will be the key to success.

WAYS OF SETTING BUSINESS PROCESS TARGETS

Once planning guidelines have been established, management can determine activity and business process targets. Management should review business processes to streamline and eliminate any duplicate activities. Example 3-3 will better illustrate this process.

Example 3-3: EZ Money's Real Cost for Securing Supplies

EZ Money Bank will be used to illustrate activity target costs for procuring office supplies. The following table identifies the activities and associated costs involved in this business process.

Business Process: Procure Office Supplies and Equipment

Activity	Workload Measures	Volume	Total Cost	Unit Cost	Activity Target Cost
Prepare quotes	Quotes	20	$1,000	$50	$45
Issue purchase order	Purchase orders	60	$1,200	$20	$19
Receive supplies	Receipts	60	$1,800	$30	$27
Pay invoice	Receipts	60	$2,400	$40	$36
Manage cost center	Staff		$20,000		
			$26,400		

EZ Money has set an activity target of $45 per quote prepared. This is a reduction of $5 from last year's cost of $50 per quote, which translates into a $100 savings. Management believes supplies can be reduced an additional $440 by keeping more information electronically.

SUMMARY

This chapter identified the process of connecting an organization's mission and strategy with critical success factors and product/service line targets. The chapter then highlighted how to relate these targets to business process targets, which can be better understood.

Part 2

ACTIVITY-BASED BUDGETING PRINCIPLES

4

TRANSLATING STRATEGY INTO A PROCESS AND ACTIVITY FRAMEWORK

This chapter will:

- Define activities.
- Discuss outputs and output measures.
- Define resources.
- Discuss how to incorporate organizational strategy into processes and activities.
- Review the impact of activity performance on strategy.

DEFINING ACTIVITIES

An activity is simply the work that is performed in transforming inputs into outputs. The easiest way to define an activity is to identify the outputs produced and the resources required for it to occur.

Activities can be classified into several categories, including primary, secondary, project activities, and subactivities.

Primary Activities

A primary activity contributes directly to the goal of a department. For example, designing and modifying product designs are two primary activities of an engineering department. Performing these and other primary activities is the reason the engineering department exists. Primary activities have a measurable output that can be quantified.

Secondary Activities

A secondary activity supports an organization's primary activities. Secondary activities are general activities such as administration, supervision, training, and secretarial work carried out in support of the primary activities.

Secondary activities are not necessarily non–value-added or unimportant but should be scrutinized when planning. An organization's major responsibility is to ensure that secondary activities increase the effectiveness of the primary activities and do not waste resources that could be more effectively used elsewhere. Example 4-1 illustrates this point.

Example 4-1: Understanding Activities of Move-It Transportation

At Move-It Transportation, Inc., a transportation business that loads and unloads containers, the activity "train operators" is a secondary activity. Machinery operators must be trained so they can load containers more effectively.

For Move-It's human resources (HR) department, however, "train operators" is a primary activity. One objective of the HR department is to design, run, and coordinate training for operators. The operators who receive training are the customers of the HR department.

Project Activities

Project activities, or one-time activities, have definite start and end dates. Generally, these activities consume significant time and resources and should be well planned to ensure that adequate resources are available.

Subactivities

Subactivities are used when there is a need for activities to be broken down into further levels of detail. The detail characteristics of a subactivity are essential when the primary definition is too broad to define a meaningful output of the activity and when it is important to plan the organization's resource requirements effectively.

For example, an automotive maintenance department's primary activity is to "provide auto maintenance." An activity such as "maintain automobile" is too broad a definition to be worthwhile for planning purposes. Instead, it is more revealing to separate maintenance activities into major types of jobs (i.e., subactivities), such as the following:

- Change oil
- Change or rotate tires
- Replace timing belt
- Replace clutch
- Perform tune-ups

Each of these subactivities has a similar outcome (i.e., an operational auto) and a distinct workload that can be planned, counted, and recorded (i.e., number of jobs). However, when an organization identifies subactivities, it should separate only the important ones and place the least important ones in an "other" category. Having too much detail is as troublesome and inefficient as not having enough detail.

Collectively, activities model an operational process. Performing activity analysis allows people to consider how they work. It focuses on tasks that are components of activities—"work."

OUTPUTS AND OUTPUT MEASURES

Outputs are the results produced by an activity, and **output measures** are a measure of the activity volume or quantity of output. For example, the output of the "pay vendors" activity would be a paid vendor invoice. The output measure for the activity could either be each paid invoice or the number of line items paid. The number of the line items might be used as individual line items that may drive the workload. This is true in cases in which invoices range in complexity. Those with multiple items purchased are more time consuming to process than invoices with a single item.

Most activities have different features. For example, the payroll department has an activity called "pay employees." The features differ based on how different types of employees are paid. For instance, features may include "pay hourly employees," "pay salaried employees," and "pay commissioned salespeople."

Paying hourly employees requires reviewing their time cards and calculating regular and overtime hours. In the case of salaried and commissioned employees, a time card is not reviewed. For commissioned salespeople, the payroll department has to calculate commissions, based on sales data including any chargebacks for returns. Thus, the features of paying these three types of employees are vastly different. If the organization wanted to better understand the work and workload in the payroll department, it would use activity features.

RESOURCES

A business needs resources to perform its work. Resources include people, equipment, material, and capital. A manager must plan how to accomplish the work with a minimum amount of resources. Opportunities are infinite, but resources are finite.

Certain resources that are considered fixed in the short term tend to continue regardless of short-term fluctuations in production activity. Examples include depreciation, rent, management salary, property taxes, and so forth. On a day-to-day or month-to-month basis, they are not sensitive to volume; however, over a longer period, they grow or shrink with the size of the business. Conversely, variable costs are resources that are directly consumed in the production process—raw materials and production labor are two examples.

A **process** is a structured set of activities that consume resources to produce an output. Typical resources consumed include employees, equipment, facilities, materials and supplies, and other resources.

COST TRACEABILITY

In activity accounting, it is important for all costs to be traced where practical and economically feasible. A rule of thumb is that 80 to 90 percent of a department's costs should be traceable to activities. Tracing less than 80 to 90 percent does not provide the visibility necessary to manage costs; tracing more could prove to be uneconomical. However, nontraceable costs should be clearly identified. The remaining 10 to 20 percent of cost which is considered nontraceable can be allocated if the accounting requirement is to have activities fully absorb all cost.

A critical factor in decision making is *relevance*, which is synonymous with traceability. In determining alternatives, relevance determines which costs and activities are to be considered and which are excluded. Traceable costs are controllable because a cause-and-effect relationship is established.

Traceability helps bring management's attention to overhead or shared costs (i.e., selling, general and administrative, engineering, and corporate costs) that are otherwise difficult to manage. When organizations allocate those costs to specific products and services or business units, it represents a charge against earnings. Managers with profit-and-loss responsibilities carefully scrutinize and challenge the charges. When costs are identified as traceable, they become more controllable.

BUSINESS PROCESS OVERVIEW

As was stated earlier, a business process is a set of related and interdependent activities that accomplish a specific objective. The activities of a business process are linked by the outputs they exchange. A specified event initiates the first activity in the process, which in turn triggers subsequent activities. An output or information flow occurs where two activities interact. The exchange of an output or information flow creates a boundary around different activities within a process and links them in a strong cause-and-effect relationship.

Most importantly, business processes transcend departmental boundaries. For example, the introduction of a new product would require a marketing assessment of needs, a design of the product, specifications of the manufacturing process, and the development of a bill of materials. This requires effort on the part of marketing, research and development (R&D), engineering, manufacturing, and finance.

A business process analysis describes the boundaries and customers and suppliers of each process, as well as the interfaces between each of the processes.

Defining process boundaries is not straightforward because processes normally cross functional areas of the organization. For example, the new product development process might begin with marketing surveys or when marketing delivers product requirements to development engineering. It could end with the release of product specifications or when the first order is manufactured.

Processes can be divided into subprocesses. For example, several subprocesses are part of the "procurement" process. Key subprocesses might include:

- Managing supplier relationship
- Purchasing material
- Managing raw material inventory
- Managing procurement process

Therefore, it is important to consider how broad or narrow should be the process definitions.

Several business process classification schemes are available. Two presented in this book include the Arthur Andersen/APQC and Davenport models.

Arthur Andersen and the American Productivity & Quality Center's (APQC) International Benchmarking Clearinghouse developed a universal Process Classification Scheme (PCS) (see Exhibit 4.1).

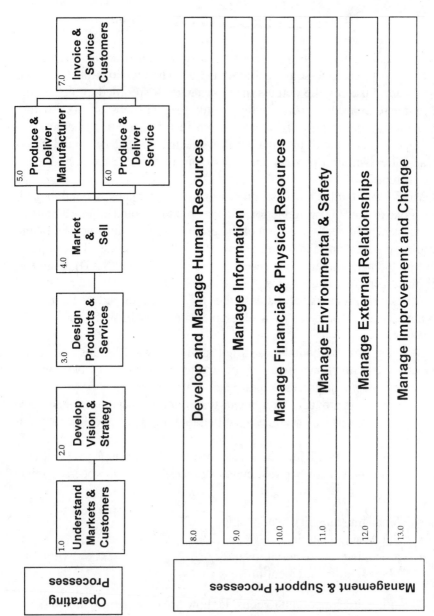

Exhibit 4.1 Process classification. *Source:* Arthur Andersen and the American Productivity and Quality Center.

The PCS is divided into two sections—one focusing on operating processes and the other on management and support processes. The classification scheme can also drill lower to various levels of subprocesses. Organizations use this tool as a guide to create their own views of critical processes customized for their industry and specific method of doing business.

The cascading process continues down to each activity that comprises a process. These individual activities are core to organizational performance. Noted strategy authority Michael Porter has stated, "Activities are the atoms of competitive advantage."[1]

Davenport suggests that the appropriate number of business processes is somewhere between 10 and 20. Exhibit 4.2 demonstrates the level at which two multinational companies define some of their business processes.

A business process view of cost is an essential adjunct to the traditional organizational structure, which equates management and accountability with a vertical manager/subordinate responsibility structure. Exhibit 4.3 provides an illustration. The traditional structure often leads to ineffective communication between departments. To be effective, management must understand how work flows horizontally across the vertical functions of the organization.

IBM	Xerox
Market information capture	Customer engagement
Market selection	Inventory management and logistics
Requirements	Product design and engineering
Development of hardware	Product maintenance
Development of software	Technology management
Development of services	Production and operations management
Production	Market management
Customer fulfillment	Supplier management
Customer relationship	Information management
Service	Business management
Customer feedback	Human resource management
Marketing	Lease and capital asset management
Solution integration	Legal
Financial analysis	Financial management
Plan integration	
Accounting	
Human resources	
Information technology infrastructure	

Exhibit 4.2 Business processes. *Source:* Davenport (1993).

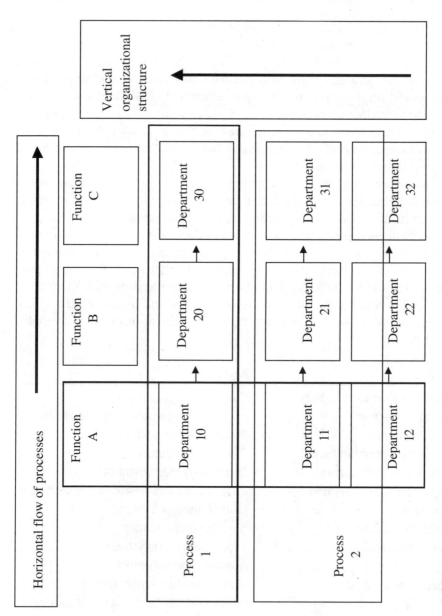

Exhibit 4.3   Horizontal flow of business processes.

Numerous examples can be found in manufacturing companies in which engineering, marketing, manufacturing, and financial activities were not coordinated for the introduction of a new product. For example, the business process to introduce a new product would set the following activities in motion:

Activity	Responsible Department
Analyze market	Marketing
Perform product R&D	R&D
Design product	Engineering
Develop prototype	Engineering
Test product design	Engineering
Plan quality	Quality assurance
Perform make/buy analysis	Industrial engineering
Plan material purchases	Procurement
Plan manufacturing process	Manufacturing engineering
Analyze financial impact	Finance

In a typical product development scenario, financial members are surprised by the additional inventory required; marketing insists on releasing the product before it is fully engineered; manufacturing spends excessive amounts of money in overtime to get the product out and make up for inadequate engineering designs. The productivity of the entire organization is affected when the new product is introduced without being well tested and, as a result, the company will receive poor customer reaction.

Business process analysis focuses management attention on the interdependencies of departments. It forces managers to realize downstream departments are their customers. Their activity performance impacts subsequent activities in the business process. An organization must also extend its definition of the business process to include links between its suppliers and customers with a view to reducing costs or enhancing differentiation.

LINKING STRATEGY TO ACTIVITIES

As previously noted, traditional budgeting does not provide a clear linkage between the organization's strategies and its budgeting process. Therefore, most operating managers do not know how to account for strategy in their budgets. Likewise, understanding how performing activities takes into account the aspects of strategy is difficult. Thus, budgeting is often seen as an abstract exercise.

Value-driven planning starts with management's defining the company vision, mission, and product and service value proposition. Through a series of steps, strategies are defined to support the performance attribute for the product and service value propositions. A cascading process can be used to articulate how strategies should be reflected in processes and activities. This process is illustrated in Exhibit 4.4.

To achieve its vision, a company identifies various strategies designed to address key areas; to be successful, these strategies must focus on critical processes. Identifying which processes are critical is based on understanding which processes are necessary to meet the customers' needs while creating a unique value proposition for the company.

Many publications exist on the subject of strategic management and planning. Therefore, this book will not go into a detailed discussion of those techniques but will assume that a strategic plan exists.

Management has the responsibility of translating the company's strategic plan into specific process goals for the organization. These goals serve as a yardstick in monitoring how well the strategies are being implemented at both the process and activity levels.

To implement activity-based budgeting (ABB), an organization needs a clear understanding of its activities. In many respects, activity analysis is a more detailed understanding of the component parts (activities) within a process classification scheme.

1. Define Enterprise Vision

2. Define Mission Statement

3. Define Organizational Goals

4. Focus on Organization's Critical Processes

5. Link Strategy to Activity

Exhibit 4.4   Link strategies to activities.

ASSESSING CURRENT PERFORMANCE

After activities and critical processes have been identified, an assessment of current performance is needed. This performance can be measured along multiple measure points, such as process cost, quality, cycle time, customer satisfaction, and employee satisfaction. The process measures selected should support the achievement of the overall corporate objectives.

DEFINING PERFORMANCE MEASURES

Activities can be measured in terms of *financial* and *nonfinancial* performance. Some organizations have created an approach to performance measures that balances a variety of measures. One approach, the balanced scorecard, suggests that an organization might divide its performance measurement system into the following categories: financial, customer satisfaction, operational, and growth and learning.

Although this approach focuses on multiple aspects of performance, it also can be complex, confusing, and expensive to maintain. As the number of measures increases, so does the probability that some of the measures will be improving while others are not. Often activity-based budgeting considers cost and nonfinancial performance targets for business processes and activities. Performance measures address questions about a business process and an activity by measuring such things as:

- Is value created for the customer and/or organization?
- What does it cost?
- Are customer characteristics changing? If so, how?
- Are product features changing? If so, how?
- How much time does it take (lead and cycle)?
- How well is the activity performed (quality)?

The relationship among different measures is tightly bonded. A change in any one activity, in many cases, affects aspects of other performance measures. A reduction in time, for example, might affect cost, quality, and flexibility because it changes the way in which the activity is performed. As a consequence of the interrelationships of performance measures, judging activity performance by any single measure is misleading.

A key to effective management is to implement changes that improve multiple dimensions of performance. This is possible only when the activity management system incorporates both nonfinancial and financial measures.

Activity management provides an easy way to maintain and to communicate whatever measures are selected. For instance, customer satisfaction can be periodically measured through customer surveys on a real-time basis. Customer dissatisfaction can be measured as follows:

- Number of complaints in customer service
- Warranty claims
- Customer support calls
- Rework in the field
- Product returns
- Market share trend

Similarly, employee dissatisfaction can be measured by employee turnover, employee disputes, and employee absenteeism.

Activity management is powerful because these factors are routinely measured within an activity-based management system. Thus, a separate data collection process is not needed.

PERFORMANCE MEASURES MUST BE FORWARD LOOKING AND TIED TO VALUE CREATION

This approach must keep a forward focus rather than just another after-the-fact scoring tool. The focus must be on how to achieve the targets set in these areas, which are tied to the organization's goal of creating economic value. A performance measure that quantifies past performance is like an inspection. Total quality has taught us that any inspection is non–valued-added. To add a more sophisticated after-the-fact performance measurement system is like adding a more sophisticated inspection system—an approach that leads to failure and added cost to collect the inspection data.

DETERMINING BUSINESS PROCESS AND ACTIVITY MEASURES

An organization must determine business process measures prior to determining activity measures. Otherwise, the organization could suboptimize the business process by improving a specific activity. For example, if purchasing buys cheaper computer paper, the purchasing cost will be low and purchasing's performance will look good. However, because lower-quality computer paper often results in tears and paper jams, the total cost to the organization could be higher than if higher-quality paper had been purchased. Therefore, it is important to start with business process measures and then create activity performance measures to meet the process targets.

Business process and activity performance measures should be based on the outputs of the processes and activities.

Consider the business process of "procuring supplies." In determining a performance measure, it may be easier to gather the total number of purchase orders rather than the number of purchase order line items. The accuracy of the cost per purchase order of supplies may not produce the level of accuracy needed for accurate costing. Therefore, management must trade off the advantages between having greater accuracy versus the cost of the increased data collection. Exhibit 4.5 illustrates the cost of collection curve related to the number of measures versus the relevance of the cost information.

In developing a performance measurement system, it is important to take into account the behavior that will occur as a result of the process or activity measure.

For example, a grounds department might define its activities and output measures and how the information might be used as follows:

Activity	Output	Output Measures
Clear snow	Cleared snow	Times/year snow cleared
Cut grass	Cut grass	Times/year grass is cut
Plant flowers	Planted flowers	Number of flowers planted
Trim trees	Trimmed trees	Number of trees trimmed
Fertilize grounds	Fertilized grounds	Times/year fertilized
Repair equipment	Repaired equipment	Number of repairs

The department could use the concept of features to further analyze these activities. For example, the trees are generally simply trimmed with shears. However, trimming trees sometimes requires a chain saw. Removing branches that were trimmed with shears is relatively easy. Removing limbs that were cut with a chain saw usually requires cutting the limbs into smaller sections to be loaded on the truck. Finally, if a storm requires removal of a tree, this is more labor intensive. As such, the following department estimate might apply:

Activity	Features	Time	Percent Change
Trim trees	Cut with shears	3 hrs.	—
	Cut with chain saw	5.5 hrs.	83%
	Remove tree	9 hrs.	300%

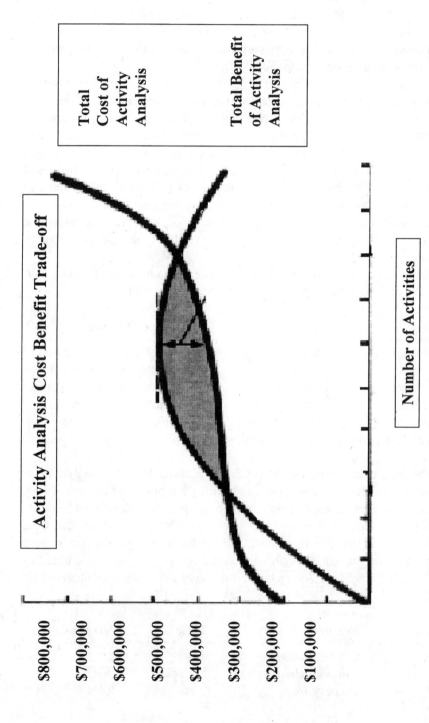

Exhibit 4.5   *Measurement: cost of data versus relevance. Source: Steve Player and Roberto Lacerda, Editors, Activity-Based Management: Arthur Andersen's Global Lessons from the ABM Battlefield, 2nd Ed., (John Wiley & Sons, 1999).*

Likewise, the concept of features or characteristics is relevant when analyzing the activity "clear snow." The same equipment is used for light and heavy snowfalls. However, it takes longer to clear the parking lots and driveways after heavy snowfalls. As such, the department estimates follow:

Activity Time	Characteristics	Extra
Clear snow	Less than 6 inches of snow	—
	7–12 inches of snow	40%
	Over 12 inches of snow	80%

This level of detail is probably more useful for planning and analysis, but may be too detailed for product and service costing. Each organization will have to decide the level of accuracy required versus the cost of collecting and analyzing data.

In the grounds department example, the concepts of features and characteristics are probably useful for planning and budgeting as well as for analysis. Severe winter weather will affect the frequency of snowfall, the amount of snow, and the number of dead limbs and trees that have to be removed.

However, for the rest of the organization, they do not need to know this level of detail. They simply want to know the cost their department is being charged for using the facilities. The facilities department would create a process budget that might look something like this:

Process Budget: Provide Facilities

Department	Activities
Grounds	Clear snow
	Cut grass
	Plant flowers
	Trim trees
	Fertilize grounds
	Repair equipment
Maintenance	Repair elevators
	Install/repair electrical
	Install/repair plumbing
	Repair heating/air conditioning
Housekeeping	Clean office space
	Clean bathrooms
Purchasing	Buy grounds supplies/tools
	Buy maintenance supplies/tools

	Buy housekeeping supplies
Rent/Utilities	Building rent/depreciation
	Building gas/electric
	Water

The budgeted costs of these activities would add up to the budgeted costs for the business process called "provide facilities." The various operating and support departments who pay for the grounds department activities in their facilities charge probably do not care about how much snow there was or how deep it was, nor do they care about whether the grounds department had to use a chain saw to trim trees or if they had to remove a tree. They probably care only about the total cost they will be charged for facilities. The grounds department must convert their activity costs into something meaningful to the people receiving their activities, which would be the cost of the grounds department per square foot of facilities.

However, the grounds department should not determine their budget based on square footage of office/manufacturing space, a commonly used metric. Determining cost of planting flowers or trimming trees per square foot of office space would not be very meaningful to the grounds department. However, determining cost of planting flowers per flower planted would be very meaningful to the grounds department.

When budgeting, it is critical to use an activity approach to budgeting and then to convert this information to a unit cost that would be useful to the user. Therefore, the grounds department would calculate the cost per flower planted. They would multiply this unit cost by the expected number of flowers to be planted. This multiplication would give them the total cost of planting flowers. They would use a similar approach for calculating the total cost of clearing snow, cutting grass, trimming trees, fertilizing grounds, and repairing equipment. These total costs would be summed and divided by total office/production square footage to derive a cost per square foot for the grounds department activities.

SUMMARY

When building an activity budget, always start with a process focus that is meaningful to the person performing the activity. Second, convert the total cost into a unit cost that might be more useful to user departments or for understanding product/service costing.

5

FORECASTING REVENUE, VOLUME, AND WORKLOAD

This chapter will:

- Define ways of forecasting revenues.
- Define ways of forecasting output volume or workload.
- Review ways of obtaining forecasted goals by using ongoing activity analysis.

INTRODUCTION

Once strategic targets are set, then product and service sales targets need to be determined, as well as other workload projections. Establishing realistic product and service price and volume targets is critical because they form the basis of planned revenue and operational costs. Many organizations, however, simplistically extrapolate a forecasted unit sales volume rather than understanding customer demand. This forecast is then formalized into "budgeted sales volume" that determines budgeted revenue. Finally, the sales forecast becomes a performance standard against which sales and marketing are measured. Unfortunately, this performance standard presumes an unrealistic level of accuracy, which is often misleading to those who need accurate information for decision-making purposes.

Activity-based budgeting (ABB) and feature costing are based on a more holistic approach to targeting a market response. These new approaches use target costing concepts to set sales prices and sales volume projections. Target costing highlights

- Required features
- Price points customers are willing to pay
- Competitive strengths and weaknesses

CONSIDERATIONS OF FORECASTING REVENUE AND VOLUME

There are many techniques used by companies to forecast revenue and volumes. Examples include exponential smoothing, linear regression, and so forth. We will not go into a discussion of a specific technique; however, we will focus on the factors required for developing a forecast. Regardless of the technique used, the fundamental element in developing realistic numbers is in hearing and understanding the voice of the customer. Frequently, cost and profitability information is introduced at this stage in the planning process. Cost information often biases the marketing analysis, resulting in an incomplete understanding of customer needs. Instead, the product or service concept should be defined in terms of price, quality, and functionality required by the customer regardless of the cost. Understanding the customer's explicit and implicit desires is the goal.

External information redirects the attention of the organization to an understanding of customer requirements and the changing competitive conditions. The credible targets delivered from the target costing process can help an organization understand why and where it needs to change.

CUSTOMER DEMOGRAPHICS AND NEEDS

Forecasting begins with an understanding of customer demographics, which involves analyzing the likelihood that a customer will purchase the product or service. Factors include the need or desire to purchase relevant geographic and statistical information. Customer demographic information is used for the purpose of separating customers into market segments.

Companies should have considerable customer information at their disposal. Sales history information contains historical patterns of orders and sales. This system can be used to determine past responses to price changes and how customers responded in anticipation of expected price changes. Did inventories pick up?

This internal data may be augmented with additional qualitative and quantitative customer information.

- Which customer segments will be more sensitive to the price/feature change?
- How will customer expectations be influenced by the price/feature change?

- Will customers perceive an emerging price trend or simply an opportunity for a short-term price discount?
- Will new market segments emerge as a result of the new price/features?
- How does the customer use our product? How important is our product to the successful delivery of the customer's product?
- What is the cost of our product relative to other product inputs?
- What are the competitors' pricing activities and their consequent effect on customer reaction?

Just like the direct sales analysis, a similar analysis should be conducted on the various distribution channels, such as value-add resellers and value-add distributors.

CUSTOMER PRODUCT CONCEPTS

For each of the targeted market segments, a **product concept** must be developed. The key elements of a product concept include characteristics that reflect customer expectations about product features, technology, delivery, and service targets.

Product Features and Technology

The product concept development processes include feedback from existing and potential customers who help define the features, functions, and relative value (including the customer's targeted product life cycle cost) that they want in products and services. This input provides an understanding of the gaps between customer expectations and current product or service design and performance.

Delivery and Service Targets

Setting delivery and service targets involves understanding how the product/service is to be used by the customer. Products and services that are critical to the customer's operations will require more rigorous targets than those that are less critical.

Economic Environment

Determining the economic environment involves assessment of economic factors for differing market segments, including industry growth rates, inflation rates, and supplier economic concerns.

Industry Technology

Budgeting must take into account all new technologies to be applied in developing and delivering new products, processes, or services. Research and development (R&D) efforts should be driven by strategy and the marketplace.

Competitive Intelligence and Analysis

Processes for obtaining and analyzing competitive intelligence play an important role in the target costing process. Product managers considering a product concept or price change need competitive intelligence to predict how and when competitors will match the price change. The following questions must be considered:

- Which competitors are more likely to respond?
- Are they financially able to sustain a significant threat to the proposed product or service change?
- What market signals have they given regarding their marketing and pricing strategies?
- Will new competitors be encouraged to enter as a result of the new price policy? If so, how will the dynamics of industry competition be affected?
- Which segments are they likely to target?
- Which segments do we want to protect and defend, and which are we willing to give up?

MULTIYEAR PROFIT AND COST TARGETS

The target costing process includes a multiyear forecast of sales and volume projections for product and service portfolios. The purpose is to plan product and service development and introductions over a 3- to 5-year horizon. These projections are set based on the customer demographics and needs, the economic environment, the industry technology, and competition.

There are many factors that affect the eventual price of a product or service. Obviously, the previously mentioned product and service features, as well as delivery and service targets, are important factors. An additional factor that must be considered is product and service maturity. There is usually less price elasticity in mature products and services than in those that will not reach the market until several years into the future. Some of the factors that managers evaluate in estimating a sales price include:

- Product and service concept
- Attributes of the targeted consumer group
- Product and service life cycle
- Expected sales quantity
- Competitors' response

It is critical that the sales price be set by market factors rather than cost data. If a sales price is set unrealistically high to cover costs, the inevitable result will be that the products or services will not sell or discounts will have to be applied. In some instances, the addition of features may be valued by a large enough portion of the market to warrant a price increase.

FEATURE COSTING: DETERMINING COST AND PROFIT TARGETS

The scope of feature costing is to support the ABB process by providing insight into special features or aspects of products or services to determine their associated costs. This knowledge is then combined with the profit targets to determine needed process improvements in primary and support processes.

A multiyear plan is also important because customers now expect continuous reductions in price, enhanced product quality, and expanded product or service features and convenience. These targets must be understood for both the short term and the long term. Ultimately, opportunities for cost improvement are likely to diminish because there is less and less waste to remove. Therefore, to satisfy customer expectations, new technologies and product or service concepts may be required, which means shifting to new profit and cost curves to remain competitive. These factors are frequently referred to as cost down (i.e., cost-reduction areas) and cost up (i.e., areas for value improvement that support price increases).

CUSTOMER REQUIREMENTS DRIVE SALES PRICE AND VOLUME TARGETS

To better understand customer preferences, one must analyze past buying patterns. It is not enough to just look at revenue or volume in total; they must be broken down further into revenue and volume by product, service, region, and so on. The sales history system is the source of this information.

Using the EZ Money Bank example from Chapter 3, we will illustrate the importance of responsibility reporting in Example 5-1.

Example 5-1: Forecasting Revenue by EZ Money's Marketing and Sales Departments

Management in EZ Money's marketing and sales departments has created forecasts for two types of mortgages and one type of auto loan. Mortgages are either standard (less than $227,000) or jumbo (greater than $227,000). They have determined that the average size of a standard loan is $100,000 and the average size of a jumbo loan is $300,000. They have forecasted $40 million in standard loans and $30 million in jumbo loans.

Calculating the Cost of Losing a Customer Instills Action

Historically, the bank has received four phone inquiries in order to secure a single mortgage. This means that for every four people who call, only one of those calls turns into a loan. Everyone should understand the cost of losing a mortgage!

Last year, EZ Money Bank charged each mortgage applicant $700. It spends about $400 processing the application. Therefore, each standard mortgage loan produces approximately $300 of profit.

Last year, EZ Money received 1,800 phone calls that did not result in a mortgage. By multiplying 1,800 mortgages by $700 of revenue per mortgage and $300 of profit per mortgage, one can see that it cost EZ Money $1,260,000 in lost revenue and $540,000 in lost profits when they were unable to convert a phone call into a mortgage or a loan.

This information was very informative to everyone. It made everyone realize that even when they are busy, each sold customer represents $300 of profit to EZ Money. They quickly determined that the best way to preserve their job was to treat each phone call as a sold mortgage. Obtaining consumer loans was no longer thought of as the responsibility of just marketing and the loan officers but as everyone's responsibility. Therefore, if the loan officers were busy, the loan application processors realized they needed to assist with potential customers. They could either learn how to handle phone inquiries, inform a loan officer of a phone call, or make sure they obtained accurate information in order to return a call.

Of course, everyone had to find ways of reducing that loss. Through brainstorming, they determined that everyone had responsibility for marketing. They could work together to improve the process of acquiring consumer loans. In reducing their process costs, they could attract more auto loan and mortgage customers because their rates would be lower and their application approval cycle shorter.

At the current average application fee of $700 per mortgage and current interest rates, they believed that they would be able to obtain only 400 mortgages (320 standard mortgages and 80 jumbo mortgages). If they raised their fees to $800, their volume would sink to 320 mortgages (270 standard mortgages and only 50 jumbo mortgages). If they reduced their fees to $600, they believed that they could obtain roughly 500 mortgages (400 standard mortgages and 100 jumbo mortgages). Based on this information, Exhibit 5.1 compares their revenue streams under these varying scenarios.

	Budgeted Rate per Mortgage		Forecasted Volume		Forecasted Revenue
Current prices	$700/mortgage	x	400 mortgages	=	$280,000
Raise prices	$800/mortgage	x	320 mortgages	=	$256,000
Reduce prices	$600/mortgage	x	500 mortgages	=	$300,000

Exhibit 5.1 Exploring financial alternatives.

To complete the profitability picture, one would need to analyze the effect volume change has on expenses.

EZ Money started the value-driven planning processes by analyzing pricing alternatives and the effects they had on volume and revenue. One possible alternative was to lower prices. Another was to keep the price the same and accept the reduced volume and revenues; or they could raise prices and thereby reduce volume further. Variable costs and possibly some fixed costs would be lowered due to less workload required to process the lower volume, but revenues would definitely be cut.

In their price-sensitive industry, they determined that to lower their prices to $600 would not jeopardize their existence. However, these prices will put them in the lower quartile of prices in the city. Therefore, the best planning alternative is to lower the price and increase the volume of loans. Increasing volume means increasing workload. Management must determine whether their existing departmental structures can handle the increased workload or how much expense they would have to add.

DETERMINING WORKLOAD

Workload is defined as the amount of output volume that an activity or process needs to produce. There are three major steps in determining activity and process workload. Organizations must forecast activities that are

- Product and service direct
- Product and service support
- Special projects

FORECASTING PRODUCT AND SERVICE-DIRECT ACTIVITIES

The first step in forecasting the total organization workload is to forecast cost object (product, services, or channel) demand and then to determine the workload for product or service-direct activities, which include all activities required to define, design, develop, test, release, produce, distribute, install, and maintain a product or service. Workload is projected by

- Identifying activities for new products or services
- Identifying product, service, and customer features
- Identifying planned changes to existing products and services
- Creating or updating a bill of activities for each product and service line
- Forecasting by product family or service line rather than individual products and services
- Exploding a bill of activities to determine process and activity quantity for each product or service line

EXPLODING A BILL OF ACTIVITIES

The concept of exploding a bill of activities is key to determining workload. A **bill of activities** is a list of activities and activity volumes required to produce a

- Product or service
- Special feature or aspect
- Project
- Business process

A bill of activities can be created to determine the cost for

- Servicing different customers (size, region, class, etc.)
- Servicing different channels of distribution—value added distributor (VAD) and value added reseller (VAR)
- Business processes
- Outsourcing
- Investment decisions

To explode a bill of activities, simply

- List each product/service line.
- List the forecasted quantity of that service.
- List the units of each activity used by each service line.
- Multiply units of service times units of each activity to calculate the activity quantity volume by service.
- Sum the total activity quantities.

We will use our EZ Money Bank example again to illustrate an exploded bill of activities for the business process "acquire consumer loans." EZ Money Bank assumes the following: In order to acquire one loan, it will have to process a certain number of mortgage and auto loan applications. Exhibit 5.2 shows the relationships between loans and applications. Exhibit 5.3 shows the relationships between applications and reports. As the exhibit indicates, the key is to identify each service line. Then, list each unit of activity used by that service.

Service	Service Volume	Business Rule Applications/Loans	Application Volume
Standard mortgages	400	1.125 applications/loan	450 applications
Jumbo mortgages	100	1.100 applications/loan	110 applications
Auto loans	500	1.080 applications/loan	540 applications
Total	1,000		1,100 applications

Exhibit 5.2   EZ Money's relationship between mortgages and applications.

Service	Application Volume	Activity	Reports/ Application	Activity Workload
Standard mortgages	450	Order report	4	1,800
Jumbo mortgages	110	Order report	4	440
Auto loans	540	Order report	2	1,080
Total	1,100			3,320

Exhibit 5.3   EZ Money's relationship between applications and reports.

DETERMINING WORKLOAD FOR SUPPORT-RELATED ACTIVITIES

The second step in forecasting workload is to determine workload for support-related activities, which are those activities performed by support departments such as human resources, management information systems (MIS), security, and accounting. Again, workload would have to be determined for each of these departments, which may be a function of

- Product/service (e.g., issue purchase order—function of type and number of parts)
- Customer (e.g., special invoicing)
- Non–product-related (e.g., number and type of financial statements)

DETERMINING WORKLOAD FOR SPECIAL PROJECTS

The third step in forecasting workload is to determine workload for any upcoming or current special projects. Examples of special projects include

- ISO 9000
- Implementing ABM/ABB
- Quality initiatives
- Installing new computer systems, telephone systems, and the like
- Expanding office space

It is a good idea to set up a Gantt chart for each special project, with the activities and tasks listed by time period in order to determine where additional resources and personnel will be needed and at what time of the year. Workload can be prioritized and budgeted for each project.

FORECASTING WORKLOAD (OUTPUT VOLUME)

Now that the three categories of workload have been discussed (i.e., product/ service related, non–product/service-related support, and project related), ways of better forecasting will be examined. The first step would be to forecast all product or service traceable activities. This can be done by

- Identifying new products or services
- Identifying planned changes to existing products or services
- Creating or updating a bill of activities for each product or service

- Forecasting product/service sales by individual product or service lines or customers
- Exploding a bill of activities to determine exact activity quantities

Exploding a bill of activities is key to determining workload. Example 5-2 illustrates how important a bill of activities is to the process.

Example 5-2: Exploding EZ Money Bank's Bill of Activities

Remember from Example 5.1 that we wanted to know whether EZ Money Bank could handle the workload of 1,000 loans at the lower average fee of $600 per loan to meet its desired placement goal of $70 million in mortgages. The question was whether the staff at EZ Money Bank could handle the additional workload. Their workload for the previous year was 900 auto loans and mortgages. Management wants to increase sales to 1,000 loans for the upcoming year, based on better target marketing and a lower application fee.

Exhibit 5.4 represents an exploded bill of activities for the business process "acquire loans." The example is broken down into three product lines:

1. Standard mortgages
2. Jumbo mortgages
3. Auto loans

Based on the forecasts for the coming year, the workload for each product line has been determined.

Product Line	Workload
Standard mortgages	400
Jumbo mortgages	100
Auto loans	500
	1,000

Under the heading "Bill-of-Activities Workload," in the first column you will notice a box entitled "Activities." This box contains a list of activities required to achieve the business process "Acquire Consumer Loans." They include the following:

- Answer phone inquiries
- Take loan application
- Evaluate loan applications
  - Mortgages
  - Auto loans
- Sell mortgages
  - Standard
  - Jumbo
- Manage branch
  - Loan processors

Product lines	Standard mortgages 400	Jumbo mortgages 100	Auto 500	Total 1,000 loans
Bill of activities workload				
1. Phone inquiries	3/loan	3/loan	3/loan	
2. Take application	1.125/loan	1.1/loan	1.08/loan	
3. Evaluate loan	1.125/loan	1.1/loan	1.08/loan	
4. Sell mortgage	1/100/loan	1/10/loan		
5. Manage branch				
6. Order reports	4/application	4/application	2/application	
7. Disperse funds	1/loan	1/loan		
Activity quantities				
1. Phone inquiries	1,200	300	1,500	3,000
2. Take application	450	110	540	1,100
3. Evaluate loan	450	110	540	1,100
4. Sell mortgage	4	10		14
5. Manage branch				
6. Order reports	1,800	440	1,080	3,320
7. Disperse funds	400	100	500	1,000

Exhibit 5.4 Forecast output volume (workload): explode bill of activities for "Acquire consumer loans."

- • Loan officers
- Order reports
- Disperse funds
  - • Mortgages
  - • Auto loan
- Miscellaneous

Next to each of these activities is a number per loan or mortgage. For instance, next to "order reports" for mortgages, there is the number four. That means, on average, four reports will be ordered by someone in the application processing department for mortgages. Next to "order reports auto loans" is the number two. That means that only two reports are required for auto loan applications.

Move below to the box titled "Activity Quantities," and you will notice that we have totaled the number of times an activity is performed for each product. For example, 450 standard mortgage applications multiplied by four reports per mortgage application equals 1,800 reports ordered.

EZ Money Bank can now break down its budget by activity and estimate how long and how many staff members it will need to process 1,000 loans and mortgages. The same can be done for the other activities in this business process.

EZ Money's management must now review their plan and budget based on this information to determine whether their staff can indeed handle the 1,000 loans. A good way of doing this is to use ongoing activity analysis.

USING ONGOING ACTIVITY ANALYSIS TO FORECAST WORKLOAD

It is a good idea to continually monitor your activity analysis, especially if you plan to change any of the variables (workload, staff size, desired revenue, etc.). You should ask yourself a few simple questions:

- • Have your outputs changed?
- • Have your customers changed?
- • Does this activity still add value?
- • Has your customers' requirements changed?

The bottom line is that you should periodically be re-evaluating your activity analysis. Requirements change at such a fast pace today that many organizations are struggling to keep up.

6

CAPACITY MANAGEMENT

This chapter will:

- Define capacity.
- Explain capacity management.

CAPACITY DEFINED

Capacity is the availability of a resource measured against a standard. A machine, for example, has a maximum run capacity (availability) of 24 hours a day. **Capacity management** is the process of creating value by assigning resources to activities to ensure that there is adequate capacity to perform an activity with the least amount of excess availability. The need for a resource must originate with a need to produce a product or service. Optimizing capacity should never be a goal by itself. Keeping a resource fully consumed without a customer demand does not create value. In other words, all "make-busy work" to achieve standard earned value does nothing but create waste.

Resources are often classified as **fixed** or **variable**. A **variable cost** or **resource** changes in proportion to production volume in the short term (All costs are variable in the long run). A fixed cost does not vary with production in the short term. Fixed costs are those items that reoccur, periodically, as part of business expenses and are not directly related to output volume. For example, a manufacturer must have a facility and equipment before products can be manufactured. These costs are incurred regardless of whether any products are produced. The cost of this equipment (depreciation or lease cost) is considered a fixed cost.

Capacity analysis is a more useful concept for taking action than fixed and variable analysis. If an organization classifies a resource as fixed, the assumption that people often make is that nothing can be done to change the resource usage. However, if an organization analyzes the components of capacity, it can determine actions that can minimize excess capacity where it exists.

To illustrate the difference between fixed and variable cost, consider the manufacturing process of inserting electronic components into circuit boards. A manual insertion process employs laborers as the primary factor of production. The technology is unsophisticated—bins of components and a workbench. In this environment, there is a direct relationship between the number of laborers and production volume. A product would absorb the laborers' cost based on the number of hours consumed multiplied by their hourly rate. Unused hours are treated as an efficiency variance.

Machine and equipment cost is treated differently. The cost of operating a machine is the sum of depreciation, property insurance, property taxes, and so forth. These costs are commonly included in overhead and allocated to products. For example, an automated manufacturing insertion process would employ machines as the primary factor of production. Machine operators, maintenance personnel, programmers, and others are important but considered secondary factors of production that support the automated process. There is a stepped relationship between the machine cost and production volume. Additional production volume, where unutilized capacity exists, can be absorbed without the need to incur additional cost until full capacity is reached. Also, machines unlike people are often inflexible and not easily changed for alternative uses.

A fixed resource has two important components: actual capacity used and unused capacity. Whereas the cost effectiveness of a machine is relative to actual volume usage, the treatment of unused capacity has a dramatic impact on cost. A machine rate based on actual usage charges the entire machine cost to current period products and buries unused capacity cost in the actual rate. For example, consider a machine with a depreciation cost of $100,000 and 7,500 actual production hours:

$$\frac{\text{Cost}}{\text{Actual usage}} = \frac{\$100,000}{7,500} = \$13.33/\text{machine hour}$$

A machine rate based on available capacity includes cost on total production hours available regardless of whether the hours are used or unused. The unused component represents either surge or excess capacity. **Surge capacity** is the additional capacity required for full production during peak times of the year. **Excess capacity** can be viewed as a non–value-added cost if there are no potential uses for the capacity, or it can represent a potential growth opportunity. In either case, the cost of the unused capacity should be separately identified and assigned to the source of the excess capacity. Common sources include plant management decisions or inadequate sales. Continuing our example, assume the available capacity is 10,000 hours:

$$\frac{\text{Cost}}{\text{Available capacity}} = \frac{\$100,000}{10,000 \text{ hrs.}} = \$10/\text{machine hour}$$

Unused capacity cost = (Available capacity – actual usage) × available capacity machine rate

$$(10,000 - 7,500) \times \$10/\text{machine hour} = \$25,000$$

Classifying cost as fixed or variable is a practice that should be abandoned. Instead, costs should be classified as used and unused. To classify fixed cost and only hold managers accountable for variable costs ignores a large potential saving. Management often ignores resources that are termed *fixed*. These costs simply appear month after month. Managers do not see these fixed costs at all because they are buried in overhead.

In addition to depreciable assets, other resources are often considered fixed. They are largely to support the ongoing enterprise, the so-called overhead of management, accounting, finance and advertising, sales, research and development (R&D), and market development. All tend to build up and are controllable as a business grows.

MANAGING CAPACITY

Capacity is an important element of an organization's profit potential. When all resources are fully deployed to value-adding activities, profitability is improved. A resource that is unused must be paid for but is not directly generating revenue and thus reduces profitability. The key to profitability is to match capacity to future needs. Having too many resources wastes capital that could be used to create value; having too few resources results in inefficient production and lost revenue. Managing capacity requires an understanding of the resources life cycle demand.

By using capacity information as part of an activity-based budget, the organization can focus on balancing flow. Traditionally, in budgeting, an organization takes the fixed costs and divides by some volume to create a fixed cost per unit. Several things might occur: The organization might downsize where volume decreases but the fixed costs do not, or the organization might increase in capacity greater than the increase in volume using the capacity.

Capacity is a concept that applies directly to resources. All resources (people, equipment, information systems, material, etc.) are limited. An important part of any manager's responsibility is to manage and allocate scarce resources to perform work.

Capacity is only indirectly related to activities. Because activities consume resources, then limitations in resources also limit the capacity of an activity. It is critical to understand the limiting resource in order to determine the capacity limits of an activity. Some organizations have incorrectly tried to express capacity in terms of the activity workload (number of output measures). This practice is valid only if the resources are totally dedicated to an activity. If resources are consumed by multiple activities, then it is not feasible to use activity workload as a measure of process capacity; at most they represent maximum possible production.

All processes produce different outputs and thus have different capacities. As in the case of activities, it is the resources, rather than the process, that have capacity limits. This limitation is less severe for process than it is for activities. The reason is that a process is a collection of several activities. Thus, as the activities are consolidated by process capacity, bottlenecks tend to be smoothed over.

CAPACITY MANAGEMENT METHODOLOGY

The following five-step methodology will help in implementing capacity management.

Step 1: Determine the Resources to Be Managed

An organization must determine the resources needed for an activity, which in turn defines the capacity utilization. The key factors are the financial significance of the resource and the degree that the resource can become a limiting factor.

Step 2: Define Capacity Basis

There are several bases for defining capacity utilization. None of these are mutually exclusive. Capacity is the output capability of an organization when it fully utilizes its limiting resources to create the maximum value with minimum waste. Effective capacity utilization starts with recognizing and minimizing idle capacity. By measuring idle capacity accurately, a company learns which assumptions, practices, and processes need to be changed. Failure to measure idle capacity makes it virtually impossible to efficiently manage capacity to create long-term value. Define available capacity to form the basis of calculating unused capacity.

Idle capacity can be caused by

- The baseline definition of capacity used (e.g., theoretical/practical versus actual)
- Management practices
- Accounting measurements
- Shifts in the work processes
- Structural slack due to the mismatch between the input and output characteristics of a resource

Capacity Measures

Theoretical capacity assumes available capacity of 365 days and 24 hours a day. Theoretical capacity is defined as the maximum output a plant can produce in a specified time period (usually one year). It allows for no downtime, waste, or idle time. Once this maximum capacity is reached, the only possible solution is to enlarge the existing plant or outsource.

Setting a theoretical limit establishes a clear and unambiguous capacity benchmark. Theoretical capacity helps an organization identify its opportunities for improvement by separating waste caused by management practices.

Practical capacity factors in lost time due to nonworking days, plant shutdowns, repairs, and maintenance. Practical capacity is theoretical capacity adjusted for normal downtime and waste. It creates an acceptable level of unavailable time by setting an upper limit on the time available for a resource to perform an activity.

Budgeted capacity is the result of the planning process. Sales forecasts, existing inventory levels, and the company's policies are combined to develop a production plan for the coming year.

Normal capacity is the actual capacity utilization that an organization has experienced over an extended period of time. It allows for human and equipment inefficiencies and idle time, which is off limits. In determining normal capacity, be sure to perform the analysis over time to smooth out cyclical patterns. Actual capacity utilization, which is often redefined in management reports as the total number of labor hours "earned," reflects work actually done.

Normal capacity refers to the average actual output of an organization over an extended period of time. It includes waste, downtime, and process variability that are currently embedded into the organization's ordinary operations.

Step 3: Define Surge Capacity

Surge capacity is the excess capacity needed to meet unpredictable and seasonal/cyclical demands. A second type of surge capacity recognizes product start-up demand. This second type of surge is temporary in nature. Typically, during the early years of a product, startup creates unused capacity until the organization reaches full production. Surge capacity due to startup shows poor profitability during the early years and higher profitability during full production. The effect of excess start-up capacity is staggering: 50 percent of existing capacity and perhaps 80 to 90 percent of new capacity can be nonproductive.

It is critical to quantify surge capacity because these are strategic costs that should be segregated, reported, and budgeted separately.

Step 4: Managing Capacity

Resource usage is determined by summing the total hours a resource is consumed in performing an activity. Wasted resource usage should be backed out of total resource usage.

The measurement of capacity is a by-product of the activity analysis process. Activity analysis captures the number of resources and the amount of resources consumed by the activities. Capacity management simply uses this data to compute resource utilization at all levels—theoretical, practical, and normal.

The important question is not how to capture capacity information as it is to understand and eliminate the root causes that create the excess capacity. Two of the common problems in managing capacity are bottlenecks and waste.

Bottlenecks

Total capacity of a process is no greater than the capacity of its most limited activity. Nonbottleneck areas always have surplus capacity, because the production process is rarely balanced. The bottleneck (or pacing) resources (or activity) limit how much volume can be pushed through an organization. Capacity, therefore, is not the total output the organization can produce, but rather the maximum total output given the bottleneck resource.

If this bottleneck is "at capacity" when the rest of the plant is running at only half its potential speed, the entire system will be constrained: No more output can be pushed through, regardless of the demand or the amount of work that gets started. Understanding and managing bottlenecks and constraints is only part of what needs to be done to effectively manage an organization.

Bottleneck analysis focuses on the areas where wasted capacity prevents the entire system from operating at a higher level of effectiveness.

Activity Waste

Eliminating waste in activities makes it possible to manage capacity more effectively. Activity performance measured at less than world class, or best practice, requires additional capacity. Conventional practice incorporates levels of scrap, downtime, and related problems to arrive at an average, or standard, level of performance that is attainable by an average worker.

When waste is built into a standard, it becomes invisible. Even more troubling is the fact that waste becomes an accepted way of doing business. Managers are essentially rewarded for wasting just the "right" amount of resources in their budget. This level of "acceptable" waste is thus built into the budgets of all department and activities. The impact on the total excess capacity is staggering to the organization. Activity improvement is the basis for identifying the root cause of wasted capacity. This problem-solving tool provides useful information for refocusing capacity-management efforts. The focus of this tool is the elimination of waste—as reflected in a company's idle capacity.

Step 5: Creating Capacity

Improving Capacity by Reducing Resource Consumption

Successful improvement programs lead to creating unused or idle capacity. Capacity is created by removing process variation, resulting in less resources employed in an activity and less corrective work such as inspections, rework, and scrap.

The continuous improvement model leads to a different set of assumptions about the best way to manage capacity: It reflects a constant pursuit of perfection (the theoretical optimum). It questions all assumptions, focuses on the creation of value, builds on a process orientation that recognizes the role of bottlenecks on system effectiveness, and tolerates zero waste. Continuous elimination of waste, wherever it is found, is the basis for competitive survival.

Increase Resource Flexibility

Resource flexibility is related to the capability of deploying a resource to multiple activities. Typically, the greater the flexibility, the less the unused or idle capacity. Conversely, the more inflexible the resource, the greater the possibility of excess capacity.

Another dimension of flexibility is the ease of acquiring and disposing of resources. A "fixed" resource cannot be purchased at the desired time or in the exact quantity needed for production. Instead, fixed resources must be purchased in fairly large quantities regardless of whether the resource can be completely consumed before it loses its productive capability.

Improve the Planning Process

Because managers lack accurate information on just how much capacity is required to meet their customers' demand, they tend to buy more capacity than is needed. An activity-based budgeting (ABB) approach minimizes this type of excess capacity.

MANAGING EXCESS CAPACITY

Once areas of excess capacity are identified, the organization can

- Utilize capacity by creating opportunities for additional work
- Dispose of the excess capacity by downsizing, selling, or outsourcing resources
- Consolidate operations to better use capacity
- Cross-train people to perform activities that have limited capacity
- Use the capacity for other activities

When a cut in capacity is proposed, it is important to give careful consideration to the cost savings that can be realized. Many infrastructure costs will not be saved. Often all that cuts in capacity achieve is to add surplus capacity to support activities.

SUMMARY

Capacity has a tremendous effect on activity output, cost, and performance. It also dramatically affects product and service costs; therefore, when addressing the topic of capacity, the following questions need to be answered:

- What are the sources of idle capacity?
- How much unused capacity is assigned to product cost?
- How large of a threat is the hidden, unused capacity?
- Who is responsible for capacity management?
- How can we obtain more capacity without buying it?

7

FEATURE COSTING: AN OVERLAY TO ACTIVITY-BASED BUDGETING

This chapter will:

- Discuss the principles of feature costing and its link to activity-based budgeting (ABB).
- Examine process structure and workload volume.
- Define cost variation versus process variation.
- Describe a feature product costing model.

This chapter discusses the principles of feature costing that are critical components of an ABB and value-based planning system. Planning and managing costs requires an understanding of the impact of planned product/ service mixes on the capacity and effectiveness of existing activities and resources to handle the mix. A varying product/service mix puts a strain on an organization's existing processes to deal with complexity that ultimately results in process variation. An organization that understands the conditions that cause its process variations can better plan the level of resources required to provide the products and services and what must change to achieve the organization's profit objectives.

INTRODUCTION

Feature costing assigns cost to activities and products/services based on the product's or service's features. Feature costing is a technique that seeks to understand the process variation caused by unique features of individual products or services. This knowledge of features enables an organization to minimize variation resulting in more predictable and manageable costs. This results in a more accurate operating plan. It also facilitates a more accurate matching of an organization's capabilities to its expected workload for products or services.

Features are major determinants of the final product/service cost. A product/service feature is important to the customer because it determines the fit, function, use, or safety associated with the product/service. For example, a significant feature of a car is the engine. Each feature should be divided into subcategories that further defines the feature's functionality. The engine in this example may be categorized as gas or diesel. Next, the gas engine may be categorized by the number of cylinders. A feature should be decomposed until the process steps no longer vary with additional subcategories.

Measuring the cost of variability is essential to both planning and controlling costs. By explicitly identifying the magnitude of costs associated with variability, managers are more likely to plan for the financial implications of variability. Furthermore, understanding the savings that result from efforts to reduce variation should stimulate the improvement process and attainment of profit objectives. These efforts may involve educating and retraining employees, redesigning the process's steps, investing in equipment, and even redesigning products or services. For instance, if a product can be manufactured using less components and parts, there is a good likelihood that the process will be simplified, resulting in less process variations.

A planning system that provides managers with information that can help them improve operations by identifying the specific sources of variability will show managers where they should focus their improvement efforts. Feature costing links the planning and budgeting process to strategic objectives by exposing causes of process variation. By quantifying the cost of these activities and then relating them back to the source of the variation, we can begin to understand the cost of variation. By reducing process variation, management reduces cost variation. Cost predictability improves as variability decreases. Thus, the key to cost control is to reduce variability in all levels of the organization.

Feature costing is based on three fundamental principles:

- Process structure and workload volume locks in a cost structure.
- Cost variation is a direct consequence of process variation.
- Process variation originates from three sources
    - poor process execution
    - product and service features
    - customer and distribution channel requirements.

PROCESS STRUCTURE AND WORKLOAD VOLUME LOCK IN A COST STRUCTURE

Feature costing is based on a **process model** of cost. According to the process model, a process is organized work designed to transform inputs into a pre-established output. Resources are the factors of production required to execute the process and are a direct consequence of the chosen work procedures. Exhibit 7.1 is an example of an input–output process model.

With a process model, an organization develops a series of procedures (activities) in order to deliver products or services to its customers. The procedures and the number of activity occurrences in turn determine the resources needed to execute the activity.

For example, the activity of purchase order processing requires a person to perform the work steps and a computer system to perform the necessary calculations and data manipulation. Other resources such as office supplies and facilities are also required. The need to process purchase orders triggers from the need for the organization to acquire the resources. The organization purchases the resources and records their cost in the general ledger. The number of purchase order clerks, data processing resources, and office supplies depends on the number of purchase orders to be processed.

The total cost of an activity is the sum of all resource costs, also known as factors of production, employed to perform an activity. Factors of production consist of people, machines, travel, supplies, computer systems, and other resources, customarily expressed as chart of account cost ele-

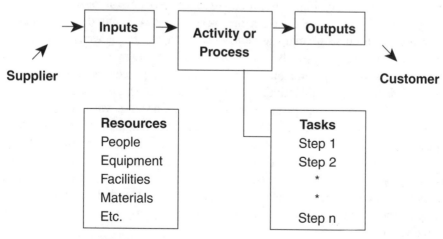

Exhibit 7.1 Input–output process model.

ments. Each significant traceable resource is included in an activity cost. In the purchase order example, the cost of the activity is determined by tracing the labor, technology, facilities, and office supplies to the purchase order activity.

The process model requires the organization to decompose the activity centers into its component activities. Thus, the activities for a production center would include those shown in the charts on the facing page.

The organization level processes are termed business processes. A business process is composed of activities, and activities are made up of tasks. What differentiates each of these is the level of detail.

COST VARIATION IS A DIRECT CONSEQUENCE OF PROCESS VARIATION

Keep in mind that, in order for a process to generate value, it must produce an output that is valued by the end users. Once a process is developed, it remains relatively unchanged over time. In other words, equipment is acquired, procedures are developed, and people are trained. Change becomes difficult once a process is locked in. However, both the demands and types of product and service features needed by customers are continually changing. Technology and competitors create changes in buying patterns. The inevitable result is process variation. New product features and demand shifts put pressures on processes to perform in ways that differ from the "optimal" original design.

Understanding and minimizing process variation is a fundamental principle of feature costing. All processes vary. No person or machine can precisely replicate a process the same every time it is executed. Wide process variation is a curse to management, because it results in varying usage of resources and varying levels of the quality of output.

From a planning and budgeting perspective, process variations cause cost variations. Understanding the source and impact of process variation is critical to achieving profitability targets. A process variation that is a direct consequence of a product feature must be managed by the marketing, product, or manufacturing development process. Yet the impact of these changes ripples throughout the organization's processes, directly impacting profitability. A process variation that is a direct consequence of a process execution should be managed at the process level and does not directly impact the specific product service that was being processed when the variation occurred.

Activity	Machinist	Supervisor	Saw	Lathe	Drill	Heat Treat	Training	Supplies	Total
Cut parts	36,000		8,000				1,500		45,500
Drill parts–manual	24,000				5,000		1,000	2,000	32,000
Drill parts–CNC*	12,000				25,000		8,000	6,000	51,000
Turn parts	23,000			6,500			1,000		30,500
Heat treat	12,500					16,500	1,000	4,000	34,000
Set up machines	8,500							3,000	11,500
Inspect parts	10,200						2,500	5,000	17,700
Move parts	7,600							1,000	8,600
Admin. tasks	4,200								4,200
Supervise group		43,000					2,000		45,000
	138,000	43,000	8,000	6,500	30,000	16,500	17,000	21,000	$280,000

*CNC: Computerized Numerical Control

Activity	Output Measure	Number of Outputs	$/Output	Time/Output
Cut parts	Number of parts cut	8,000		
Drill parts–manual	Number of holes drilled–manual			
Drill parts–CNC	Number of holes drilled–CNC			
Turn parts	Number of parts turned			
Heat treat	Number of parts heat treated			
Set up machines	Number of setups			
Inspect parts	Number of parts inspected			
Move parts	Number of moves			

Assume the average cost of a drilled part was $0.05 per hole drilled. This cost was derived by studying the resources assigned to the process and number of process outputs over a period of time. It represents an average of both good and poor process performance as illustrated here:

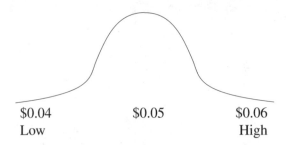

| $0.04 | $0.05 | $0.06 |
| Low | | High |

The wider the process variation, the greater the cost variation. If the cost per output was closer to $0.06 during the period, then the financial reports for the group would have significant unfavorable variances.

A further problem with process variation is that it causes variability in the output. Inconsistent output causes problems in downstream processes and ultimately to customers. The cost of process variation shows up in activities that deal with the consequence of the variation. Often, these activities are later steps in the business process. Downstream activities that receive the output must adjust their processes to compensate for the output variation. Best case is that these adjustments slow down the process, resulting in unfavorable cost variances. Worst case, the output must be scrapped or reworked, resulting in wasted resources. Repeated variations cause additional activities such as inspection that are not necessary if the output had been produced consistently. These costs are termed non–value-added and are typically "hidden" in traditional budgeting systems.

The financial and operational impact of all process change must be understood. It is important to keep in mind that corrective action to prevent process variation by removing the root cause of the variation is often a one-time cost. However, the costs of internal failure (scrap, rework, downtime, etc.) as well as external failure are ongoing costs. The longer the variation problem remains unresolved, the greater the non–value-added costs.

The implication is that if management decides not to incur the voluntary expense of reducing variation, they will ultimately incur several times that amount in the form of warranty costs, lost contribution because of customer ill will, and so forth. If there is variation in the output of the drill hole activity, then the assembly process is going to incur additional costs because of rework, adjustments to process, reduced throughput, and so on.

PROCESS VARIATION ORIGINATES FROM THREE SOURCES

The three sources of process variation are:

1. Poor process execution
2. Product features
3. Customer requirements

Knowing the magnitude of process variation is incomplete by itself. It is critical to also understand why the process varies. This requires identifying and managing the root causes of variation. Stable process performance is possible only when the root causes of variation are removed. This requires a systematic and continuous problem-solving effort to find and eliminate the root causes. The planning and budgeting process is important because it formalizes this root cause identification and management process.

What Causes Variation?

Products/Services and Process Capability

Variation occurs because each process has certain physical limits and capabilities. Where a product or service is a good fit for the process, then minimal variations occur. However, where there is a bad fit, the probability of process variation is increased. Keep in mind that a process is a unique configuration of material, method of work, man, and machine. The limits that are rationally achievable from a process are based on the process technology and procedures employed. Anytime a product/service characteristic is outside the bounds of the normal characteristic for which the predetermined process (under predetermined work conditions) was designed, it will slow down or abort a process. Thus, a product or service feature that exceeds a process limit causes a process variation resulting in additional work, longer processing time, and/ or quality problems. These variations are directly attributable to specific products or services and should be planned for or eliminated during the budgeting process.

Chance Causes

Process variation can also be due to chance causes. Chance causes occur because there is always some process variation that occurs even when the process is performed by the same worker, the same work procedures, and even with the same material and equipment. This is because the process is affected by changes in the environment or process that cannot be controlled. Chance variations include the sum of all chance causes acting simultaneously on a process. They reflect the inherent "normal" characteristics of the process. Such variations can be influenced only by changing the process, by changing the technology, or by new procedures. In feature costing, chance variations are included in the average of the activity/process cost.

Noncompliance with Activity and Process Procedures

A third type of process variation occurs because of noncompliance with activity and process procedures or inadequate procedures. These problems result in non–value-added activities or tasks. For example, a machine breaks down. When this occurs a process can no longer deliver its expected output, which in turn causes schedule disruptions. In our example the maintenance department must quickly fix the problem, which results in inefficient maintenance, and the finance department must resolve the resulting cost variances. Consequences of this lead to high cost and poor performance. It is management's responsibility to act and remove as many of the root causes of these problems as possible and thereby render the process more efficient and error free. This can be done by constantly improving the process.

Poor Process Execution

Non–value-added costs are incurred when a process is not executed properly. Errors must be detected by inspection and reworked. If a product can be sold as a first-quality unit after the rework, then these out-of-pocket rework costs are the total costs of variability. If the reworked unit cannot be sold as a first-quality unit, then the cost of variability also includes sales discounts.

If a product falls outside the specification limits, and cannot be reworked, it must be scrapped. The cost of variability for this includes materials, labor, and other costs incurred in producing the product service. In addition, any disposal cost incurred is also a cost of variability. Poor quality products and services result in customer complaints, sales returns, warranty costs, and lost sales.

All processes must be continually evaluated to understand the root cause of the variation.

Product Features

One paramount factor that impacts product or service cost is how their characteristics impact a process. A product or service that utilizes the existing process capabilities will be efficient to produce. Conversely, a product or service that pushes the limits of a process can cause significant disruption and consequently high cost.

Characteristics that exceed a process's limits cause process variations. Variation results in additional work steps, longer processing time, and/or quality problems. Thus, it is important to understand the impact of each characteristic. In the case of a sewing machine operation sewing jeans, thin material often jams the machine, causing the operator to feed the material at a slower speed. The number of sewing errors increases because the machine guides cannot hold the required tolerances. Efficiency loss due to the thin material is assessed on the basis of the calculated amount of variability or influence that the process characteristic (thin material) caused to the base process.

For example, a company in feature costing analysis determined that the production of uncoated paperboard resulted in a much larger proportion of defective units than that of coated paperboard. By attaching a cost to those products exhibiting high rates of variability, it helped the company analyze the strategic implications of manufacturing a product that exhibits extreme variation in the quality of production.

Customer Features

Another major source of variation is customers and distribution channels. Some customers require unique product features or services. Typical requirements include specified delivery schedules or packaging. These changes may disrupt the normal production and distribution process, which increases cost.

Distribution channels affect cost. A company that sells through brokers, telephone sales, or direct sales will have a significantly different process to sell a product. Each channel may require different ordering, packaging, and shipping. The same could apply to an insurance company that sells through their own agents, through direct mail or telesales. The way policies are processed and updated and statements created also vary by distribution channel.

FEATURE PRODUCT COSTING MODEL

Feature costing uses features and characteristics to assign cost to activities and processes in order to differentiate product and service cost. Attributing cost and value, based on how product/service characteristics impact a process is the most proficient tool available for accurately assigning cost. A step-by-step procedure for computing a product or service feature cost follows.

Step 1: Determine the Product Features

In our sewing example, the important product features would include the following:

Product Feature	Product Feature Subcategory
Product style	Pant
	Shorts
Watch pocket	
Fly	Zipper fly
	Button fly

Step 2: Determine the Activity Routing Associated with Each Product Feature

As mentioned in Step 1, a product or service feature should stop being decomposed when the process steps no longer vary. Creating a feature involves a unique routing or step-by-step procedure. At this stage, it is important only to recognize the activity steps involved, even though different products and services may have unique physical characteristics that may require different processing time. For example, the color of the car does not impact the fact that every car is painted.

In our sewing example, the work steps associated with the watch pocket features would include the following:

Product Feature	Activity Routing
Watch pocket	Cut pocket
	Hem pocket
	Attach pocket

Step 3: Determine the Cost of Each Activity

During this step, an activity analysis is performed to establish a per unit activity cost. In our sewing example, the activity cost associated with attaching a pocket feature is determined:

Activity	Activity Resources	Cost
Attach pocket	Sewer	$0.0755
	Sewing machine	$0.0032
	Thread	$0.0100
	Space	$0.0001
		$0.0888

Keep in mind that the activity cost represents an average cost based on actual performance. This cost is not an engineered standard, nor does it necessarily represent good performance.

Step 4: Determine Product Characteristics That Will Cause a Process to Vary

During this step, the product characteristics that impact the sewing process are determined. In our sewing example, the product characteristics are:

Product Characteristics	Product Characteristics Subcategories
Fabric color	White
	Blue
	Black
Fabric thickness	< .05" (Thin)
	.05"–.07"
	> .07" (Stiff)
Size	Small size (children's jeans)
	Normal
	Large
Waist size	30"–40"
	40"+
Thread color	Standard
	Nonstandard

Step 5: Determine How Much Product Characteristics Cause the Process to Vary

During this step, the process loss associated with each product characteristic is determined. In our sewing example, the process loss associated with each product characteristic is determined as follows:

Product Characteristics	Process Loss	Hem Watch Pocket adj.
< .05" Thin	15%	0.0133 (0.0888 × 15%)
.05"–.07"	—	
> .07" (Stiff)	10%	0.0088 (0.0888 × 10%)

Step 6: Associate Product Features and Characteristics to Products

During this step, the previously identified product features and characteristics are associated to products. Each unique product is assessed to determine its product features and characteristics. For example, assume you are manufacturing a pair of blue jeans with a watch pocket and a zipper using thick denim and standard thread for a 34-inch waist size. These data are associated to the product.

Product: Blue Jeans

Product Feature	Product Characteristics
Pants	Fabric color: blue
Watch pocket	Fabric thickness: .08"
Zipper fly	Size: 34
	Thread color: standard

Step 7: Adjust Activity Cost Based on the Product's Features and Characteristics

The final step is to compute a product cost. All activities necessary to produce the product are derived from the product features. This step creates the bill of activities. Next, each activity uses the average activity cost and then adjusts the cost of the activity based on the product's characteristics. All costs are then summed to calculate a product cost.

Product Feature	Standard	Adjusted	Total Adjusted Cost
Cut watch pocket			
Hem watch pocket	.0888	.0089	0.0977
Set back pocket			

SUMMARY

Once organizations understand the causes of variation on a formal basis as part of their activity budget, they can strive to:

- Improve or reduce sources of variation
- Understand how customers, products, and services and distribution channels cause variation and whether they should:
  - Charge differently for customer-caused sources of variation
  - Simply take variation into consideration when budgeting
  - Explain to customers how they caused variation that increases costs

Part 3

METHODOLOGY

8

CREATING AN ACTIVITY BUDGET WITH FEATURES

This chapter will:

- Define the business process and activity hierarchy.
- Provide an overview of why business processes and activities are an appropriate basis for driving value using activity-based budgeting (ABB) and features.
- Define and discuss business processes and how they can be implemented and improved using an activity-based budget.
- Provide a step-by-step analysis of an ABB plan.

BUSINESS PROCESS AND ACTIVITY HIERARCHY: UNITS OF WORK DEFINED

Activities and business processes form the foundation of any organization. Business processes and activities describe the way an enterprise employs its time and resources in order to achieve its organizational objectives. The goal is to produce an **outcome**. An outcome is a satisfied customer, a paid vendor, a safe neighborhood, a hip replacement patient who is now walking. In order to achieve these outcomes, the organization must produce certain outputs.

Outcomes	Output
Satisfied customer	Product/service that meets customer needs
Paid vendor	Vendor payment (check, electronic data interchange [EDI])
Walking hip replacement patient	Patient visited by physical therapists

Outcomes Require Outputs Produced by Business Processes and Activities That Consume Resources

Outputs are produced by **activities** that consume resources (materials, labor, and technology). The principal function of an activity is to convert resources into outputs (products or services). For example, the primary activities of a manufacturing engineering department might include developing and maintaining bills of material, conducting capacity studies, suggesting process improvements, and designing tools.

Functions are a combination of activities related by skills and common experiences. Such activities would be related by a common purpose or goal such as material procurement, security, and quality. Most organizations are already organized functionally. This functional structure interferes with the connection between all of the interwoven activities of separate departments. For example, the responsibility of quality control activities historically was often assigned to the quality control department. Yet many other quality activities have taken place before the product enters the quality control department (i.e., quality planning during the design stage, in-process inspections, rework, customer services activities, etc.) There is no guarantee that the interdependency among the activities relating to the common purpose will be understood and streamlined if the organization manages itself solely based on functions.

A **business process** is a series of related and interdependent activities linked by the outputs they exchange. The activities are related because a specific outcome is desired. This outcome requires certain outputs that initiate the first activity in the process, which, in turn, triggers subsequent activities. An output or information flow occurs where two activities interact. The exchange of an output or information flow draws a boundary between different activities within a process and links them into a strong cause-and-effect relationship.

A **task** is a combination of work elements, or operations, that make up an activity. Organizations may accomplish the same activities using different tasks and operations.

For example, a bank has an activity to evaluate loan applications. The application can be for an auto loan, a standard (less than $227,000) mortgage, or a jumbo (greater than $227,000) mortgage. In the case of a standard mortgage and a jumbo mortgage, the tasks are the same. The credit history of the applicant, the survey, the title, and the appraisal are reviewed. The interest rates are higher for jumbo mortgages than for standard mortgages because it is more difficult to sell jumbo mortgages, not because there is any difference in processing standard and jumbo applications and buyers require higher interest.

Meanwhile, when an auto loan application is evaluated, there are some different tasks, which might include reviewing the credit history and the Motor Vehicle Report (MVR). These tasks are different than for a standard or jumbo mortgage. However, both sets of tasks make up the activity to evaluate a loan application.

Historically, some organizations would actually create subactivities: evaluate standard mortgages, evaluate jumbo mortgages, and evaluate auto loans. Theoretically, there is nothing wrong with creating subactivities. However, subactivities complicate product and service costing.

We suggest that the organization consider defining one activity—"order reports"—and use the concept of features. A feature is a different step required by an activity. For example, in the "order reports" activity, the features for ordering mortgage reports include evaluating four reports: survey, appraisal, credit history, and title. The features for ordering auto loan reports involve two reports: a credit history and an MVR.

If the difference in time for ordering reports for auto loans and mortgages is significant, then the concept of features is very useful. The volumes for mortgages and auto loans can be weighted to reflect the different amount of time needed to order reports for these different types of loans.

Some activities have different characteristics. The concept of characteristics says that tasks and/or operations take more time or less time. For example, if the bank chooses to sell its mortgages, it has an activity entitled "sell mortgages." Whether these mortgages are standard mortgages or jumbo mortgages, it may still choose to sell them. However, there is a difference in the time connected with selling these two types of mortgages. A standard mortgage is generally sold to two major buyers: Freddie Mac and Fannie Mae. These are quasi-federal agencies that buy residential mortgages. The selling is mostly automated, and the requirements are straightforward.

Jumbo mortgages are sold to private investors. Because there are less private investors for jumbo mortgages, the bank must look for additional investors. This takes longer than looking for buyers of standard mortgages. Each buyer may have different requirements. Therefore, although the bank must prepare resell documents for both standard and jumbo loans, the time to create them is longer for the nonstandard jumbo mortgages and shorter for the standard mortgages.

Finally, the market for jumbo mortgages may or may not have funds and/or interest in buying jumbo mortgages at the time the bank wants to sell them. The selling of jumbo mortgages has characteristics that require more resources versus selling standard mortgages. The tasks are the same, but it takes longer to execute the tasks.

Therefore, features is the concept of using different tasks or operations to complete an activity. **Characteristics** is the concept where the activities are the same, but it takes different amounts of time to complete the activities. Using the concepts of features and characteristics instead of subactivities will make the planning process and budgeting model easier to understand and less cumbersome.

An **operation** is the smallest unit of work. It is the very detailed work elements. An organization would traditionally not cost at this level of detail except as part of an improvement initiative. Steps do help the organization understand the procedures it follows. They are a useful analysis tool. However, they are too detailed for monthly or quarterly costing and budgeting.

WHY ACTIVITIES?

Activities and business processes form the basis of a driving value. They are the appropriate level of detail to drive value. They support an ongoing activity-based budget, which drives value. Examples include:

Department	Activity
Marketing	Research market
Engineering	Design concept
Marketing	Design concept
Engineering	Create prototype
Operations	Create prototype
Regulatory	Obtain regulatory approval

An activity is what the organization does to accomplish its work. For example, a salesperson's selling of a product is an activity within the sales and marketing function. The activity of selling a product is distinct from the activity research market for new product ideas. Both are part of the sales and marketing function. A salesperson might perform a number of activities, including selling a product, pricing a product, and processing an order.

The business process of selling a product might consist of activities such as traveling to the customer, making a general presentation about the organization, preparing a specific proposal, presenting a specific proposal, and processing the order. This entire business process is contained within the sales and marketing function. Many business processes cross functions.

The business process of developing new products would include researching the market (marketing); designing the concept (engineering and marketing); creating the prototype (engineering and operations); and obtaining regulatory approvals (regulatory).

Business Process: *Sell Product   (All within sales and marketing function)*

Travel to customer
Make presentation about organization
Prepare a specific proposal
Present specific proposal
Process order

Business Process *(Cross-functional): Develop Product/Service*

Function	Activity
Marketing	Research market
Engineering/Marketing	Design concept
Engineering/Operations	Create prototype
Regulatory	Obtain regulatory approval

Managing business processes and activities is a powerful tool for managing an enterprise successfully. A management system structured on activities ensures that plans are transmitted to a level at which action can be taken. The traditional practice of budgeting by extrapolating historical costs to the future does not provide the detailed information needed to make appropriate changes. An activity-based budget defines the business processes and activities to achieve the necessary strategic objectives. It is a more forward-looking system than traditional budgets.

BUSINESS PROCESSES AND ACTIVITIES HELP FOCUS ORGANIZATIONAL STRATEGY

Activities and business processes are what organizations do. Strategic goals represent what the organization needs to accomplish. Recognizing goals determines what needs to change from what is being done today and what activities are needed to accomplish that change. Goals help to better perform the business processes and activities that relate to those goals. By examining activities, the organization can make changes and move forward toward achieving its goals.

Business Processes and Activities Work Toward Continuous Improvements

Business process and activity analysis provides management with the tools needed to identify redundant, duplicate, and wasteful tasks or activities.

Managing business processes and activities helps everyone cut waste, make improvements, ensure quality, and simplify tasks.

Business Processes and Activities Help Improve Decision Making

Value-driven plans using ABB and features provide information that paint a very real picture of the impact of decisions on current processes. This "clear view" lets managers get feedback in a timely fashion so that changes can be made ahead of the fact, rather than merely reporting historical information, thus creating a far more useful system.

The Importance of Business Processes in Value-Driven Planning Using ABB and Features

A business process is how an organization creates value. How a business process is structured determines how value is created. The key is to structure business processes in alignment with strategic objectives and the market-place. Only by thinking about this alignment can an organization effectively achieve its goals.

For example, look at the procurement process. One approach is to store items that are bought and then pick them from inventory when they are needed. The organization buys raw materials, stores these raw materials, and issues them to production.

The consequence of this approach is large dollar amounts tied up in raw materials, high storage costs, and large material handling costs. A second approach is where vendors deliver just in time. There is minimal need to store and very little picking and material handling. However, there could be extreme disruptions and cost if material is not available. These disruptions and cost could offset savings from not carrying inventory.

The key to success is to structure an organization's business processes in alignment with business conditions in its industry. Either of these two approaches to procurement could make sense for an organization. However, it is critical that the organization understand which approach makes the most economic and customer satisfaction sense so that goals are achieved.

Business process analysis helps determine the interdependencies among activities, their costs, and their outcomes. These interrelationships help provide a clearer view into the events that trigger different business processes.

By controlling the initial trigger of a nonvalue process, an organization can help to reduce or eliminate unnecessary work. Simultaneously, it can improve the outcome of required processes.

CREATING AN ACTIVITY BUDGET FOR YOUR DEPARTMENT: AN EXAMPLE

When an organization creates an activity-based budget, it must start with a business process workload that results from the customers of any business processes for which a department performs activities. In some cases, such as in a sales department, the customers of the business process are the same as the customer for the entire organization. In other cases, the customer of the business process will be internal customers from other departments. Example 8-1 will show how workload and activities drive the department's budget.

Example 8-1: Creating EZ Money Bank's Loan Officer Department Budget

The loan officer department has forecasted a total of 1,000 loans: 400 standard mortgages (less than $227,000), 100 jumbo mortgages (over $227,000), and 500 auto loans.

Creating an Activity Budget for Loan Officer Department

To achieve these outputs (evaluated, dispersed, and sold loans), the loan officer department must perform the following five activities:

1. Answer phone inquiries.
2. Take loan applications.
3. Evaluate loans.
4. Sell mortgages.
5. Manage loan officers and processors.

The loan officer department consists of three employees. They have expected benefits of 25 percent of salaries and the following expected salaries:

Position	Salary	#	Total Salary	Benefits %	Benefits Dollars	Grand Total
Loan officers	$32,000	2	$ 64,000	25%	$16,000	$ 80,000
Branch manager	$40,000	1	$ 40,000	25%	$10,000	$ 50,000
		3	$104,000		$26,000	$130,000

By focusing on outputs (budgeted loan volume), ABB can be used to forecast workload and thus more effectively and accurately create a meaningful budget. We will show how to budget for salaries, benefits, space, equipment, supplies, and phone.

Budgeting the Activity "Answer Phone Inquiries"

The first activity handled by the loan officer department is "answer phone inquiries." The loan officers estimate that the department will average three inquiries in order to obtain one loan. This business rule of three phone inquiries per loan is the same for mortgages and auto loans. In this example, the salaried branch manager and loan officers estimated that they will average 2,000 hours per year after vacations, holidays, and sick days:

2,088 hours (261 work days per year × 8 hours per day)
+   96 hours (unpaid overtime)
−   80 hours (vacation)
−   80 hours (holidays)
−   24 hours (personal/sick days)
2,000 hours budgeted per person

So how many people does this department need to perform the activity "answer phone inquiries"?

In order to budget for this activity, the loan officers develop some business rules:

1. Calculate the total workload (i.e., total number of loans they expect to process)

    400 standard mortgages
    100 jumbo mortgages
    500 auto loans

    1,000 loans
2. Multiply the total workload (i.e., 1,000 loans) by the average of three phone inquiries per loan to obtain the total workload for the activity "answer phone inquiries":

    1,000 loans × 3 phone inquiries per loan = 3,000 phone inquiries

The average phone inquiry requires 15 minutes for a loan officer to answer. Therefore, 3,000 phone inquiries, with a standard of 15 minutes per inquiry will require 45,000 minutes. Then divide 45,000 minutes by 60 minutes per hour to obtain 750 hours of loan officer time to answer phone inquiries.

    15 minutes standard per phone inquiry × 3,000 phone inquires
       = 45,000 minutes divided by 60 minutes per hour
       = 750 loan officer hours for answering phone inquiries

Now, we have determined that the workload to "answer phone inquiries" is 750 hours. We have already stated that the loan officers average 2,000 hours per year per full-time equivalent (FTE) loan officer. They earn $40,000 per year in salaries and benefits. Therefore, their hourly salaries and benefits are $20 per hour.

$40,000 in annual salaries and benefits ÷ 2,000 hours per year
= $20 per hour for loan officers

Once we have calculated that the loan officers earn $20 per hour for salaries and benefits, we can then calculate the budget for the activity "answer phone inquiries." To make this calculation, we multiply the 750 budgeted hours for the activity "answer phone inquiries" by the $20 per hour rate for salaries and benefits to derive a budgeted total of $15,000 of salaries and benefits for this activity.

750 loan officer hours for answering phone inquiries x $20 per hour
= $15,000 budgeted dollars for salaries and benefits

Thus, we created an activity budget in which we budgeted $15,000 for the activity "answer phone inquiries."

Budgeting the Activity "Take Loan Applications"

The second activity in the loan officer department is "take loan applications." With our forecasted number of 1,000 new loans, we must figure out how many applications the loan officers must take in order to have 1,000 new loans. Historically, approximately .889 of standard mortgage applications, .909 of jumbo mortgage applications, and .926 of auto loan applications are converted into loans. Therefore, to obtain 1,000 new loans, the loan officers will have to divide 1,000 new loans by the conversion ratio for each type of loan to determine the number of applications that must be taken.

400 standard mortgages ÷ .889 = approximately   450 applications
100 jumbo mortgages ÷ .909 = approximately   110 applications
500 auto loans ÷ .926 = approximately   540 applications

Total 1,100 applications

EZ Money Bank considers the features connected with loans. For the activity "take loan applications," the loan officers decide that the only feature that differs among loans is whether the bank is required to order private mortgage insurance (PMI). Only standard mortgages require PMI if the down payment is low.

The activity "take loan applications" takes only 30 seconds more time to record on the application when PMI is required. Because this is a small amount of time, the loan officers decide not to create a separate activity for marking on the loan application that PMI is required.

An average loan application is budgeted to take two hours to complete. Therefore, to determine the total workload (hours) required to perform the activity "take loan applications," multiply 1,100 loan applications by two hours per loan application to derive a workload of 2,200 hours for taking loan applications.

1,100 applications x 2 hours per application
= 2,200 loan officer hours taking applications

Previously, we budgeted that salaries and benefits for loan officers were $20 per hour. Now, we can multiply 2,200 budgeted hours for taking applications by our budgeted rate of $20 per hour to derive budgeted salaries and benefits of $44,000.

Budgeting the Activity "Evaluate Loan Applications"

The third activity for the loan officer department is "evaluate loan applications." From the budget for taking loan applications, they forecasted that 1,000 loans would require 1,100 applications. Therefore, the branch manager and two loan officers will have to evaluate 1,100 loan applications.

EZ Money Bank explores the features connected with different types of loans. It is determined that the features connected with standard mortgages and jumbo mortgages are the same. However, there are certain features connected with mortgages that are not present with auto loans.

For example, evaluating an auto loan application requires looking at the:

- Credit history
- Income
- Car value/blue book of car appraisals

Evaluating a mortgage requires looking at the:

- Credit history
- Income
- Appraisal
- Survey
- Title policy

These features for evaluating mortgages require significant extra time. This example assumes that mortgages take each loan officer and the branch manager an average of .893 hour to evaluate and that auto loans take each loan officer and the branch manager an average of .463 hour to evaluate. If the difference in time for different types of customers or loan officers with different experiences is small, using an average time for budgeting may make sense. If the differences in time for different types of customers or for loan officers with different types of experience is significant, then it may make sense to look at the features and characteristics of these different types of customers and incorporate them into the budgeting process.

There were 450 standard mortgage applications and 110 jumbo mortgage applications for a total of 560 mortgages. There were 540 auto loan applications. Each of the two loan officers and the branch manager evaluate loans. Therefore, to calculate the total workload, we must determine the total hours for both the loan officers and the branch manager.

First, multiply the 560 mortgage loans by .893 hour per mortgage by two loan officers and one branch manager to come up with the number of hours of workload for evaluating mortgages.

$$560 \text{ mortgages} \times .893 \text{ hour per mortgage} \times 2 \text{ loan officers}$$
$$= 1,000 \text{ hours of loan officer workload}$$

560 mortgages × .893 hour per mortgage × 1 branch manager
= 500 hours of branch manager workload

Second, multiply the 540 auto loans by .463 hour per auto loan by two loan officers and one branch manager to come up with the number of hours of workload for evaluating auto loans.

540 auto loans × .463 hour per auto loan × 2 loan officers
= 500 hours of loan officer workload to evaluate auto loans

540 auto loans × .463 hour per auto loan × 1 branch manager
= 250 hours of branch manager workload to evaluate auto loans

Then, add the total hours needed to evaluate the two major classes of loans. In this case, add the 1,000 hours of loan officer workload for evaluating mortgages and the 500 hours of loan officer workload for evaluating auto loans for a total of 1,500 hours of loan officer time.

	Workload (hours)	
Product	**By loan officers**	**By branch manager**
Mortgages	1,000	500
Auto loans	500	250
Total	1,500	750

Then multiply 1,000 budgeted loan officer hours for evaluating mortgages and 500 budgeted loan officer hours for evaluating auto loans by a budgeted rate of $20 per loan officer hour to derive budgeted loan officer salaries and benefits of $20,000 for evaluating mortgages and $10,000 for evaluating auto loans.

1,000 budgeted loan officer hours for mortgages × $20 per loan officer hour = $20,000

500 budgeted loan officer hours for auto loans × $20 per loan officer hour = $10,000

Then, multiply 500 budgeted branch manager hours for evaluating mortgages by a budgeted rate of $25 ($50,000 annual salaries and benefits divided by 2,000 hours) per branch manager hour to derive $12,500 budgeted branch manager salaries and benefits for the activity "evaluate mortgages."

500 branch manager hours × $25 per branch manager hour = $12,500

Then, multiply 250 budgeted branch manager hours for evaluating auto loans by a budgeted rate of $25 ($50,000 annual salaries and benefits divided by 2,000 hours) per branch manager hour to derive $6,250 budgeted branch manager salaries and benefits for the activity evaluate auto loans.

250 branch manager hours × $25 per branch manager hour = $6,250

This example illustrates that there are two types of loans (mortgages and auto loans) that must be evaluated. These loan types can be referred to as features. This example showed how to budget for these features: mortgages (both standard and jumbo) and auto loans.

Branch Manager Budgeting for the Activity "Sell Mortgages"

EZ Money Bank does not sell its auto loans. It only sells its mortgages. Budgeting for the activity "sell mortgages" involves understanding the different characteristics of selling standard versus jumbo mortgages. The tasks are the same for both types of mortgages. The tasks include:

Activity	Sell mortgages
Tasks	Identify buyer of mortgages
	Prepare mortgage documents for sale

However, even though the tasks are the same, it takes longer to perform the tasks for selling jumbo mortgages than for standard mortgages.

Each branch sells its own mortgages. There are 400 standard mortgages and 100 jumbo mortgages. Standard mortgages average about $100,000 each or a budgeted total of $40 million (400 mortgages multiplied by $100,000). They are usually bundled into $10 million batches for sale. Therefore, $40 million in total budgeted mortgages divided by $10 million batches results in four batches being sold this year. Each batch takes about 50 hours to prepare or approximately one-half hour per standard mortgage.

($40,000,000 in standard mortgages) / ($10,000,000/batch) = 4 batches

50 hours per batch × 4 batches = 200 hours or

1/2 hour per mortgage × 400 mortgages = 200 budgeted branch manager hours

The bank calculates the budgeted salaries and benefits for selling standard mortgages. This calculation is made by multiplying the budgeted workload of 200 hours for selling standard mortgages by the budgeted rate of $25 per hour to come up with $5,000 of budgeted branch manager salaries and benefits.

There are 100 jumbo mortgages. Jumbo mortgages average about $300,000 each or a budgeted total of $30 million (100 jumbo mortgages multiplied by $300,000). They are usually bundled in $3 million batches for resale. Therefore, $30 million in total budgeted jumbo mortgages divided by $3 million results in 10 batches being sold this year. Each batch takes about 30 hours to prepare or approximately three hours per jumbo mortgage.

($30,000,000 in standard mortgages) / ($3,000,000 per batch) = 10 batches

30 hours per batch × 10 batches = 300 budgeted branch manager hours

The bank calculates the budgeted branch manager salaries and benefits for selling jumbo mortgages by multiplying the budgeted number of hours required for selling jumbo mortgages by the budgeted rate of $25 per branch manager hour to yield $7,500 of budgeted salaries and benefits.

Three hundred budgeted branch manager hours times $25 per hour equals $7,500 of budgeted salaries and benefits. Therefore, the following budgeted salaries and benefits are required to sell standard and jumbo mortgages:

Salary Budget for Branch Manager to Sell Mortgage

Mortgage Type	FTEs	Workload	Hourly Rate	Salary & Benefits	Number of Mortgages
Standard	.10	200	$25	$5,000	400
Jumbo	.15	300	$25	$7,500	100
Total	.25	500	$25	$12,500	500

Therefore, the budgeted workload looks like the following:

Activity	Loan Officer Workload	Loan Officer FTE	Branch Manager Workload	Branch Manager FTE
Answer phone	750	.375		
Take application	2,200	1.1		
Evaluate:				
Mortgages	1,000	.50		
			500	.25
Auto loans	500	.25		
			250	.125
Sell mortgages:				
standard			200	.10
jumbo			300	.15
Manage loan processors			200	.10
Manage loan officers			200	.10
Total	4,450	2.225	1,650	.825
Available	4,000	2.0	2,000	1.0
Over/Under available	450 O		350 U	

This preliminary budget shows that there is more work than the two loan officers can handle given the above conditions. The branch manager has more hours available than workload. After reviewing options and process improvements, the loan officers and branch manager agree that the branch manager will take some loan applications.

The branch manager sees that there are 450 hours of workload that must be addressed in the preliminary budget.

4,450 budgeted hours for loan officers – 4,000 available hours for loan officers = 450 hours of workload that require capacity

Taking mortgage applications takes two hours per mortgage. The branch manager currently has a workload of 1,650 hours. If she budgets herself for the entire 450 hours of capacity required for helping the loan officers take applications, she will be working 2,100 hours.

Branch Manager

1,650	current hours budgeted
+ 450	hours budgeted to take loan applications
= 2,100	hours of workload for revised budget

Because the spring and summer are heavy mortgage periods, she has requested that the loan officers and herself take their vacations in the fall or winter. She thinks this will address the seasonality issues. She plans to create a monthly budget of workload based on previous years to check her assumptions. The revised budget now looks like the following:

	Loan Officer		Branch Manager		Grand
Activity	**Workload**	**FTEs**	**Workload**	**FTE**	**Total**
Answer phone	750	.375			750
Take application	**1,750**	**.875**			
			450	**.225**	**2,200**
Evaluate loans:					
Mortgages	1,000	.50			1,000
			500	.25	500
Auto loans	500	.25			500
			250	.125	250
Sell mortgages:					
Standard			200	.10	200
Jumbo			300	.15	300
Manage loan					
processors			200	.10	200
Manage loan					
officers			200	.10	200
Budgeted total	4,000	2.0	**2,100**	1.05	6,100
Available	4,000		2,100	with overtime	6,100

Now that the budgeted workload has been matched with the available resources, EZ Money Bank can now calculate the updated budget for salaries and benefits. The budgeted loan officer rate for salaries and benefits remains at $20 per hour ($40,000 divided by 2,000 hours). The budgeted branch manager rate for salaries and benefits is now $23.81.

$50,000 ÷ 2,100 (2,000 + 100 overtime) budgeted hours
= $23.81 per hour for salaries and benefits

Activity	Loan Officer		Branch Manager		Salary Dollars	Total
	Workload	Rate	Workload	Rate		
Answer phone	750	$20			$15,000	$15,000
Take application	1,750	$20	450	$23.81	$35,000 $10,714	$45,714
Evaluate mortgages	1,000	$20	500	$23.81	$20,000 $11,905	$31,905
Evaluate auto loans	500	$20	250	$23.81	$10,000 $5,952	$15,952
Sell standard mortgages			200	$23.81	$4,762	$4,762
Sell jumbo mortgages			300	$23.81	$7,143	$7,143
Manage loan processors			200	$23.81	$4,762	$4,762
Manage loan officers			200	$23.81	$4,762	$4,762
Total	4,000		2,100		$130,000	$130,000

Budgeting the Cost of Space, Equipment, Supplies, and Phone

When budgeting expenses for space, equipment, travel/meals, and other miscellaneous items, keep in mind that it is very common for some activities to occur independent of an organization's resources. Resources should be budgeted only for those activities that are directly related to that department.

In this example, EZ Money Bank pays rent of $20 per square foot per year for the space it occupies. This rent figure includes all maintenance. EZ Money Bank believed that it should budget facilities (rent) costs based on square footage to the department and then assign rent cost with a department based on hours within a department. The branch manager's office is the same size as the offices of the loan officers and loan processors. The square footage for the loan officer department is 600 square feet, or 200 square feet per person. This 600 square feet is evenly distributed between the two loan officers and the branch manager and equals 200 square feet per person.

The total budget for the loan officer department is $12,000 (600 square feet multiplied by $20 per square foot). Therefore, the rent budget for each person in this department is $4,000 (200 square feet multiplied by $20 per square foot). This department believes it is valuable to budget all expenses based on hours worked. Therefore, they develop a rental rate for each position: loan officers and branch managers. This rental rate is calculated by dividing the total budgeted rental rate per person ($4,000) by the budgeted hours worked:

Position	Budgeted Rental/Person	Budgeted Hours	Budgeted Rate/Hour
Loan officer	$4,000	2,000	$2.00
Branch manager	$4,000	2,100	$1.905

Therefore, the budgeted rent can be traced to the activities in this department as follows:

Loan Officer Department: Rental Space Budget

Activity	Workload in Hours	Rental Rate/ Hour	Loan Officer	Total Branch Manager Budget $
Answer phone inquiries	750	$2		$1,500
Take loan	1,750	$2		$3,500
applications	450	$1.905		$857
Evaluate:				
Mortgages	1,000	$2		$2,000
Auto loans	500	$2		$1,000
Mortgages	500	$1.905		$953
Auto loans	250	$1.905		$476
Sell mortgages:				
Standard	200	$1.905		$381
Jumbo	300	$1.905		$571
Manage loan officers	200	$1.905		$381
Manage loan processors	200	$1.905		$381
Total loan officer space budget			6,100	$12,000

Now that the space budget has been determined, we will move on to EZ Money's equipment budget for the loan officer department. The equipment budget includes a desk, chair, cubicle, and computer. Total depreciation and computer maintenance charges for equipment are budgeted as follows for the coming year:

Department	Equipment Budget
Loan officers	$30,000

There are different models of personal computers, varying in age, in these depart-ments. Some are fully depreciated and some are brand new. EZ Money Bank de-cides that it is not worth breaking out the more expensive computers from the other computers.

The total budget for the loan officer department is $30,000. Therefore, the equipment budget for each person in this department is $10,000 per person ($30,000 divided by three people). Again, this department believes that it is valuable to budget all expenses based on hours worked. Therefore, they develop an equipment rate for each position: loan officers and branch managers. This equipment rate is calculated by dividing the total budgeted equipment rate per person ($10,000) by the budgeted hours worked.

Position	Budgeted Rental/Person	Budgeted Hours	Budgeted Rate/Hour
Loan officer	$10,000	2,000	$5.00
Branch manager	$10,000	2,100	$4.76

Therefore, the budgeted rent can be traced to the activities in this department. Based on this budgeted information, they create a budgeted hourly rate for the loan officer department as follows. Each person in the loan officer department is budgeted $10,000 for his or her equipment and computers. Therefore, take $10,000 divided by 2,000 loan officer hours to derive a rate of $5 per loan officer hour for budgeted equipment and computer charges. Follow the same procedure for calculating the branch manager's budgeted equipment rate per hour.

Loan Officer Department: Equipment Budget

Activity	Workload in Hours	Rate/Hour Officer	Rate/Hour Manager	Total Budget $
Answer phone inquiries	750	$5		$3,750
Take loan applications	1,750	$5		$8,750
	450		$4.76	$2,143
Evaluate:				
Mortgages	1,000	$5		$5,000
Auto loans	500	$5		$2,500
Mortgages	500		$4.76	$2,381
Auto loans	250		$4.76	$1,190
Sell mortgages:				
Standard	200		$4.76	$952
Jumbo	300		$4.76	$1,428
Manage loan officers	200		$4.76	$953
Manage loan processors	200		$4.76	$953
Total loan officer equipment budget	6,100			$30,000

The supplies budget will be budgeted only for the activity "take loan applications." This department estimates that each loan application costs about one dollar. The use of other supplies is minimal and not to be budgeted for separately. Therefore, $1 per application multiplied by a budgeted 1,100 applications equals $1,100 of budgeted supplies for the activity "take loan applications."

Loan Officer Department: Supplies Budget

Activity	Volume	Unit Cost	Total Budget $
Answer phone inquiries			
Take loan applications	1,100	$1	$1,100
Evaluate loans			
Sell mortgages			
Manage loan officers			
Manage loan processors			
Total supplies budget			$1,100

Budgeting Telephone Expenses

Finally, EZ Money Bank must budget for telephone expenses. The telephone budget for this department is $600 per person. Again, this department believes it is valuable to budget all expenses based on hours worked. Therefore, they develop a telephone rate for each position: loan officers and branch managers. This equipment rate is calculated by dividing the total budgeted equipment rate per person ($600) by the budgeted hours worked:

Position	Budgeted Rental/Person	Budgeted Hours	Budgeted Rate/Hour
Loan officer	$600	2,000	$.30
Branch manager	$600	2,100	$.286

Loan Officer Department: Telephone Equipment Budget

Activity	Workload	Loan Officer	Branch Manager	Total Budget $
Answer phone inquiries	750	$.30		$225
Take loan applications	1,750	$.30		$525
	450		$.286	$128
Evaluate:				
Mortgages	1,000	$.30		$300
Auto loans	500	$.30		$150
Mortgages	500		$.286	$143
Auto loans	250		$.286	$72

Loan Officer Department: Telephone Equipment Budget

Activity	Workload	Loan Officer	Branch Manager	Total Budget
Sell mortgages:				
Standard	200		$.286	$57
Jumbo	300		$.286	$86
Manage loan officers	200		$.286	$57
Manage loan processors	200		$.286	$57
Total loan officer phone budget				1,800

Long distance charges are placed mainly to corporate and to sell the mortgages. Based on historical experience, there will be daily calls to corporate, averaging $10 day for 240 days or $2,400. There will be weekly calls to investors, which also average $10 each for a total of $500. The following table shows the average time per phone call for the various activities performed in the department.

Loan Officer Department: Telephone Equipment—Long Distance Charges

Activity	Workload	Loan Officer	Branch Manager	Total Budget
Answer phone inquiries				
Take loan applications				
Evaluate loans				
Sell mortgages	50 calls	$10		$500
Manage loan officers	240 calls	$10		$2,400
Manage loan processors				
Total loan officer long distance budget				$2,900

Now that the various expense elements for each activity have been budgeted, the departments can total all of these budgeted cost elements to obtain the total budgeted cost for each activity. It also can determine the total budgeted cost to complete all of the activities of this department. (See table on following page.)

The branch manager decides to assign her secondary activities based on the loan officers' and loan processors' workload. The two loan processors each have a workload of 2,000 hours per year for a total of 4,000 hours. Therefore, she takes the total cost of the secondary activity "manage loan officers" ($6,153) and divides it by 4,000 loan officer hours to come up with an assignment rate of $1.54 per budgeted loan officer workload. Therefore, the assignment of this secondary activity would be calculated as follows:

Loan Officer Department Budget By Activity

Activity	Workload	Salaries/ Benefits	Rent	Equipment	Supplies	Telephone	Phone (Long Distance)	Subtotal	Total
Answer phone inquiries	750	$15,000	$1,500	$3,750		$225		$20,475	20,475
Take loan applications	1,750	$35,000	$3,500	$8,750	$1,100	$52		$48,875	
	450	$10,714	$857	$2,143		$128		$13,842	$62,717
Evaluate:									
Mortgages	1,000	$20,000	$2,000	$5,000		$300		$27,300	
Mortgages	500	$11,905	$953	$2,381		$143		$15,382	$42,682
Auto loans	500	$10,000	$1,000	$2,500		$150		$13,650	
Auto loans	250	$5,952	$476	$1,190		$72		$7,690	$21,340
Sell mortgages:									
Standard	200	$4,762	$381	$952		$57	$400	$6,552	
Jumbo	300	$7,143	$571	$1,428		$86	$100	$9,328	$15,880
Manage loan processors	200	$4,762	$381	$953		$57	$2,400	$8,553	$8,553
Manage loan officers	200	$4,762	$381	$953		$57		$6,153	$6,153
Total	6,100	$130,000	$12,000	$30,000	$1,100	$1,800	$2,900		$177,800

Assigning Budgeted Secondary Activities to Budgeted Primary Activities for EZ Money Bank Loan Officer Department

Activity	Workload	Primary Total	Secondary	Total With Secondary
Answer phone inquiries	750	$20,475	$1,154	$21,629
Take loan applications	1,750	$62,717	$2,692	$65,409
Evaluate:				
Mortgages	1,000	$42,682	$1,538	$44,220
Auto loans	500	$21,340	$769	$22,109
Sell mortgages:				
Standard	200	$6,552		$6,552
Jumbo	300	$9,328		$9,328
Manage loan processors	200	$8,553		$8,553
Manage loan officers	200	$6,153	(6,153)	
Total		$177,800		$177,800

Now the branch can enter the various workload volumes for each activity in order to calculate the budgeted activity unit cost. Some activities, such as "answer phone inquiries" and "take loan applications," take the same amount of time regardless of the type of loan. Other activities, such as "evaluate loans" and "sell mortgages," require more or less time, depending on the type of mortgage or loan. For example, it takes .893 hour to evaluate a mortgage—standard or jumbo—but it takes only .463 hour to evaluate an auto loan. There were 560 mortgages and 540 auto loans.

Loan Officer Budgeted Activity Unit Cost

Activity	Workload Total	Total	Budgeted Volume	Output Measure	Unit Cost
Answer phone inquiries	750	$21,629	3,000	Inquiries	$7.21
Take loan applications	2,200	$65,409	1,100	Applications	$59.46
Evaluate:					
Mortgages	1,500	$44,220	560	Applications	$78.96
Auto loans	750	$22,109	540	Applications	$40.94
Sell mortgages:					
Standard	200	$9,328	4	Batches	$2,332
Jumbo	300	$6,552	10	Batches	$655

Loan Officer Budgeted Activity Unit Cost

Activity	Workload Total	Total	Budgeted Volume	Output Measure	Unit Cost
Manage loan processors	200	$8,553			
Manage loan officers					
Total budget		$177,800			

The budget would be submitted to the process manager as well as senior management for review. The branch manager should also review their activities to determine if they are still part of the same business processes as they were last year. In this department, all activities are considered part of the business process entitled "acquire loans."

Budgeting For the Loan Application Processing Department

The loan application processing department consists of two people. They have two activities:

1. *Order reports*
2. *Dispense funds*

For mortgages, they order four reports:

1. Credit history
2. Title
3. Survey
4. Appraisal

For auto loans, they order two reports:

1. Credit history
2. MVR

Budgeting for the Activity "Order Reports"

The activity "order reports" has different features for mortgage versus auto applications. For mortgages, the bank orders four reports. For auto loans, the bank orders only two reports.

There are 560 mortgage applications. Each mortgage application requires four reports: credit history, title, survey, and appraisal. Each report takes about 15 minutes to order and review. Therefore, the workload for ordering reports for mortgages is 560 mortgage applications multiplied by 15 minutes per report multiplied by four reports per mortgage equals 560 loan processor hours.

560 applications × 15 minutes per report × 4 reports per application
= 560 loan processor hours

There are 540 budgeted auto loan applications. Each auto loan application requires two reports: credit history and MVR. Each report takes about 15 minutes to order and review. Therefore, the workload for ordering reports for mortgages is 540 auto loan applications multiplied by 15 minutes per report multiplied by two reports per mortgage equals 270 hours.

540 applications × 15 minutes per report × 2 reports per application
= 270 loan processor hours

Therefore, the total workload for ordering reports is the sum of 560 loan processor hours for mortgages and 270 loan processor hours for auto loans for a total of 830 loan processor hours.

Loan processors earn $24,000 in salaries plus $6,000 (25 percent of salaries) in benefits for a total of $30,000. As an alternative to calculating a rate per hour, this department decides to budget by looking at FTEs. They calculate the number of loan processor FTEs required to order reports by dividing 830 budgeted hours for ordering reports by 2,000 hours per year to yield .415 FTE.

830 loan processor hours / 2,000 loan processor hours per year = .415 FTE

They multiply .415 loan processor FTE by loan processor annual salaries and benefits of $30,000 to yield $12,450 of budgeted loan processor salaries and benefits for the activity "order reports."

.415 FTE × $30,000 = $12,450 in budgeted loan processor salaries and benefits

Based on the above calculation, they created the following activity budget:

Activity	Workload Hours	FTEs	Salary Dollars
Order reports	830	.415	$12,450

Budgeting the Activity "Order Reports Using Features"

Another way to budget for this is to use the concept of features. The example will assume that it takes about the same amount of time to order each of the reports. Therefore, if it takes 15 minutes to order a report, mortgages take 1 hour (4 reports multiplied by 15 minutes) and auto loans take one-half hour (2 reports multiplied by 15 minutes per report). The average time of mortgages (1 hour) and auto loans (one-half hour) is 45 minutes. Next, calculate the percentage that the budgeted time is over or under the average time. For example, the budgeted time for mortgages is 1 hour and the average time of mortgages and auto loans is 45 minutes. Therefore, the budgeted time of 1 hour is 33 percent over the average time (60 minutes divided by 45 minutes equals 133 percent).

Loan Type	Number of Reports	Average Time/ Report	Budgeted Time	Average Time	% Budget Is From Average Time
Mortgages	4	15 minutes	1 hour	45 minutes	1.3333
Auto	2	15 minutes	1/2 hour	45 minutes	.6667

Knowing that the average time is 45 minutes and the percentage difference, EZ Money Bank can now calculate the workload. They would multiply the number of mortgage applications (560) by the average time of 45 minutes by the fraction that budgeted time is over or under the average time.

$$560 \text{ mortgages} \times 45 \text{ minutes average} \times 1.333 = 560 \text{ hours}$$
$$+ \; 540 \text{ auto loans} \times 45 \text{ minutes average} \times .6667 \quad = \quad \underline{270 \text{ hours}}$$
$$830 \text{ hours in total}$$

Obviously, using the concept of features allows the organization to use only one activity—"order reports." It gives insights into what features cause the organizations to spend more time and money in ordering reports. Using features may give the organization different insights into its processes. It can start asking why it takes more time to order reports for one type of loan than for another. In this example, we knew that answer ahead of time. However, if we did not know the answer, features may give us additional insights into the features of different products and services that drive our cost.

Budgeting for the Activity "Disperse Funds"

The second activity for the loan processing department is dispensing funds to the approved loan applicants. EZ Money Bank budgeted 1,000 total loans, of which 500 were auto loans, 400 were standard mortgages, and 100 were jumbo mortgages.

Dispersing funds includes all tasks connected with dispensing the funds to mortgagors. An average loan closing for a mortgage takes a loan processor 3.2 hours whether it is a standard or a jumbo mortgage. An average loan closing for an auto loan takes a loan processor one hour. These times include preparation and paperwork after the closing. Dispersing funds for a mortgage takes more time than for an auto loan because there are more legal documents. For example, an auto loan requires only recording the lien. A mortgage requires recording the mortgage and the loan lien, ordering the title policy, and preparing the appraisal, survey, lien, and mortgage for storage.

Therefore, the loan processor workload for dispersing funds for mortgages would be 500 mortgages multiplied by 3.2 hours per mortgage, or 1,600 loan processor hours.

$$500 \text{ mortgages} \times 3.2 \text{ hours per mortgage} = 1,600 \text{ loan processor hours}$$

The loan processors like to analyze their operations in terms of FTEs. This is a different approach than that of the loan officer department, which wanted to look at everything in terms of hours worked.

The loan processors convert the workload of 1,600 loan processor hours for dispersing mortgages divided by 2,000 budgeted loan processor hours per loan processor, which equals .8 loan processor FTE.

1,600 hours / 2,000 hours per FTE = .80 loan processor FTE

They then multiply .80 FTE by the average budgeted salaries and benefits for loan processors of $30,000 to derive $24,000 of budgeted salaries and benefits for dispersing funds for mortgages.

The workload for dispersing funds for auto loans would be 500 auto loans multiplied by 1 hour per auto loan, or 500 loan processor hours.

500 auto loans x 1 hour per auto loan = 500 loan processor hours

The loan processors convert the workload of 500 loan processor hours for dispersing auto loans divided by 2,000 budgeted loan processor hours per loan processor equals .25 loan processor FTE.

500 hours / 2,000 hours per FTE = .25 loan processor FTE

They then multiply .25 FTE by the average budgeted salaries and benefits for loan processors of $30,000 to derive $7,500 of budgeted salaries and benefits for dispensing funds for mortgages.

Therefore, the budgeted workload, FTEs, plus salaries and benefits would look like the following:

Activity	Workload	FTEs	Salaries & Benefits
Disperse funds:			
Mortgages	1,600	.8	$24,000
Auto loans	500	.25	$7,500

The branch decided to break out dispersing funds into two activities, because dispersing funds for mortgages takes different amounts of time than dispersing funds for auto loans. Using an average of the two types of loans would distort the cost of mortgages and auto loans. Therefore, the branch divided this activity into two subactivities called "disperse mortgages" and "disperse auto loans."

Budgeting for the Activity "Process Private Mortgage Insurance"

One of the features of standard loans is that loan applicants who have a small down payment are required to purchase private mortgage insurance. EZ Money Bank only allows small down payments on standard loans. EZ Money's purchasing of jumbo loans does not permit small down payments.

The loan officers estimate that half of the 400 standard mortgages (200) will require private mortgage insurance. The loan processors set a target of two hours to process the private mortgage insurance. Therefore, 200 standard mortgages requiring private mortgage insurance multiplied by two hours to process the private mortgage insurance equals a budgeted workload of 400 hours to process private mortgage insurance.

200 standard mortgages requiring private mortgage insurance
x 2 hours to process private mortgage insurance
= 400 loan processor hours to process private mortgage insurance

They then calculate the number of loan processor FTEs processing private mortgage insurance would require. They divide 400 loan processor hours by 2,000 hours per FTE to yield .2 loan processor FTE.

400 loan processor hours / 2,000 annual hours per FTE
= .2 loan processor FTE

They then multiply the number of FTEs by the loan processors' annual budgeted salary and benefits of $30,000 to obtain $6,000 of budgeted salaries and benefits for processing private mortgage insurance.

.2 loan processor FTE × $30,000 per loan processor
= $6,000 of budgeted loan processor salaries and benefits

Therefore, the total workload for this loan processing department is:

.415 FTE for ordering reports
.80 FTE for dispersing mortgages
.25 FTE for dispersing auto loans
.2 FTE for processing PMI
1.665 FTE total

This is a budgeted total of 1.665 FTEs. The loan processors feel they have a variety of miscellaneous activities that take up the rest of their time. The branch manager and loan processors decide to budget this .335 FTE for miscellaneous activities.

They also decide to investigate during the year what work is being done in this miscellaneous activities category. Then they can decide if these miscellaneous activities are the best use of the loan processors' time.

Activity	FTE Loan Processor	Annual Salaries & Benefits	Activity Salaries & Benefits
Order reports	.415	$30,000	$12,450
Disperse funds—mortgages	.80	$30,000	$24,000
Disperse funds—auto loans	.25	$30,000	$7,500
Process PMI	.20	$30,000	$6,000
Subtotal	1.665	$30,000	$49,950
Miscellaneous	.335	$30,000	$10,050
Department total	2.000		$60,000

Budgeting Loan Processor Space, Equipment, Supplies, and Phone

In this example, EZ Money Bank pays rent of $20 per square foot per year for the space it occupies. This rent figure includes all maintenance. EZ Money Bank believed that it should budget facilities (rent) costs based on square footage to the department and then assign rent cost with a department based on hours within a department. The square footage for the loan processors is 400 square feet for two loan processors, or 200 square feet per loan processor. When the budgeted rent of $20 per square foot is multiplied by 200 square feet per FTE, this calculation yields $4,000 per person.

Therefore, budgeted rent can be traced to the two loan processors as follows:

Determination of Budgeted Rent (Space): Loan Processor Department

Activity	Workload in FTEs	Rental Rate/FTE	Total Budget $
Order reports	.415	$4,000	$1,660
Disperse funds:			
Mortgages	.80	$4,000	$3,200
Auto loans	.25	$4,000	$1,000
Process PMI	.20	$4,000	$800
Miscellaneous capacity	.335	$4,000	$1,340
Total processor space budget	2.00		$8,000

Now that the space budget has been determined, we will move on to EZ Money's equipment budget for the loan processor department. The equipment budget includes a desk, chair, cubicle, and computer. Total depreciation and computer maintenance charges for equipment are budgeted as follows for the coming year:

Department	Equipment Budget
Loan processors	$20,000

There are different model personal computers, varying in age, in these departments. Some are fully depreciated and some are brand new. EZ Money Bank decides that it is not worth breaking out the more expensive computers from the other computers.

Based on this budgeted information, they create a budgeted equipment rate per FTE for the loan processor department as follows: Each person in the loan processor department is budgeted $10,000 ($20,000 divided by two loan processors) for his or her equipment and computers.

Determination of Loan Processor Equipment Budget

Activity	Workload in FTEs	Rental Rate/FTE	Total Budget $
Order reports	.415	$10,000	$4,150
Disperse funds:			
Mortgages	.80	$10,000	$8,000
Auto loans	.25	$10,000	$2,500
Process PMI	.20	$10,000	$2,000
Miscellaneous capacity	.335	$10,000	$3,350
Total processor equipment budget	2.00		$20,000

The supplies budget will be budgeted only for the activity "disperse funds." The use of other supplies is minimal and to be budgeted for separately. The supplies budget for the activity "disperse funds" is $5 per loan times 1,000 loans, or $5,000.

Determination of Loan Processor Supplies Budget

Activity	Workload	Activity $ per FTE	Total Budget $
Order reports			
Disperse funds:			
Mortgages	500	$5/mortgage	$2,500
Auto loans	500	$5/auto loan	$2,500
Miscellaneous activities			
Total supplies budget			$5,000

Finally, EZ Money Bank must budget for telephone expenses. The phone charge is $600 per year per person for a phone on each desk and local calls.

Budget for Loan Processor Telephone Equipment

Activity	Workload in FTEs	Activity $ per FTE	Total Budget $
Order reports	.415	$600	$250
Disperse funds:			
Mortgages	.80	$600	$480
Auto loans	.25	$600	$150
Process PMI	.20	$600	$120
Miscellaneous activities	.335	$600	$200
Total phone budget	2.00		$1,200

Now that the various expense elements for each activity have been budgeted for, the loan processor department can total all of these elements together to obtain the total budgeted cost for each activity. It also then can determine a total budgeted cost of resources needed to complete all of the activities of this department. (See table on the following page.)

Now the loan processor department can enter the various workload volumes for each activity in order to calculate the budgeted activity unit cost. For the activity order reports, the loan processors use the following calculation to determine the activity volume:

Loan Type	Number of Loan Applications	Number of Reports/ Loan	Budgeted Volume
Mortgages	560	4	2,240
Auto	540	2	1,080
			3,320

Now the branch manager must assign her budgeted amount for managing loan processors as a secondary activity to the primary activities in the loan processing

Loan Processor Budget for Each Activity

Activity	FTEs	Salaries/ Benefits	Rent	Equipment	Supplies	Phone	Total
Order reports	.415	$12,450	$1,660	$4,150		$250	$18,510
Disperse funds:							
Mortgages	.80	$24,000	$3,200	$8,000	$2,500	$480	$38,180
Auto loans	.25	$7,500	$1,000	$2,500	$2,500	$150	$13,650
Process PMI	.20	$6,000	$800	$2,000		$120	$8,920
Miscellaneous	.335	$10,050	$1,340	$3,350		$200	$14,940
Total budget	2.00	$60,000	$8,000	$20,000	$5,000	$1,200	$94,200

department. She does this by assigning this secondary activity to all primary activities based on FTEs, including the FTEs for the miscellaneous activities.

The total cost of the secondary activity "manage loan processors" is $8,553. This amount is assigned from the loan officer department to the loan processor department. This amount is assigned based on two FTEs. The manager simply divides $8,553 by two FTEs to derive an assignment of $4,276.50 per FTE.

Assigning Budgeted Secondary Activities

Activities	FTEs	Total	Secondary Activities	Total $ with Secondary
Order reports	.415	$18,510	$1,775	$20,285
Disperse funds:				
Mortgages	.80	$38,180	$3,421	$41,601
Auto loans	.25	$13,650	$1,069	$14,719
Process PMI	.20	$ 8,920	$855	$9,775
Miscellaneous	.335	$14,940	$1,433	$16,373
Manage loan processors		$ 8,553	($8,553)	$0
Total budget	2.00	$94,200	$0	$102,753 includes $8,553

Budgeted Activity Unit Cost: Loan Processor Department

Activity	FTEs	Total	Budgeted Volume	Unit Cost
Order reports	.415	$20,285	3,320	$6.11
Disperse funds:				
Mortgages	.80	$41,601	500	$83.20
Auto loans	.25	$14,719	500	$29.44
Process PMI	.20	$9,775	200	$48.88
Miscellaneous	.335	$16,373	1	
Total budget	2.00	$102,753		

This budget would be submitted to the process manager as well as senior management for review. The branch manager should also review their activities to determine if they are still part of the same business processes as they were last year. In this department, all activities are considered part of the business process entitled "acquire loans."

Activity	Business Process
Answer phone inquiries	Acquire loans
Take loan application	Acquire loans
Evaluate loans	Acquire loans
Sell mortgages	Acquire loans
Manage loan processors	Acquire loans

Activity	Business Process
Manage loan officers	Acquire loans
Order reports	Acquire loans
Disperse funds	Acquire loans
Process PMI	Acquire loans
Miscellaneous	Acquire loans

The department has assigned the secondary activities "manage loan processors" and "manage loan officers" to each of the primary activities:

Department	Primary Activities
Loan officers	Answer phone inquiries
	Take loan applications
	Evaluate mortgages
	Evaluate auto loans
	Sell mortgages—standard
	Sell mortgages—jumbo
Loan processors	Order reports
	Disperse funds—mortgages
	Disperse funds—auto loans
	Process PMI

All activities are connected with the one business process, one channel of distribution, and only one major service/product line (i.e., consumer loans).

For now, they decide to leave miscellaneous activities as a nontraceable activity. This will not be added into the cost of the service they provide. Instead, it will be treated like other nontraceable expenses such as the president of the bank, the tax department, public relations, etc. If the bank decided it wanted fully loaded costs for product costing purposes, it would treat miscellaneous activities as a secondary activity and assign it to the primary activities in a manner similar to "manage loan processors." They might assign it based on FTEs, dollars spent on primary activities, or logic.

In this example, miscellaneous activities were found. There are two loan processors in the loan processor department. Of this amount, 1.665 FTEs were needed to perform the workload that was forecasted. In many departments/cost centers, miscellaneous capacity will exist. When this is found, the organization must decide what is the best action to take concerning miscellaneous activities. In some cases, miscellaneous activities are really just excess capacity in disguise. In other cases, the budget will allow for a variety of activities that take a small amount of time and may not be worth tracking individually.

As a result of the budgeting process, the EZ Money Bank branch can now produce both a traditional cost element budget and an activity and business process budget. The traditional cost element budget shows salaries, rent, equipment, supplies, phone equipment, and phone long distance. The activity budget shows the various activities for this department/cost center.

Only the activity budget would be shown to the process manager and/or senior management. If either the process manager or senior management had questions about the activity budget, the methodology for creating the activity budget would be shown to them. However, the traditional cost element budget would not be shown to them unless they asked. What is important is to think in terms of activities and business processes rather than cost elements.

CREATING A PRODUCT OR SERVICE COSTING BUSINESS PROCESS BUDGET

Once the unit costs for each activity in a product or service have been budgeted, then the organization can create a budgeted bill of activities for those products and services. For EZ Money Bank, we have budgeted the branch portion of the business process " acquire loans." The budgeted bill of activities shows the following:

- All the activities for the product or service
- The budgeted activity unit cost
- The budgeted volumes for each activity
- The total cost for each activity
- The grand total

Budgeted Bill of Activities for Business Process "Acquire Loans" for 400 Standard Mortgages

Activity	Rules Budgeted Volume	Budgeted Factor Unit Cost	Budgeted Total Cost
Answer phone inquiries	3/mortgage = 1,200	$7.21	$8,652
Take loan applications	1.125/mortgage = 450	$59.46	$26,758
Evaluate loans	1.125/mortgage = 450	$78.96	$35,533
Sell standard mortgages	100/ Batch = 4	$2,332 (batch)	$9,328
Order reports	4/application = 1,800	$ 6.11	$10,998
Disperse funds	1/loan = 400	$83.20	$33,280
Process PMI	50% × 400 loans = 200	$48.88	$9,776
Total budgeted cost for standard mortgages			$134,325
Budgeted standard mortgages			400
Budgeted cost per unit for standard mortgages			$336

Budgeted Bill of Activities for Business Process "Acquire Loans" for 100 Jumbo Mortgages

Activity	Rules Budgeted Volume	Budgeted Unit Cost	Budgeted Total Cost
Answer phone inquiries	3/mortgage = 300	$7.21	$2,163
Take loan applications	1.1/mortgage = 110	$59.46	$6,542
Evaluate loans	1.1/mortgage = 110	$78.96	$8,687
Sell mortgages	10/Batch = 10	$655	$6,550
Order reports	4/application = 440	$6.11	$2,688
Disperse funds	1/loan = 100	$83.20	$8,320
Process PMI			
Total budget cost for jumbo mortgages			$34,950
Total budgeted jumbo mortgages			100
Budgeted cost per unit for jumbo mortgages			$349

Budgeted Bill of Activities for Business Process Acquire Loans for 500 Auto Loans

Activity	Rules Budgeted Volume	Budgeted Unit Cost	Budgeted Total Cost
Answer phone inquiries	3/mortgage = 1,500	$7.21	$10,815
Take loan applications	1.08/loan = 540	$59.46	$32,109
Evaluate loans	1.08/loan = 540	$40.94	$22,108
Sell mortgages			
Order reports	2/application = 1080	$6.11	$6,599
Disperse funcs	1/loan = 500	$29.44	$14,720
Process PMI			
Total budgeted cost for auto loans			$86,351
Total budgeted auto loan volume			500
Total budgeted unit cost for auto loans			$173

To check this, the branch adds up the budgeted total product costs for all three types of loans: standard and jumbo mortgages plus auto loans. This total corresponds with the total budgeted resources for the two departments: loan officers ($177,800) and loan processors ($94,200).

Loan Type	Product Cost
Standard mortgages	134,325
Jumbo mortgages	34,950
Auto loans	86,351
Miscellaneous*	16,373
Total	272,000

*Miscellaneous is treated as nontraceable

The purpose of producing a budgeted product cost is to compare this amount with the organization's targeted cost. The marketplace tells the bank what they are willing to pay for mortgages and auto loans. Senior management tells the branch what targeted profit they desire. The targeted cost is simply the market price minus the targeted profit set by senior management. It is up to the employees to budget to meet the targeted cost.

SUMMARY

Example 8-1 gave a step-by-step procedure for creating an activity-based budget for a mortgage branch office of a bank. Breaking down this department's budget into activities and business processes helps management get a clear view of the actual costs involved in this portion of their business process of acquiring loans. These techniques can be applied to any department or cost center. Just follow the same procedures outlined here.

The reader should complete this section by realizing that:

- An activity-based budget is a more logical approach to budgeting. It is defined by the organization's activities rather than just resources (salaries, rent, equipment, supplies).
- An activity-based budget is based on workload versus a traditional budget, which is often based on increasing or decreasing budgets as sales increase or decrease.
- Management must consider workload as the key to a successful value-driven plan.

Once management obtains its clear view of a budgeted business process and activity cost, it can then turn its attention to ensuring that the organizational strategy has been incorporated into its business processes and activities. Successful organizations have found ways to make every employee's role a necessary and invaluable part of the overall workings of the organization. This success is achieved by "cascading" organizational strategies down through their activities and business processes. This philosophy states that all process workers have important jobs. They must understand how their activities contribute to organization goals.

Introducing the Concept of Customer Characteristics

In the previous example, we assumed that all jumbo and standard mortgages and auto loan applications took an average time to evaluate them. This may not be a good assumption if it takes longer to evaluate some mortgage applications than it does other mortgage applications. Although there is an average time to evaluate mortgages, there may be significant customer characteristics that drive this average time.

To illustrate this, we will revisit EZ Money Bank using the concept of customer characteristics. EZ Money Bank reviews a sample of loans and determines that two major customer characteristics affect the amount of time it takes to evaluate a mortgage: monthly loan payments as a percentage of monthly income and marketable assets as a percentage of loan.

The mortgage applications that take the least amount of time are those applications in which the applicant will spend less than 25 percent of his or her monthly income on mortgage payments and his or her marketable assets exceed the amount of the loan. Conversely, those mortgage applications that take the longest and result in the most rejections are ones in which the applicant has monthly loan payments in excess of 35 percent of his or her monthly income and he or she has less than 25 percent of the mortgage value in marketable assets. The bank has analyzed these factors and come up with the following table:

Factor	Incremental time
Monthly loan payments as a percentage of monthly income	
< 25%	—
26–34%	15%
> 35%	25%

Factor	Incremental time
Marketable assets as a percentage of loan	
> 50%	—
25–50%	10%
< 25%	20%

They created a table that shows what the loss factor is for different combinations of the above factors.

	Loan Payments as a Percentage of Income		
Assets as a Percentage of Loan	< 25%	26–34%	> 34%
> 50%		15%	25%
25–50%	10%	20%	30%
< 25%	20%	30%	35%

They created a cost table that shows what percentage of loans fall in these various categories.

	Loan Payments as a Percentage of Income		
Assets as a Percentage of Loan	< 25%	26–34%	> 34%
> 50%	5%	8%	10%
25–50%	6%	11%	23%
< 25%	7%	10%	20%

By understanding what drives their cost better, EZ Money Bank can make better decisions. For example, if the mix of loan applicants changes so that more applicants have characteristics that require more time, this will increase the cost of acquiring loans. This change may also increase the rejection rate, which drives up cost while reducing loans put on the books. If these characteristics were significant, the organization may want to build them into its budget. However, it may be sufficient to identify these characteristics and use them for planning and understanding rather than incorporating them into the budget.

Characteristics help organizations understand the causes of variations in the process better. One cause of variation is that the process is not in control. Other sources of variation are the products, services, distribution channels, and customers. All causes of variation must be understood and effectively managed.

9

REVIEWING AND FINALIZING THE BUDGET

This chapter will:

- Discuss the steps required in finalizing the budget.
- Show how business process reviews are key to senior management reviews.
- Compare budgeted performance to targets.
- Discuss costing for activities and business processes.
- Discuss ways of handling foreign currency.
- Outline ways to use business process reporting to finalize the budget.
- Review implementation plan.

Finalizing a budget consists of a series of steps such as the following:

- Create plans and budgets for all business processes and each activity within the business processes, and activities within each department.

The process manager and process workers who are part of the business process agree to the business process plan and budget. The process workers coordinate their activities with all activities performed in their department.

- Compare the budgeted performance to the strategic targets.
- Evaluate performance and cost tradeoffs.
- Finalize activity and business process cost and performance targets.

See Exhibit 9.1 for a visual breakdown of these steps.

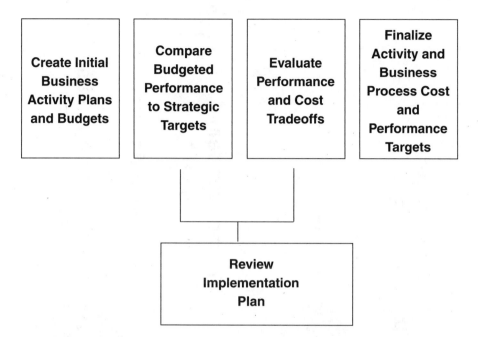

Exhibit 9.1 Finalize activity budget.

PLAN AND CREATE A BUSINESS PROCESS BUDGET FIRST

When budgeting by business processes and activities for the first time, it may make sense to experiment with one department. Run the department through this business process and activity budgeting approach before setting up many different review panels and finalizing all budgets. Use this one budget as a pilot to test the review and implementation procedures.

The pilot budget should be reviewed by the steering committee and someone who will have responsibility for the business process budget. This steering committee should be composed of three to five members. Once approved by the steering committee and the person responsible for the business process, the budget should be sent to the department or unit manager for clarification. The **pilot budget** should be tested, using an adequate number of employees and/or units to get an accurate reading of its usefulness and applicability to the organization. See Exhibit 9.2 for a clarification of this pilot program.

Steering Group — 3-5 members

Panels — 5-6 members

Unit Manager — 1 manager per planning unit

Pilot Team — 20-40 planning units / consultant
10-20 planning units / coordinator

Exhibit 9.2   Activity planning and budgeting pilot.

BUDGET REVIEW PANELS

Budget reviews should take place on three levels:

1. Business process reviews of all activities in the business process
2. Departmental reviews of all activities within the department
3. Senior management reviews of business processes

Everything should key off the business process and activity budgets. (See Exhibit 9.3.)

Business Process Budget Review Panel

The first panel to review the business process plan and budget should be the **business process review panel**. This panel

- questions the business process team about their assumptions,
- offers alternatives, and
- approves the business process plan and budget.

A business process review panel may consist of the following:

- Business process owner sponsor, director, and/or manager involved with the business process
- Relevant process workers (i.e., any process workers, or a representative sample, who perform activities within the business process)
- Relevant support process representatives (i.e., representatives from human resources, training, information systems, accounting, etc.)
- Suppliers and customers of the business process. (i.e., internal and external suppliers and customers for that business process)

The purpose of the business process review panel is to ensure that:

- All activities are synchronized from the beginning to the end of the business process.
- A representative from each activity in the business process represents his or her activities.
- They achieve understanding and agreement on performance measures for the business process.
- They achieve understanding and agreement on performance measures for all activities in the business process.

Departmental Reviews

Business Process Reviews

Senior Management Budget Reviews

Exhibit 9.3   Budget reviews.

- The business process performance measures are in alignment with organization goals and strategy.
- Proactive process controls are established.

By obtaining this understanding and agreement up front, a number of problems should be prevented. There should be a clearer understanding of how each activity fits into the overall business process.

See Exhibit 9.4 for an outline of such a panel.

Head of Business Process	Sponsor, director, or manager of business process
Relevant Process Workers	Any process worker who is part of business process
Relevant Support Processes	Relevant support processes might include technology, people, information sytems
Suppliers/Customers of Business Process	Internal and external suppliers and customers of business process

Exhibit 9.4   Business process review panels.

Department Review Panels

The next step is to have the plan and budget reviewed by the department or function. The department budget review panels consist of the department director (head of function), managers within the department, and the department process workers (all process workers or a representative sample of process workers in that department). (See Exhibit 9.5 for an illustration.)

The purpose of the department review panel is to coordinate all activities

Head of Department	**VP, department director**

Cost Center Managers	**Managers within that department**

Function Process Workers	**All process workers or a representative sample who are in that department**

Exhibit 9.5   Department review panels.

within their department, understand the workload demanded by different business processes, and coordinate process improvement projects.

It is important that this review follow the business process review panel. The business process review panel needs to understand the hand-offs between departments. The department review panel needs to understand and staff the demand of the various business processes. The department needs to understand and participate in process improvement projects that might affect their department.

Senior Management and Business Process Owners Review Panel

The final review is by senior management and the business process owners. This review panel consists of the following:

- President
- Business process owners or sponsors for the major business processes of the organization (e.g., acquire customers, provide customer service, order fulfillment, etc.)
- Support business process sponsors/owners (i.e., provide people, provide technology, provide information, provide new products and services, etc.)

See Exhibit 9.6 for an illustration.

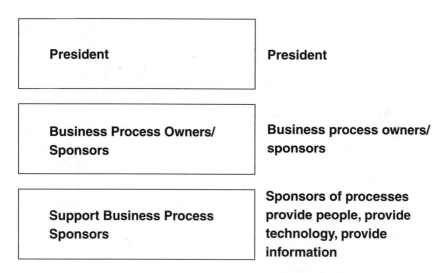

Exhibit 9.6   Senior management and business process owners review panels.

COMPARE BUDGETED PERFORMANCE TO TARGETS

After the business process and department review panels have completed their analysis of business processes, senior management, and the business process owners can review their business processes and activities.

The preliminary budget should be compared to the strategic targets. Any gaps between budgeted performance and strategic targets should result in modifications to the budgeted activities and their resulting resources. Where cost targets are not being met, the activity and business process managers should identify additional improvement opportunities.

This phase is complete when managers have met both the performance and cost targets or have documented why they are unable to meet these targets.

Evaluate Performance and Cost Tradeoffs

When gaps still exist between activity and business process performance and cost targets, tradeoffs must be made.

The best way to handle this will depend on the culture and size of the organization. One convenient way of ranking business processes and activities is through a rating system in which the budget requests are analyzed in comparison to customer needs.

Another useful tool is to classify the budgets according to whether they support the current level of service or whether they are at the minimum, intermediate, or expanded service levels.

Current implies that this is the cost of the activities as they are presently performed. *Minimum* implies that this is the minimum level of service for an activity. *Intermediate* implies that this is not a final solution. *Expanded* implies enlarging the level of service.

Then the organization should look at the impact of projects in terms of the change in workload. The organization should also review projects in terms of the changes in activity/business process cost, cycle time, quality, and outcomes.

See Exhibit 9.7 for an example of how to rank budgets. In this example, the budget for the activity "evaluate loans" has been given a rank of "1." This is not because it has the largest budget. Other activities may have a larger budget. It is ranked first because without evaluating loans, there would be no rational way to determine who to loan money to.

This ranking approach is less concerned with the difference between two ranks that adjoin each other. Therefore, it is more important to disperse loans or evaluate loans. This approach, at least initially, does not pretend to be that sophisticated. Instead, this approach wants to separate what the organization thinks is really important from other activities that this senior management and business process owners team feel are less important such as the following:

- answer phone inquiries.
- take loan applications.
- order reports.
- evaluate loans.
- disperse loans.
- sell mortgages.

In the case of EZ Money Bank, it is thought that monthly closings should be in the category of activities that do not get funded. Management believes that quarterly financial statements are sufficient. They feel that during the other eight months (nonquarterly financial statements), the accounting staff's time is better spent improving processes rather than preparing financial statements every month.

Likewise, the activity of extended hours was rejected for funding. The extended hours were determined in the customer survey to be not that important to justify the additional cost. Therefore, extended hours were not funded.

The budget reviews should be used extensively to rank budgets. Refer back to the original implementation plan to rank important activities for each

Activity	Department	Required/ Discretionary	Rank	Value	Nonvalue	Total $
Evaluate loans	**Loan officer**	**R**	**1**	**206,800**	**233,200**	**440,000**
Disperse loans	**Loan processor**	**R**	2	463,000		463,000
Sell mortgages	**Loan officer**	**D**	3	133,200	136,800	270,000
Order reports	**Loan processor**	**D**	4	65,023		65,023
Take application	**Loan officer**	**R**	5	30,000	14,000	44,000
Answer inquiries	**Loan officer**	**D**	25	7,100	345	7,445
Bill customer	**Operations**	**R**	37	40,000	7,332	47,332
			112		77,000	77,000
		FUNDING	**LINE**	4,058,000	1,947,000	6,000,005
Close monthly	Finance	D	150		94,668	94,668
Extended hours	Branch	D	166	180,000		180,000
TOTAL				5,500,000	3,000,000	8,500,000

Exhibit 9.7 Rank and select activities for budget.

department. Also, review the original business process targets. Keeping targets in mind will help when finalizing the budgets.

FINALIZE ACTIVITY AND BUSINESS PROCESS COST AND PERFORMANCE TARGETS

An organization should start budgeting by activities. It should hold employees responsible for their activity results and tie promotions and salary increases to business process and activity results. However, in the short term (i.e., less than one year), the organization has two options for activity budgeting:

1. It can budget and report by business processes and activities.
2. It can budget by business processes and activities and convert the activity budget into a traditional cost element budget while waiting for its activity budgeting system to be installed.

In this second costing approach, the organization plans on an activity and business process basis, but managers would use activity costs per unit to determine cost elements. Then they summarize by cost elements.

COST BUDGETED ACTIVITIES AND BUSINESS PROCESSES

There are three methods for capturing the needed data on cost elements:

1. There are resources dedicated to specific activities in each department. These resources are a known quantity. The department simply defines workload measures at the activity and business process level.
2. There are shared resources. Each person tracks what percentage of time he or she spends or plans to spend on specific activities and then calculates the amount of resources spent on different activities.
3. There is the use of surrogates in which actual outputs are used at a standard activity cost. In this approach, actual costs would be compared to total department earned costs.

Dealing with Foreign Currencies

There are a few points to keep in mind when finalizing a budget if the organization works in the overseas markets or has acquired any revenue or debt in foreign currencies. Before finalizing any budget, current rates of exchange should be factored in along with any duties, tariffs, or taxes that may not have been accounted for. When budgeting for future years, future rates of exchange will have to be predicted and plotted for any affected service along with any known changes in tariffs or tax laws.

It is important to understand what is actually happening before the effects of currency fluctuations. Is the entity becoming more effective or is it just being helped by a favorable foreign currency swing? Is the organization becoming less effective or is it just an unfavorable currency swing? Therefore, activity planning and budgeting should be done in local currency first, and then adjusted for foreign currency fluctuations.

USE BUSINESS PROCESS REPORTING TO FINALIZE THE BUDGET

For best results, use business process reporting to finalize the budget and to plan for future budgets. Remember, in business process reporting, activity costs should be shown for each department, as well as for each business process that delivers a service or product.

10

USING THE INFORMATION

This chapter will:

- Discuss the need for continuous department improvement.
- Define value-added and non–value-added activities.
- Discuss ways of implementing continuous improvement procedures.

ACTIVITY ANALYSIS IS THE BASIS FOR CONTINUOUS IMPROVEMENT

With every activity analysis, and as part of setting planning guidelines, you should keep in mind the need for continuous improvement of value-added business processes and activities plus elimination of nonvalue activities and tasks.

Activities are what an enterprise does. **Strategic goals** represent what the enterprise wants to achieve. Planning guidelines and activity analysis help the organization achieve its goals. Activities and business processes must be continuously evaluated to ensure that the activities contribute to the achievement of organizational strategies and objectives. Poor structuring of business processes leads to missed deadlines, unfinished projects, disappointed customers, and non–value-added costs.

WHAT ARE NON–VALUE-ADDED COSTS?

Non–value-added costs are costs or activities other than the minimum amount of equipment, materials, parts, space, and workers' time that is absolutely essential to add value to the enterprise. In a word, non–value-added costs are **waste**.

In daily operations, many activities are non–value-added and secondary to the organization's mission. Visibility of these non–value-added and secondary activities provided by an activity-based cost management system is the basis for continuous improvement.

Seeing these non–value-added activities during the budgeting processes helps to facilitate action plans to eliminate or reduce nonvalue. These action plans can be incorporated into everyone's performance appraisal to help ensure the action plans are worked on and the nonvalue eliminated and reduced. The resources formerly spent on nonvalue can now be transferred to value-creating activities.

HOW CAN ACTIVITY ANALYSIS HELP REDUCE WASTE AND SPUR CONTINUOUS DEPARTMENT IMPROVEMENTS?

Activity analysis provides information used to identify redundant, duplicate, and wasteful activities together with the factors that drive cost. Understanding activities provides a basis for determining whether to continue performing or to restructure an activity. Continuous improvement has several objectives:

- Elimination of waste (non–value-added activities)
- Improvement of performance of value-added activities
- Synchronization of lead time within cross-functional business processes
- Improvement of quality
- Elimination of process variance by correcting the source cause of the variance
- Simplification of activities

Continuous improvements of activities or business processes does not come automatically with experience or the passage of time. Continuous improvement requires constant attention by management. Example 10-1 shows how continuous department improvement could help EZ Money Bank's mortgage branch.

Example 10-1: How Continuous Improvement Could Save Time and Money in Evaluating Loans

EZ Money Bank conducted a customer survey regarding its loan processing procedures. Its objective prior to the survey was to process loans within two days of receipt of the application. During crunch times, hitting that two-day objective required additional staff from corporate and overtime expense.

The survey posed the question, "How long do you think it took to process your loan application?" The possible answers were:

- Less than 1 week
- 1 week
- 2 to 3 weeks
- 4 to 6 weeks
- Don't know

To EZ Money Bank's surprise, most respondents answered that they did not know. The second most popular answer was 4 to 6 weeks because that is how long it took to actually receive the money. So why was EZ Money Bank spending extra time and resources to process loans quickly if the public did not know how long it took to actually get loan approval? EZ Money Bank decided to either spend less resources by processing loans over a longer period of time or to create an advertising program showing they had the fastest loan approval time in the city.

Look what happens to the department budget when those additional resources are removed:

	Salaries & Benefits	Space	Equipment	Other	Total
Current	$160,000	$7,500	$10,000	$2,500	$180,000
Revised	$144,000	$6,700	$9,000	$2,300	$162,000

By increasing the amount of time they take to process a loan, the loan department can reduce its overall cost and still meet customer requirements for timely service.

In Example 10-1, the 1- or 2-day turnaround was a cost driver. A **cost driver** is considered a factor whose occurrence creates cost. A cost driver or root cause represents a prime cause of the level of activity (e.g., quick turnaround, cumbersome procedures, high turnover). Determining and eliminating cost drivers/root causes is only one step in the continuous department improvement process. There are four more.

CONTINUOUSLY IMPROVING ACTIVITIES: A FIVE-STEP PROCESS

There are many ways of improving activities and business processes. Some methods of improvement are industry specific. However, the following five general steps can be applied to any organization:

1. Determine cause and effect: cost drivers/root causes.
2. Determine customer needs.
3. Determine solutions by applying creative thinking.
4. Redesign business processes and activities.
5. Manage the newly redesigned process.

See Exhibit 10.1 for an illustration of this process.

Determine Cause and Effect: Cost Drivers/Root Causes

As shown in Example 10-1, unnecessary processes or requirements can be cost drivers. In the warehouse example later in this chapter, MegaStorage finds that it could save time and money by not inspecting the furniture received at its warehouse. MegaStorage did not need to inspect it because it

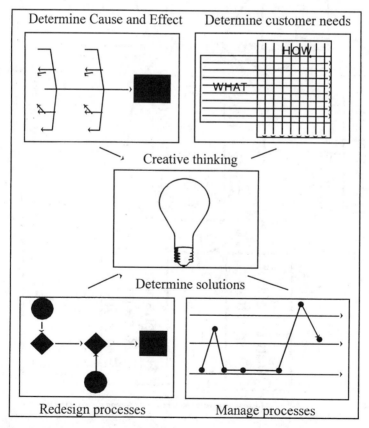

Exhibit 10.1 Continuously improve business processes and activities.

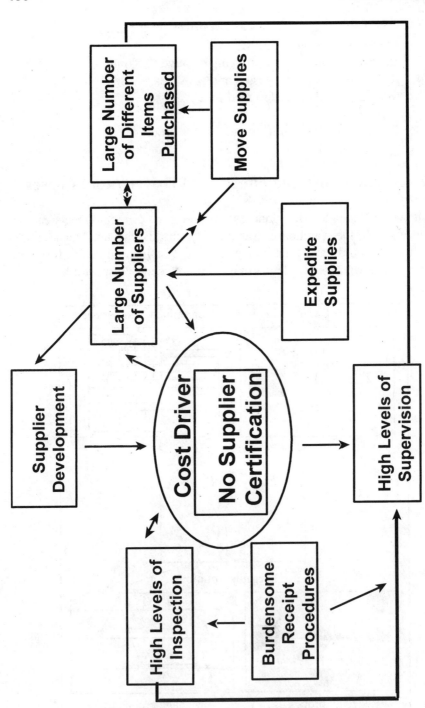

Exhibit 10.2   No supplier certification of inspection creates a cost driver at MegaStorage warehouse.

had already been inspected by the furniture manufacturer. There was a certification from the furniture manufacturer/supplier that the furniture had been inspected. That preinspection saved MegaStorage tremendous amounts of time and resources. Exhibit 10.2 illustrates what would happen if there were no supplier certification of inspection. The lack of inspection translates into more required tasks, resources, and workload.

By insisting that the furniture manufacturer/supplier be responsible for inspections, MegaStorage was able to reduce its costs. The inspections, or lack thereof, were the cost drivers.

Organizations should determine their business processes and activities. They should try to identify as many cost drivers as they can. Some organizations like setting up categories of cost drivers. The following are examples of these categories of cost drivers:

- Cost driver source:
  - External to department
  - Internal to department
  - Technology
- Controllable:
  - By a department
  - By someone outside the department
  - By someone outside the organization
- Require investment of:
  - Capital dollars
  - Employees' time

Determine Customer Needs

In Example 10-1, we saw how EZ Money Bank could still meet its customers' needs, but save time and resources by lengthening the time it took to process loans. EZ Money Bank saved money but did not sacrifice its customers' need.

An organization should perform market surveys to determine its customers' (both internal and external) needs. Based on the customers' answers, the organization can improve its business processes to meet their needs but reduce its costs. If appropriate, questionnaires can be sent out to the top customers. Including questionnaires or suggestion forms with mailed correspondence is a good idea. Then, the organization should listen to its customers!

Determine Solutions by Applying Creative Thinking

Many of us get caught up in our day-to-day existence, and we seldom look for ways of improving that existence. If we were to take the time to "brainstorm" or truly think creatively about the tasks we perform on a daily basis, we could indeed come up with other ways of performing those tasks. It just takes a little creative thinking. What is creative thinking and how do we start?

The first step is to look and think differently about your work. The following is a list of possible ways of seeing your activities and processes differently:

- Challenge your assumptions about your activities and business processes. Do they truly need their current levels? Could someone else provide those services and products? Could the location where the activity takes place change? Could part of the service take place somewhere else?
- Look outside your industry to see how other industries perform their activities. Maybe some of their activities do not relate to your industry, but maybe the principles behind their business processes and activities could be applied.
- Perceive patterns from other divisions, offices, products/services, and departments. Some of these patterns could be translated into profits for your department.
- Make connections with other divisions and departments. They may be of some future use.
- Establish networks between your suppliers, your suppliers' suppliers, you, your customers, and their customers.
- Exploit failures. Do not hide your failures—use them as a training tool. However, do not sacrifice an employee's feelings or morale to do so.
- Perform your activities or processes backwards and/or from the middle. Your process should work wherever it is started.
- Set up idea triggers (i.e., articles, suggestion boxes, customer questionnaires, employee forums).
- Create superheroes (i.e., superman/woman, etc.).
- Become the product, service, activity, and/or business process. Envision yourself as you go through each step. Where and how would you change the process?
- Use a positive future vision. State future plans to both employees and customers. Stress results, not downfalls. Use activity descriptions

that capture the essence of what output you want to achieve rather than the current way you perform the activity (i.e., instead of describing the activity as "issue a check to supplier," say "compensate supplier"). Capturing the essence of what result you are trying to accomplish (compensate supplier) will open up your thinking to other possibilities.

- Shift paradigms. Break molds and shift work flow patterns.
- Question everything. It never hurts to be overly inquisitive. Do not assume that just because a process has been performed one way for a number of years that it is the most efficient way.
- Change the boundaries of your business processes both within and outside your organization.
- Just as important as positive reinforcement is the use of positive language and words when dealing with customers and employees (i.e., *delight, satisfy, combine, change, gratify, invert, enlarge, minimize, substitute, rearrange, rotate*, etc.). Positive words strengthen relationships.
- Employ "otherness"—pretend to be the other person, service, place, or thing.
- Never blame; focus on learning and improving.
- Read at least one magazine outside your industry and/or outside business for ideas.

Redesign Business Processes and Activities

Once the problem areas in an organization's business processes or activities have been identified, possible solutions must be outlined and "plugged" into the business processes to see if they fit. Some solutions may work, and others may not. Try to learn from each failure. Remember, Sony is known for product successes, yet it has one of the highest failure rates. Yet, most of us remember the successes rather than the failures.

Once the solutions that work have been found, the business processes or activities to make them work more effectively may have to be redesigned. This means performing an additional activity analysis once the business process is redesigned. (See Example 10-2 for an illustration of how this is accomplished.)

Keep in mind, too, that a solution may work for one activity and not another. Use trial and error for learning rather than for blame or disappointment.

Manage the Newly Redesigned Process

Once the business processes and activities have been improved, the management techniques to maintain such improvements may need to be changed. If the old business processes were not working, why would the old management style work? Progress with the improved business processes can be tracked by keeping logs and journals accounting for the savings in time, resources, and workload.

CONTINUOUS IMPROVEMENT CAN HELP
ANY BUSINESS PROCESS OR ACTIVITY

Implementing continuous improvements is not difficult if each business process is broken down to individual activities. One approach is to examine each activity for waste and then start the improvement from that point. If waste is eliminated in each activity, the business process will be improved, as shown in Example 10-2.

Example 10-2: Improving MegaStorage's Procurement Process

MegaStorage wants to find ways to improve the workings of its purchasing department. It has been determined that there may be waste in the procurement process. The purchasing department manager breaks down the procurement process into the following steps:

1. Issue purchase order (PO).
2. Receive supplies.
3. Move supplies.
4. Expedite supplies.
5. Certify the supplier.
6. Pay the invoice.

Currently, the procurement process ensures quality in order processing, but because of the amount of time it takes the department to complete all of the steps, the unit cost for the department is quite high. (See Exhibit 10.3.)

Look what this business process actually costs. In Exhibit 10.4, each activity has been broken down into its value-added cost, non–value-added cost, total cost, output workload, and cost per output. The total cost is $301,500. Of this total, $195,000 is value-added.

This view should stimulate everyone's thinking to determine why there is $106,500 of nonvalue costs. What could be done to reduce that cost? Does the organization still need so many invoices, or could this be reduced?

As part of the budgeting process, it is helpful to compare budgeted unit cost and budgeted workload volume with the current year's figures (See Exhibit 10.5.) This figure

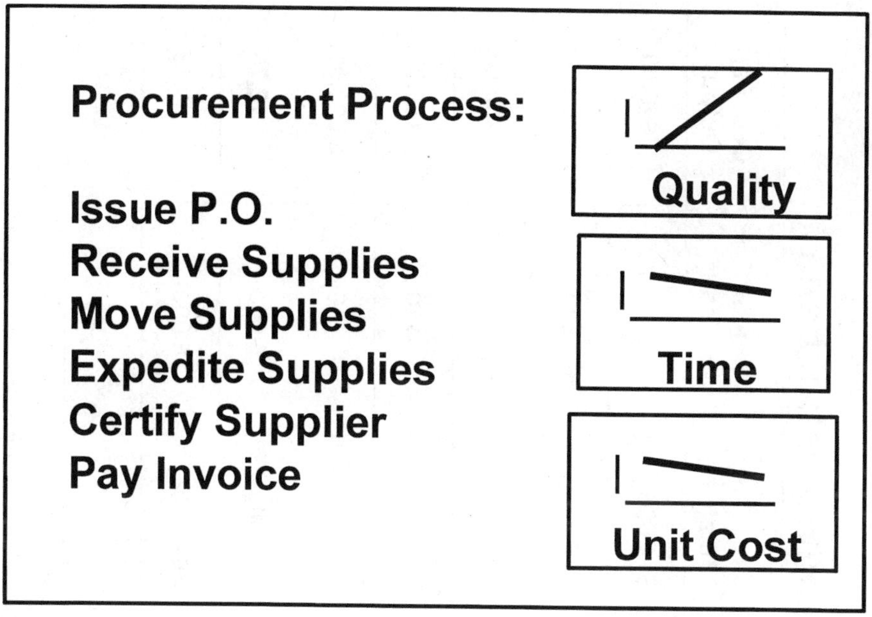

Procurement Process:

Issue P.O.
Receive Supplies
Move Supplies
Expedite Supplies
Certify Supplier
Pay Invoice

Quality

Time

Unit Cost

Exhibit 10.3 Continuously improve business processes: MegaStorage's procurement process.

gives anyone looking at this analysis an understanding of what is happening to workload and unit cost trends. Is someone playing games by increasing volume in order to reduce unit cost? It is true that if someone decided to put less items on a purchase order and create more purchase orders, the unit cost may go down as the organization spreads fixed costs over more units. However, because more purchase orders are being generated, the total cost will probably increase for this activity even though unit cost is decreasing. Therefore, this type of analysis gives everyone insight to what the trends are in terms of budgeted output volume and budgeted unit cost as compared with history and best practices.

Management determines that a new system of electronic data interchange (EDI) would improve the work flow of the department and reduce non–value-added expenses. It would eliminate redundant steps, as well. Look at one specific activity—"pay invoice"—to illustrate how it can be improved by implementing improvement. The organization decides to pay vendors from purchase orders and receivers rather than by matching invoices, purchase orders, and receivers.

Exhibit 10.6 breaks out the activity "pay invoice" before the implementation of this change. You can see that the total cost for the activity "pay invoice" is $150,000 with $50,000 of that money being used by non–value-added tasks. The system of paying from receivers and purchase orders will eliminate two activities ("receive vendor invoice" and "match purchase order, receipt notice, and vendor invoice"). There will no longer be a need for someone to do these tasks. The new software will handle the activities "post supply receipt notice," "match purchase order/receiver notice," and "enter data" electronically, thereby reducing the amount of non–value-added activities performed by the purchasing department's staff.

Process Manager: Eve
Process Team Members: Leo, David, Emily, Austin, Lana

	Value	Non-Value	Total	Output Workload	Cost per Output
Issue Purchase Order	$30,000	$14,000	$44,000	1,100	$40.00
Receive Supplies	20,000	6,000	26,000	520	50.00
Move Supplies		29,700	29,700	165	180.00
Expedite Supplies		19,800	19,800	110	180.00
Certify Supplier	65,000	15,000	80,000	10	8,000.00
Pay Invoice	80,000	22,000	102,000	8,000	12.75
	195,000	106,500	301,500	10,000	30.15
	65%	35%			

Exhibit 10.4 Continuously improve business processes for budget year: MegaStorage's procurement process.

Current Year Budgeted Year

Activity	Workload	Unit Cost	Workload	Unit Cost
		$		$
Issue Purchase Order	1,600	50	1,100	40
Receive Supplies	586	58	520	50
Move Supplies	150	200	165	180
Expedite Supplies	100	200	110	180
Certify Vendor	10	10,000	10	8,000
Pay Invoice	8,000	18.75	8,000	12.75

Exhibit 10.5   Continuously improve business process: MegaStorage's procurement process current year versus budgeted year.

Compare the total cost for the activity "pay invoices" before and after the implementation of the new process. Exhibit 10.6 breaks out the costs before this improvement, and Exhibit 10.7 illustrates costs after the implementation of the improvement. MegaStorage's total cost was reduced to $102,000 from $150,000, with only $22,000 in non–value-added activities. That is a significant improvement!

SIX METHODS FOR IMPROVING ACTIVITIES AND OUTPUT

As shown in Example 10-2, management and the process workers should implement improvements to each business process so that the overall business process improves. The focus must be on improving the business processes, because focusing on resources or activities can result in suboptimization. A few tips to help you on your way to business process and activity improvement are:

Task	Total	Non–Value Added	Value- Added	Best Practices
Receive purchase order	0.50	0.50		
Record supplies receipts notice	0.50	—	.50	.50
Receive vendor invoice (VI)	0.50	0.50		
Match PO/RN/VI	2.00	2.00		
Enter data into computer	6.50		6.50	3.00
Determine errors	2.50	2.50		
Expedite payment	.75	.75		
Generate computer payment	4.00		4.00	2.50
File documentation	1.50		1.50	
TOTAL	$18.75	$6.25	$12.50	$6.00
Units	**x 8,000**	**x 8,000**	**x 8,000**	**x 8,000**
	$150,000	$50,000	$100,000	$48,000

Exhibit 10.6   Continuously improve activities: pay vendor invoice before improvement.

Task	Total	Non–Value Added	Value- Added	Best Practices
Receive purchase order	0.50	0.50		
Record supplies receipts notice (RN)	0.50	—	.50	.50
Receive vendor invoice (VI)	—	—		
Match PO/RN/VI	—	—		
Enter data into computer	4.50	—	4.50	3.00
Determine errors	2.50	1.50	1.00	
Expedite payment	.75	.75		
Generate computer payment	4.00		4.00	2.50
File documentation				
TOTAL	$12.75	$2.75	$10.00	$6.00
Units	**x 8,000**	**x 8,000**	**x 8,000**	**x 8,000**
	$102,000	$22,000	$80,000	$48,000

Exhibit 10.7   Improving MegaStorage's activity: pay vendor invoice—after improvement.

1. Reduce business process and activity volume wherever possible.
2. Eliminate activities, tasks, and steps that are non–value-added or that do not support a value-added activity.
3. Coordinate each activity with customers, suppliers, other cost centers, and other divisions.
4. Automate activities wherever possible. (You saw what it did for MegaStorage's purchasing department.)
5. Improve internal methods and/or change the sequence in which activities are performed.
6. Start with a current cost per unit of business processes and activities. Then back flush to individual cost categories (e.g., salaries, supplies, etc.) by reviewing the activity and tasks involved in each activity.

If these six methods are employed, improvement in both activities and business processes is guaranteed. Improvements result in money available for growth, cost and workload savings, and elimination of frustration.

11

GAP ANALYSIS AND PLANNING GUIDELINES

This chapter will:

- Define ways of using gap analysis.
- Discuss ways of instituting planning guidelines.
- Define ways of performing market targeting.
- Discuss ways of setting up a plan that will ensure continuous improvements.

INTRODUCTION

In this chapter, gap analysis and how to develop planning guidelines will be discussed. **Gap analysis** is the study of the difference between an organization's goal or strategy and its current working levels. Once this gap is recognized, planning guidelines can be drafted to bring the organization's working level closer to its goals. Throughout the chapter are planning tips and guidelines in display boxes. These tips are designed to assist the reader when setting up his or her own plan.

GETTING STARTED

Determining the current levels of work being performed through activity analysis is the basis from which one can begin to analyze and plan better ways of achieving an organization's goals.

After determining the work being performed by the department, the next question is "How efficiently is the work being done?" There are five criteria for judging work efficiency:

1. Is the work a consequence of a customer requirement?
2. Is the work wasteful?
3. Are best practices followed in doing the work?
4. How much unused capacity (space and personnel resources) exists?
5. How much time does it take to complete the activity?

GUIDELINE: *Determine the effectiveness of work being performed using five criteria.*

Is the Work a Consequence of a Customer Requirement?

Work should be undertaken only to satisfy some customer need for which the customer is willing to pay. The "customer," in this sense, may be either an external customer or an internal one (another department). The output of work must be of a quality that is of value to the customer, at a cost that the customer is willing to pay, and within a set amount of time. Work done without the customer's need in mind results in waste and a deterioration of competitive position. (See Example 11-1.)

Example 11-1: MegaStorage's Customer's Needs

MegaStorage's current customer, Quality Furnishings, stated two primary needs:

1. Furniture must be at their store at the exact time needed.
2. Furniture must arrive undamaged 100 percent of the time.

Look at the list of activities for the receiving department below. How can management meet the customer requirements using the outputs for the receiving department? The customer needs must be mapped to the receiving department's activities as follows:

Activity	Need
Receive goods	Goods in store at time needed
Inspect goods	Guarantee of 100% undamaged goods
Move goods to storage	NA
Move goods to stores	Goods delivered to store on time
Expedite goods	NA
Train associates	NA
Manage employees	NA

When the receiving department's activities are looked at in this way, it is evident that several of the department's activities are a consequence of management decisions on how the work should be accomplished, rather than being a direct result of a customer need.

> **GUIDELINE:** *Management must determine which activities are most important at the current time to meet customer needs and achieve profits.*

Is the Work Wasteful?

Several of MegaStorage's receiving department activities are wasteful. Waste occurs where the activity can be limited with the organization continuing to meet customer needs. Waste results from errors (correction, detection, and interruption of operations), useless paperwork, ineffective policies and procedures, mismanaged capacity, and ineffectual physical/organizational structure. (See Example 11-2.)

Example 11-2: MegaStorage Determines Which Activities Are Wasteful

MegaStorage's receiving department manager identified three activities as wasteful: (1) inspecting goods, (2) moving goods to storage, and (3) expediting goods.

The manager believes that even though the customer wants delivery of undamaged goods 100 percent of the time, inspecting them in the warehouse was wasteful because they have already been inspected once before leaving the supplier. This activity duplicated an activity already performed.

Moving goods to storage was considered wasteful because the goods should not be in the warehouse for any length of time. An excellent warehouse could synchronize the receipt of goods with its use and eliminate the need for storage.

Finally, the need to expedite goods was a primary result of the failure to meet the time expectations of the customer. Certifying vendors for quality and timeliness is key. Using only these certified vendors would eliminate much of the need to expedite.

> **GUIDELINE:** *Determine whether any waste exists by looking at each activity and its relationship to customer need.*

Are the Best Practices Followed in Doing the Work?

When determining the performance of an activity, it is critical to think of it in terms of the best practices. Is there a better way of performing this activity? Management should be able to set up a plan so that all activities are being performed in the most efficient, cost-effective way that still ensures product or service excellence.

GUIDELINE: Determine that best practices are being utilized. Are there more effective ways to achieve this output and more efficient ways of handling this activity that would still meet customer needs but be more profitable for the organization?

How Much Unused Capacity Exists?

Excellent managers continuously convert underutilized capacity into utilized assets and redeploy or sell any unused capacity. Profitability is highest when the minimum necessary capital is employed to accomplish a task. (See Example 11-3.)

Example 11-3: MegaStorage Determines Its Unused Capacity

The equipment used by MegaStorage's receiving department remained idle for significant amounts of time. Few organizations would allow their employees to remain idle for longer than a few minutes, but these same organizations often think very little about their equipment. Why pay a lease fee or monthly payment for a piece of equipment that may sit idle for, say, 40 hours of a 160-hour work month. Management must develop a plan not only to keep their employees busy for the 160 hours per month, but also to best utilize their equipment.

GUIDELINE: All resources, both human and equipment, should be put to use at all times to meet customer needs, ensure quality, and achieve profitability.

How Much Time Does It Take to Complete the Activity?

Doing work quickly, without unnecessary delays, is essential to producing good results and profitability. The greater amount of time a piece of furniture is held in MegaStorage, the more information is needed to keep track of the status of operations, resulting in more employee involvement and cost to the company. A delay increases the possibility of a piece of furniture becoming lost. The longer the period of time before the customer pays for the goods, the longer the receiving department is losing money. Therefore, it is in the receiving department's best interest to get the goods moved in and out as fast as possible.

GUIDELINE: Reducing the time required to perform activities increases flexibility, lowers costs, and improves customer satisfaction.

PERFORMING MARKET TARGETING

A key element in activity-based planning is the continuing assessment of customer needs. The key is to set operational targets to meet those needs. A department manager's role is to plan the resources needed to achieve strategic goals, meet customer needs, and institute controls to ensure the consistency in plan performance. This process is known as **strategic deployment.** In order for it to work, it requires a strong target cost system.

Planning future workload is key when setting these targets. Workload is derived from numerous sources and services (i.e., reports are often triggered by a specific date in the month or year, or project work may be a once-a-year thing). (See Example 11-4.)

Example 11-4: MegaStorage Uses Market Targeting to Determine Workload

MegaStorage's receiving department manager can determine the anticipated workload by evaluating next year's sales forecast. The initial study showed that total sales were forecasted to be lower by 7 percent, but there would be a shift to specialty items (e.g., oak desks) rather than items sold in bulk (office furniture packages). Typically, specialty items have features that require much greater receiving activity because goods are bought in smaller quantities. The manager estimates that the total workload for the following year would be equivalent to this year's workload. The lower bulk item receipts would be offset by higher specialty item receipts.

The department manager also meets with personnel from the stores taking delivery of the furniture to discuss their level of satisfaction. The store personnel stated that the time from goods receipt to store delivery needed to be reduced from three days to one day. Here is how the manager broke out his future workload plan:

Activities	Workload Measure	Current Workload	Future Workload
Receive goods	Number of goods received	150,000	150,000
Inspect goods	Number of goods inspected	60,000	60,000
Move to storage	Number of goods moved	100,000	70,000
Move to stores	Number of goods delivered	50,000	80,000
Expedite goods	Number of goods expedited	15,000	15,000
Train associates	Number of training days	20	100
Manage employees			

In order to meet these market-driven targets, the receiving department must improve the way it works. It does that by instituting business process improvement.

---

*GUIDELINE: **Determine future workload using next year's sales forecast and input from customers.***

---

*GUIDELINE: **Develop a plan for continuous improvement in all activities.***

SETTING ACTIVITY-PLANNING GUIDELINES

By using activity-based planning's six basic steps (activity analysis, market targeting, business process improvement, continuous activity improvement, process controls, and activity planning), one can easily determine the guidelines required for a specific plan. We used this six-step process for MegaStorage's receiving department in our example. From this, we can glean the following planning guidelines:

- Determine the efficiency of activities and tasks being performed using five criteria:
  1. Is the work a consequence of a customer requirement?
  2. Is the work wasteful?
  3. Are the best practices followed in doing the work?
  4. How much unused capacity exists?
  5. How much time does it take to complete each activity?

- Management must determine which activities are most important at the current time to meet customer needs and achieve profits.
- Determine whether any waste exists by looking at each activity and its relationship to customer need.
- Determine department best practices. Are there more efficient ways of handling this activity that would still meet customer needs but be more profitable?
- All resources, both human and equipment, should be managed effectively and unused capacity monitored and managed at all times to ensure quality and profitability.
- Reducing the time required to perform activities increases flexibility, lowers costs, and improves customer satisfaction.
- Determine future workload using current numbers, adjusting for next year's sales forecast and input from customers.
- Plan for improved business processes and activities using a simple five-step process:
  1. Eliminate wasteful work.
  2. Eliminate root causes of problems.
  3. Reduce workload.
  4. Improve working methods by simplifying tasks, emulating best practices, and employing alternative resources.
  5. Minimize unutilized or underutilized capacity.
- Research and develop process controls for all department activities to ensure efficiency and profitability.
- Develop a plan for continuous improvement in all activities.

Try using these guidelines and develop a plan for your department or cost center. Some of these guidelines may need to be modified to meet your specific needs and those of your organization. Be creative and determine more of your own guidelines to satisfy your organization's specific needs.

12

PERFORMANCE REPORTING AND ANALYSIS

This chapter will:

- Define earned value measures and reporting.
- Define proactive process control principles and show how they may be used at the business process and activity level to monitor effectiveness.
- Illustrate how resources can be shifted effectively using *best practices.*

WHAT ARE PERFORMANCE REPORTS?

Earned value reports monitor actual performance against planned performance. Because the budget was prepared at the activity level, performance reporting must also be managed at the activity level. Where variation exists in outcomes, workload, cost, and quantity, management can use performance measures to determine the root cause of the problem and quantify its financial impact.

Proactive Process Control Principles

Process controls can be used to monitor for the planned levels of performance. These process controls can be broken down into two categories:

1. Proactive process controls
2. Reactive inspections (cost monitoring)

Proactive Process Controls

Proactive process controls are processes designed to monitor activity performance as the activity is being performed. The power of proactive process controls is that they can prevent problems because the problem is detected immediately during execution. In contrast, most accounting controls wait until the end of the month and then report an unfavorable variance. This is too late to take corrective action.

Process controls should be established at both the business process and activity levels. A business process manager and those process workers who perform activities that make up a business process must work together closely. The process workers must coordinate their department activities with the higher-level business process. They must select and agree to activity measures that maximize the effectiveness of the business process rather than just their activity. Together, the process manager and the process workers from various departments should be able to design process controls to ensure that quality, cycle times, and cost targets for the business process are achieved. These business process targets should satisfy the customer requirements as well as the goals of the organization. These activity measures should facilitate comparison with **best practices** for both the business process and the department.

Selecting an activity measure requires three steps:

1. Determining the activity measure
2. Gather statistics on business process and activity output and transactions
3. Validate business process and activity measure for reasonableness

Determining Activity Measure

An organization should use an activity measure that will support strategy. It should use a measure that is meaningful to the process worker. The measure should be relatively easy to calculate.

Gather Statistics on Business Process and Activity Outputs and Transactions

After a business process and relevant, integrated activity measures have been selected, the frequency of its occurrence is determined. The following are common sources of activity volume information:

- Information systems transaction statistics
- Department records (If service orders are numbered sequentially, for example, an approximation of the number of service orders is determined by subtracting the beginning number from the ending number.)
- Sampling

Validate Business Process and Activity Measure for Reasonableness

The activity measure must be validated to ensure that relationships between the business processes and activities are reasonable. Alternative business process and activity measures should be selected in cases in which the lack of homogeneity (commonality) would make the measures meaningless. The following are the primary techniques used to validate business process and activity measures for reasonableness:

- The high–low approach, which examines cost behavior at the highest and lowest levels of the business process and related activities
- Curve fitting, which determines the line that best explains the relationship between changes in cost and the business process and activity level by graphing historical relationships
- Multiple regression analysis, which is similar to curve fitting but is used when changes in costs are a function of multiple independent variables
- Refinement of features and characteristics that may affect business process and activity costs

Using Activity Measures to Design Proactive Process Controls

Once the process manager and relevant process workers have determined business process and activity measures, proactive process controls should be designed to understand the factors that cause variation in a process. (See Exhibit 12.1.)

Reactive Inspections Put a Bandage on the Problem

Traditional accounting controls are reactive in nature. Measuring the variance between actual and budgeted performance is an inspection.

Postmortem cost monitoring procedures plot actual activities and busi-

**The most effective reports are those that
do not have to be made**

**Introduce Proactive Process Control rather than reactive
cost monitoring wherever possible**

**Activity Planning & Budgeting encourages
proactive process control**

Exhibit 12.1   Performance reporting proactive process control principles.

ness process costs versus their budgeted costs. This approach leaves the
process manager and process worker who work on the business process
powerless to make changes in business processes or activities as needed. This
is because that data is too late and too aggregate to take action. All the
manager does in this situation is to plot costs. By using performance reporting with proactive process controls, the process manager and process workers
have a set plan to go to in case the workload or the business process changes.

AN ACTIVITY PERFORMANCE REPORT
SHOWING EARNED VALUE

It is far more actionable to manage by using proactive performance measures
rather than after-the-fact measures. Management will continue to want global
measures. However, after-the-fact reports need only be done monthly or
quarterly at most.

An activity-based performance report should show the following:

- Budgeted activity unit cost
- Budgeted activity workload
- Total budgeted activity cost
- Actual cost
- Actual activity volume

- Earned value (actual volume times budgeted unit cost)
- Earned value variance (earned value minus actual cost)

See Exhibit 12.2 for an example.

In this sample budget, the organization budgeted the activity "issue purchase orders" at $50 per purchase order. It budgeted 3,000 purchase

Department Total

Expense	Budget ($)	Actual ($)
Wages	80,000	80,000
Supplies	40,000	38,000
Space	30,000	30,000
Equipment	18,000	18,000
Travel	22,000	20,000
Other	10,000	8,000
Total	200,000	194,000

Earned Value Activity Performance Report

Output Measure	Issue Purchase Order — Number of POs	Certified Vendor — Number of Certified Vendors	Expedite Order — Number of Expedited Orders	Other — Other	Total
Activity Budgeted rate	$50	$2,000	$10	$9,000	
Budgeted volume	3,000	20	100	1	
Budget	$150,000	$40,000	$1,000	$9,000	$200,000
Actual volume	2,700	18	90	1	
Earned value	$135,000	$36,000	$900	$9,100	$181,000
Actual					$194,000
Earned value variance					$13,000

Exhibit 12.2 Activity-based budget report.

orders. This yielded a budgeted value for the activity "issue purchase orders" of $150,000. The same activity budgeting process was followed for the remaining activities. This yielded a total activity budget for this department of $200,000, which was back flushed into expense categories.

Earned value is calculated for each activity by multiplying the actual volume for each activity by that activity's budgeted rate. For the "issue purchase order" activity, the actual volume of 2,700 purchase orders yields $135,000. The same calculation is made for all activities and the answers added for each department. This earned value total of $181,000 is compared to actual expenses of $194,000 to yield an earned-value variance of –$13,000. This is a different picture than simply comparing actual with budget. Business process managers and process worker can use this as a planning tool as well as a means to operate their organization more efficiently.

FINDING THE BEST PRACTICE IS KEY TO PERFORMANCE REPORTING

Exhibit 12.3 shows a graph indicating the performance of EZ Money Bank. The branch budgeted workload is 1,000 loans per year divided by 50 weeks per year, which translates into 20 loans per week. The graph shows that during the first nine weeks of the year, the workload ranged from a low of 10 loans per week to a high of 50 loans per week. Filling 50 loans per week with a staff designed to handle 20 loans per week is a burden on the department. The business process "acquire loans" is obviously out of control.

How does the process manager fix this? If the process manager and process workers have proactive business process controls in place and ready to go, the increased workload will already be handled. They might have hired part-time staff until the workload returns to normal. Costs for this contingency could have been built into the budget to reflect peaks and valleys in workload. For example, they might find that workload peaks in the spring and summer and put this into their budget to reflect part-time staff during peak spring and summer months. (See Exhibit 12.4.)

The concept of "best practice" plays an important role in performance reporting. Using business process and activity measures and proactive process controls, a process manager and relevant process workers can readily anticipate and plan for expected changes in workload. Also, if volume is down, they can use process controls to indicate the lower volume. They can come up with contingency plans to generate the volume that they need to achieve their goals rather than being caught off guard.

Performance reporting gives a process manager and the relevant process workers a clear view of what is truly taking place in their business

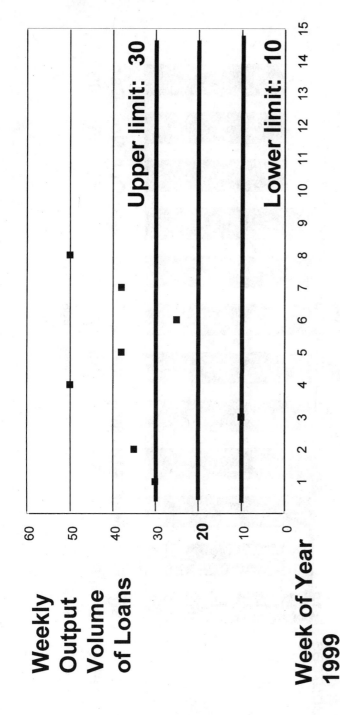

Weekly Output Volume of Loans

Week of Year 1999

1,000 loans/ 50 weeks per year = 20 loans per week

More than 30 loans/week or less than 10 loans/week indicate activity is out of control. Need to research reasons for this business process.

Exhibit 12.3   Performance reporting for business process "acquire loans."

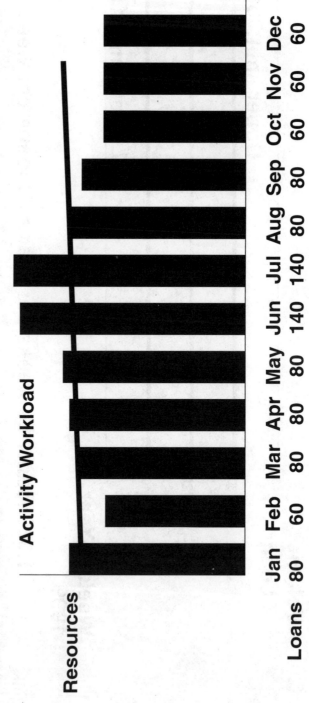

ENSURE RESOURCES CAN BE SHIFTED WHEN WORKLOAD VARIES

Activity Workload

Resources

	Jan	Feb	Mar	Apr	May	Jun	Jul	Aug	Sep	Oct	Nov	Dec
Loans	80	60	80	80	80	140	140	80	80	60	60	60

Exhibit 12.4   Performance reporting—ensures resources can be shifted when workload varies.

process. If a performance report indicates that a business process or an activity is out of control (not staying within its budget), proactive process controls should:

- Provide a basis for anticipating and planning for changing workload
- Give the manager alternatives that will solve the problem
- Reduce costs
- Ensure quality

INSTITUTING PROCESS CONTROLS

The way an activity is done will vary, even if only slightly, each time the process is done. But a uniform and predictable process is required to produce good quality and meet customer needs. Processes that produce excessively variable results will also produce defects, errors, and waste. Inconsistency in work leads to unacceptable outputs and often additional activities to rectify the problem.

The objective of MegaStorage's "receiving" activity is to receive an item in a proper package, unpack it, deliver it on time to the user, and notify the system of the receipt. Consider the consequences of an inconsistent process. First, if the item is delivered to an incorrect location, the item would have to be found and the information updated in the system. Store efficiency would also be lowered while they are waiting for the item. The resulting worker's time necessary to chase down the item results in higher costs and no value to the customer.

An inconsistent process could also result in the high cost of detecting errors that would not be necessary if process consistency was established. An inconsistent process may not result in an unacceptable output, but it increases the cost and loss of profitability as a consequence of excessive goods being held, frustration and ineffective processes, and potential customer dissatisfaction. An inconsistent process could also result in late delivery.

The receiving department manager needed to understand how consistently the current processes were being performed. Consistency was measured in three different ways. First, errors were measured by approximating the amount of time spent correcting errors. Second, the time detecting internal errors was estimated, Third, the manager calculated the amount of time it would take to do the work if there were no errors. The error-free work time was compared to actual work time and then the effect of output variability was approximated.

Using these approaches, the manager estimated the impact of inconsistent work on the department as follows:

Activities	Time Correcting (%)	Time Detecting (%)	Wasted Time (%)
Receive goods	5	1	25
Inspect goods	5	1	10
Move to storage	8		7
Move to stores	2		10
Expedite goods	3		15
Train associates			25
Manage employees	10		30

The only way to ensure consistent output is to minimize the factors that cause inconsistency by implementing process controls. A process control monitors the process to ensure that it is operating effectively to produce a consistent output. The process must be studied to determine where a potential error might occur. A study of the "receive goods" activity reveals the following possible weakness:

Activity	Task	Potential Error
Receive goods	Unload goods	Goods damaged due to mishandling

Once the potential weakness is determined, the manager identifies potential improvements to the activity to minimize the occurrence of the problem:

Activity	Task	Potential Solution
Receive goods	Unload goods	Improve equipment used Improve working environment

Process controls also monitor other key factors that would cause the activity to function inconsistently, such as deviations in weights of shipments, equipment problems, storage space problems, and so on.

PLANNING GUIDELINE: Research and develop process controls for all department activities to ensure efficiency and profitability.

COMPUTER SYSTEMS

As they are being performed, activities both consume and create transactions. In most organizations, the amount of data created by these transaction process systems is extremely large. Most managers need summarized data (often termed information) to make decisions.

Traditionally, data has been summarized by combining transactional data. Thus, one would determine the cost of a product by adding together all the transactions related to the product, labor, material, overhead, and so forth.

An activity-based budgeting (ABB) system requires a system to monitor cost and performance at the activity level. Unfortunately, transaction processing systems do not collect activity information. This creates a disconnect between the planning and monitoring system. Actual activity information is required to complete the planning and budgeting cycle. Thus a new module must be added to enterprise resource planning (ERP) systems to perform this translation. This module is termed a **process translator.** (See Exhibit 12.5.)

Enterprise resource planning systems provide transaction data. They explain the "what's happening?"

Data warehouses summarize transaction data. They give a vertical view of data.

Process translator systems convert transaction data to processes (horizontal) data process rules.

Management information systems are decision support systems that use process data and summarized vertical data.

**Management
Information**

**Process
Translator**

**Data
Warehouse**

**Enterprise Resource Planning (ERP)
(Translation Data)**

Exhibit 12.5   Management information system.

SUMMARY

Organizations should use earned value measures and reporting. They should use proactive process controls rather than after-the-fact monitoring. They should shift resources using best practices. They need a process translator that converts ERP type transaction data into management information.

13

ORGANIZATION-WIDE IMPROVEMENTS

This chapter will:

- Discuss the importance of re-engineering to achieve organization-wide improvement.
- Present a four-phase process to implement re-engineering.

IMPORTANCE OF RE-ENGINEERING

Re-engineering is an intensive, customer-focused, top-down management effort to establish breakthrough in the performance capabilities and value of processes. Because few companies are as updated on process research and development (R&D) as on product R&D, re-engineering rethinks business processes. The approach is to re-examine the way an organization does business to produce dramatic improvements in performance through an alignment of process, people, technology, measurement, and organizational structure in support of shared vision and values.

The underlying principles of the re-engineering process include creating a sense of urgency attributable to external influences; recognizing the need to develop and implement solutions aligned with customer needs; and ensuring clear, consistent communication for effective project management and focused efforts. Re-engineering also creates awareness and opportunity for organizational learning and change with a focus on high-value opportunities utilizing cost/benefit analysis.

FOUR PHASES FOR IMPLEMENTATION

A four-phase implementation process can be used to achieve business process re-engineering. The four steps are:

1. Create re-engineering strategy
2. Develop detailed design
3. Implement solutions
4. Evaluate results

Create Re-engineering Strategy

During this phase, the organization must ensure that the senior management team shares a common understanding of what business process re-engineering is and the role senior management must play in its implementation. Often, the many stakeholder expectations of the project outcomes are not aligned. The organization must recognize and create a meaningful dialogue on this issue in order to recognize problems that need re-engineering.

Through training, discussion, and meetings, the company must ensure that management understands:

- Basic business process re-engineering (BPR) concepts
- BPR methodology
- Importance of management's commitment to the effort
- Necessity to act as leaders, to move from an autocratic management style to a participative, team-building style
- Vital importance of effective cross-functional teamwork to the success of the initiative

The objectives of creating a re-engineering strategy are to build an authentic relationship within the company, including project sponsor and key stakeholders; determine the implications of differences of opinion among stakeholders; develop a shared understanding of the real problems among sponsors; and identify range of desired outcomes. The creative stage goes through these steps:

- Develop shared vision
- Determine business problems

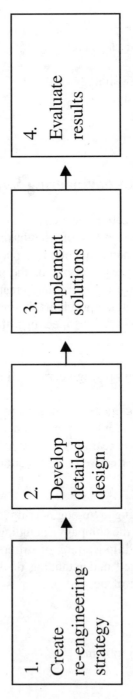

Exhibit 13.1   Four phases of re-engineering.

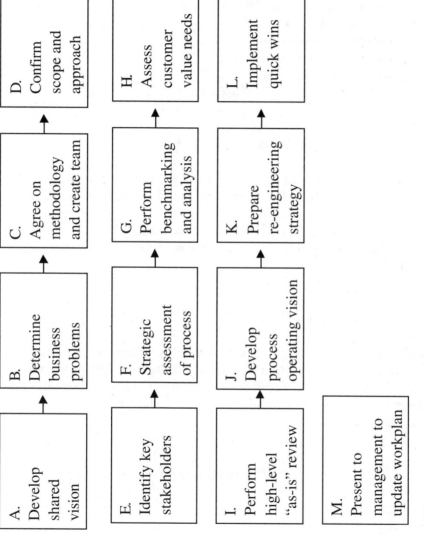

Exhibit 13.2 Steps to phase 1—create re-engineering strategy.

- Agree on a methodology and create a team
- Confirm scope and approach
- Identify key stakeholders
- Strategic assessment of the process
- Perform benchmarking analysis
- Assess customer values/needs
- Perform high-level "as is" review
- Develop process operating vision
- Prepare re-engineering strategy
- Implement "quick-wins"
- Present to management to update work plan

Develop Shared Vision

Companies should strive to develop a shared vision throughout their organization. This process includes determining the participants in the initiative, identifying and clarifying management's vision for the future, and understanding the extent to which the vision is shared among key stakeholders. In addition, informal meetings with management help to give context to the project.

Determine Business Problems

Next, the organization determines its business problems by examining the organization's current situation by studying organization history, competitor analysis, and examining supplier relationships. In addition, complications and consequences must be identified, as well as the range of desired stakeholder outcomes.

Agree on a Methodology and Create a Team

This action is established to determine the appropriate methodology to address the problems and to establish the team with various skills needed to accomplish project objectives. Resource issues are brought to the attention of the steering committee, and project team training is used to get the project team up to speed.

Confirm Scope and Approach

This process is used to gain consensus on broad boundaries of project scope to ensure project relevance and organizational focus. The project team must tailor the methodology and detailed approach to the company's structure and protocol based on team members' feedback. Then, finite project goals are set. At the conclusion of this activity, the project team and leadership should explicitly agree on the scope, desired outcomes, and approach.

Identify Key Stakeholders

Project teams identify influential individuals and assess how to involve them in the project to add value and avoid potential barriers in later phases. During this step, the teams determine how key individuals and segments of the organization are impacted by the project. Then, a plan is designed to meet their needs based on commitment.

Strategic Assessment of the Process

Strategic assessment ensures consensus on what the current process produces, including its boundaries and its relative value to the organization. In this step, project teams prepare a high-level view of the process to ensure team consensus. However, the definition of the processes to be re-engineered must be thoroughly debated because a relatively narrow definition may limit the achievement of quantum leaps in performance. Processes must be defined broadly in order to reach stretch targets.

Perform Benchmarking Analysis

Benchmarking analysis is conducted through a survey focusing only on the key performance measures addressing quality, time, profitability, and cost factors. Data-collection alternatives are reviewed and a survey implementation process is designed to conduct the benchmarking and activity analysis efforts.

Assess Customer Values/Needs

This information brings the project team closer to understanding internal and external customer requirements and the processes' performance in order to prioritize re-engineering opportunities. During this step, customers are interviewed, focus groups are conducted, and other data-gathering methods are used to obtain an understanding of customer profiles, critical buyer values, and key performance indicators.

Perform High-Level "As Is" Review

The purpose of this review is to analyze and document existing processes and uses of technology. Process deficiencies can vary depending on the organization's culture and the nature of the project.

Develop Process Operating Vision

Developing vision of how the process should be performed creates conceptual and pictorial descriptions of the envisioned future state that will serve to guide the detailed process design. The goal of this step is to identify those capabilities that the company can use to add unique value to the customer. Knowledge of these core competitive competencies offers the leverage points to determine how the organization can strengthen its competitive position and offer a unique value proposition to its customers.

Prepare Re-engineering Strategy

This step encourages the project team to filter the opportunities for re-engineering and develop a hypothesis to achieve a quantum leap in performance. During this step, it is critical to surface creative tension. Creative tension is a result of the gap between the desirable future and the present state. Discrepancies between the present and desired states create gaps. A natural tension is felt from those gaps, and energy is created. Creative tension is surfaced by acknowledging the weaknesses in current reality and recognizing and creating the image of the preferred future.

Implement "Quick Wins"

This step works to identify and implement those initiatives that would quickly realize benefits and sustain momentum. Quick wins typically represent process inefficiencies that are readily evident and require minor resources to implement the change. By definition, these initiatives are aligned with the organization's strategies, and the purpose is to get some early successes so others will see the benefits.

Present to Management to Update Work Plan

This is the step to reconfirm the project's success factors and obtain project leadership commitment to results to date and to future phases.

Develop Detailed Design

The detailed design of the BPR project is the "blueprint" that guides the implementation of the re-engineered system. Typically, process re-engineering efforts focus on cost reduction with inadequate understanding of those processes that deliver real value to the customer. By understanding the drivers of customer satisfaction, process redesign efforts gain the necessary insight to focus on elimination of low-value activities and on growing revenues and profitability.

The development of a detailed design goes through three steps:

1. Validate, design, and develop detail
2. Refine business case
3. Present to management and update work plan

Validate, Design, and Develop Detail

First, the organization builds upon the initial visioning framework and designs the prototype processes. This validate, design, and development detail involves obtaining regular feedback from the organization's stakeholders, setting goals linked to stakeholder wants, and setting performance measures linked to those goals. In addition, it involves feeding back information to the

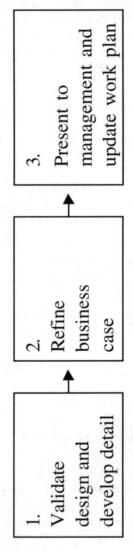

Exhibit 13.3 Steps to phase 2—develop detailed design.

appropriate people, taking corrective action when performance is off target, and resetting goals in response to continuously changing stakeholder expectations.

Refine Business Case

Second, the economic analysis and reasoning for implementing the re-engineered processes must be finalized for the company. The cost estimates include systems, training, relocation, and resource requirements. This step is necessary for the company to make decisions, and, therefore, it is essential to fully understand the cost and benefit elements in the plan.

Present to Management and Update Work Plan

Finally, the project is presented to management and the work plan is updated. This process ensures checking expectations, updating deliverable formats, validating key elements of new process design, and obtaining commitment to implementation.

Implement Solutions

The third phase of re-engineering is implementing solutions. This phase migrates the company to the redesigned environment and develops a continuous improvement process. The critical objective of this phase is to install systemic changes that will last. To achieve the critical objective requires

- Sound planning on how to migrate to the new operating model
- Comprehensive plans for each re-engineering initiative
- Frequent communications
- Wide-ranging training programs
- A dedication to operating in a new environment. A focus on project management is necessary to accomplish the migration.

The pattern to implement solutions goes through several steps, including the following:

- Develop transition plans
- Prepare communication plan

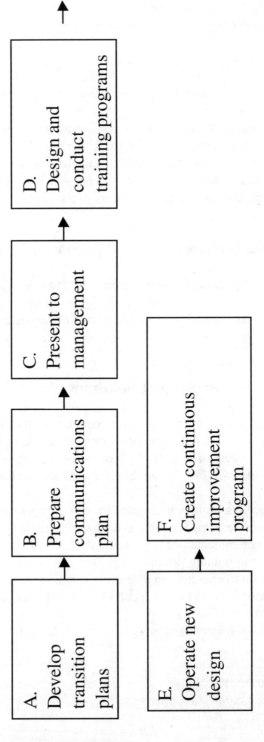

Exhibit 13.4 Steps to phase 3—implement solutions.

- Present to management
- Design and conduct training programs
- Operate new design
- Create a continuous improvement program

Develop Transition Plans

During the development of the transition plans, the project team prepares to implement change by developing a time-phased action plan. The action plan describes all activities necessary to move to the new design (e.g., training, organizational changes, process documentation).

Prepare Communication Plan

The communication plan is used to manage the change. An open and continuous communication system supports the transition process. In contrast, lack of information can lead to resistance to change and rumors about potential threats, especially when redundancies are a result of the new design. Therefore, the communication plan involves determining who needs to be targeted, determining the mode of communication, and involving the action team in defining the key messages.

Present to Management

This presentation to management is used to gain management's commitment to persevere during the implementation of the new operating model. During this stage, an outline of how normal business operation will be maintained during the implementation is created. In addition, management's express commitment and support to the program is secured.

Design and Conduct Training Programs

Employees are prepared during this step for operating the new design by developing and conducting appropriate training. The training content should be focused on the redesigned process as well as specific activities that employees will be performing. This approach enables process employees to see how their work effort impacts the whole system.

Operate New Design

When operating the new design, the organization should ensure that the re-engineering environment is operational and that the expected quantitative and qualitative benefits are achieved. This activity is successfully achieved by using a project management tool to track the realization of implementation costs and benefits.

Create a Continuous Improvement Program

Once the process has been implemented, it is important to encourage lasting change by installing a systematic program focused on customer satisfaction. The objectives of this step are to

- Explain strategies for ensuring continuous improvement.
- Identify principles to use in managing change for continuous improvement.
- Identify ways to ensure lasting change.

Responsibilities related to continuous improvement should be clearly examined, and the company's readiness for and resistance to change should be addressed. Ways to address this include the following:

- Use feedback to surface dissatisfaction.
- Communicate a clear image of the future.
- Create a roadmap for change.
- Assess individual transitions.
- Re-evaluate the company and leadership's commitment to and/or ownership of the change process.

Evaluate Results

In this last phase, the organization must ensure that expected benefits are realized in accordance with the overall plan. The primary objective of this phase is to drive for continuous improvement by monitoring and making enhancements based on key performance indicators.

Then, monitor the results by comparing the results being achieved to those anticipated. It is important to develop a formal procedure to monitor results, inform responsible individuals, and assign accountability for modifying implementation activities.

14

LET'S GET STARTED

This last chapter will get you started on driving value into your organization using activity-based budgeting and feature costing. There are two paths you can take—beginning either in a single area or on an enterprise-wide basis. If you choose the option to pilot in a single area, you can later expand the use of ABB and feature costing for the entire enterprise.

ENTERPRISE-WIDE IMPLEMENTATION

Part I: Activity-Based Budgeting and Feature Costing Overview

For the enterprise-wide implementation, begin with selling top management on the benefits of changing to an activity-based budgeting (ABB) and feature costing approach. Start with obtaining an agreement on how management is trying to drive value into the organization. Chapter 1 emphasizes focusing on how activities create value. Senior management must look at how their collection of activities and business processes drive value and give them a sustainable competitive advantage (à la Michael Porter).

The second step is to then compare how well the existing budgeting process supports the efforts to create value. Chapter 2 helps this evaluation by identifying common problems many organizations experience with traditional budgeting techniques. Management should ask, "If the traditional budgeting techniques do not help us create value, what changes do we need to make?" This chapter helps sharpen the focus on how the budgeting process can create value. These include management focusing on eliminating waste, reducing workload, and reducing unused or wasted capacity. Value is also created by synchronizing operations with both customers and suppliers, identifying root causes, creating action plans to reduce and eliminate non-value, and focusing on outcomes.

Chapter 3 stresses the importance of linking strategy and the budgeting process. It discusses defining organization goals, translating customer requirements to targets, planning guidelines, and setting business process targets. The key is to set stretch targets and ensure that workers believe that they are achievable. Planning guidelines are a key tool in translating the strategic direction into specific measurable actions. Everyone must understand how his or her activities support the strategic direction of the organization. They must understand how they create value in the organization.

Part II: Activity-Based Budgeting and Feature Costing Principles

For an enterprise-wide implementation, it is important for a project team to fully understand the principles of ABB. Because managers will focus on how the work (or activity) is performed, the budgeting process will yield more actionable information for operating managers. With a firm grasp of the business needs and the underlying principles of ABB, the team is ready to move forward with implementation.

Part II explains ABB principles that provide the process to put these techniques into practice. The principles of ABB are the foundation for implementation. It begins in Chapter 4 with translating a strategy into processes and activities. From this framework, strategic objectives can be cascaded down into specific activity and process targets.

Chapter 5 provides an overview of activity and business process analysis. It discusses forecasting volumes and revenues combined with forecasting of activity workloads. This is the heart of the ABB methodology. It differs from traditional budgeting in that it focuses on customer demand for products and services and the workload that is required to serve those customers and produce those products and services. This workload is translated into business process and activity workload and finally into required resources to perform those activities. It provides operational managers with clear visibility of what activity will be needed to provide the expected volumes of products and services.

Chapter 6 helps one to understand the impacts of capacity and how capacity impacts the value-creating capability. Organizations should calculate capacity utilization during ABB and during the year. They should also communicate available capacity to marketing and sales so that available capacity can be sold.

Chapter 7 provides insights on how features and characteristics impact activity performance. It shows an innovative way to make an activity analysis more robust while reducing the data collection effort by focusing on similarities. Features and characteristics help guide your organization not to just use best practices alone, but to use it in conjunction with understanding product features and customer characteristics.

Part III: Activity-Based Budgeting and Feature Costing Methodology

Chapter 8 shows a full example using EZ Money Bank. It presents a methodology for implementing ABB. The strategic plan feeds the ABB process. At the corporate level, this drives:

- The development of the planning guidelines
- Forecasting of volumes and revenues
- Forecasting of activity workloads
- Consideration of enterprise-wide improvement projects

Steps 3 and 4 are executed several times until enterprise-wide activity workloads and improvement projects are agreed to. This corporate level feeds the department level. The departments begin step 5 by reconciling the departmental targets supplied by corporate to existing activity performances. Gaps in performance lead to step 6—identification of department improvement projects. After these iterations, step 7 is taken to finalize and consolidate the budgets.

Chapter 9 explains reviewing and finalization of the budget. Chapter 10 discusses how to improve activities and business processes. In most cases, the departmental performance needs to be continually improving. This is both to cover the gaps and to use improved productivity to enhance market position.

Chapter 11 presents ideas on how to perform gap analysis. As targets are passed from the senior management to the departmental level, there is an immediate need to reconcile these targets to existing activity performance. These gaps represent both over- and underutilized capabilities. The overstaffed areas must be redistributed to cover the gaps or to find ways to otherwise realize value from them.

The tie-in to ongoing performance is illustrated in Chapter 12. Performance reports were illustrated as well as earned value reporting. The emphasis on instituting process controls rather than after-the-fact reporting was discussed. A brief review of computer systems of the future was provided.

Chapter 13 provides guidance on the importance of business process reengineering and other enterprise-wide initiatives. As all organizations must be changing to meet the changing environment, there is a need to consider the impact of enterprise-wide improvement projects as part of driving value in your organization.

Target-setting techniques are discussed in Appendix A and specific company examples are reviewed in Appendix B. This is followed by a glossary of terms.

DEPARTMENTAL OR WORK GROUP IMPLEMENTATIONS

Virtually any manager can apply these techniques directly to the area he or she supervises. You can do this by focusing solely on the area under your control.

The hardest part of this approach is to understand how your department supports your company's mission and strategic objectives. The overview in Chapter 4 should assist you. In many cases, it is just a matter of persistent asking of the question, "How do we fit into what our organization is trying to achieve?"

Activity analysis of a department or work group can be completed in one or two sessions using a storyboard technique. The key processes supported by the group can be posted. Then each work group can add their activities in process sequence. The guidance in Chapter 4 as well as the additional texts, which are referenced, can aid in this process.

The methodology is the same for an individual department; however, there is more converting of the inputs from the corporate level into an activity-based format. Using ABB will provide all the same feedback to the traditional budgeting process, but it will also yield much richer information.

Overall, the ABB process transforms the budgeting process from financial abstraction into a tool for operational clarity. The combination with features costing permits robust detail at an affordable maintenance costs. You and your organization will continue to face trade-offs, but with ABB, you will be able to see the future much more clearly.

Call us with your experiences and your suggestions. Call us if you need some additional insights or some coaching. We look forward to creating value for you.

John Antos 972.980.7407 valucreate@aol.com
Jim Brimson 817.275.6677 abm.institute@airmail.net

___Appendix A___

TARGET-SETTING TECHNIQUES

This appendix will:

- Explore five techniques to set targets.
- Give examples of how these techniques can be easily implemented.

FIVE PROVEN TECHNIQUES TO HELP SET TARGETS

There are many proven techniques for setting targets for business processes and activities. Some of the more common include the following:

- Customer satisfaction and loyalty surveys
- Core competency analysis
- Benchmarking
- Business process and activity deployment
- Reverse engineering competitor's products and services

Although the reader is familiar with most of these techniques, we want to show how to use these techniques for creating value in the planning and budgeting process. Let's discuss each technique and illustrate how to set business process and activity targets with an example.

CUSTOMER SATISFACTION AND LOYALTY SURVEYS

Customer satisfaction surveys question customers concerning how well the organization is meeting their needs. Some surveys are designed for "external and internal customers" and others are designed for "internal and external suppliers." An **external customer** would be one who buys your organization's products or services. The salesperson would be considered your **internal customer**. The customer or a dealer or broker would be considered an **external customer**. An **internal supplier** is someone who produces materials directly for your organization, whereas an **external supplier** is a separate firm producing just one component or part for your product or service.

Most surveys are designed to measure overall customer satisfaction. Recently, organizations have been migrating to *customer loyalty* surveys. Customer loyalty surveys can be used instead of or in addition to *customer satisfaction* surveys. It does not really matter to what degree your customer is satisfied if he or she will never buy your product or service again. Repeat business is key to growth, so more and more organizations are working on garnering customer loyalty.

One company, Toyota, learned the importance of customer loyalty quickly and used it to their advantage. Toyota came out with its high-end luxury car. This luxury car was constantly ranked at or near the top of J. D. Powers Customer Satisfaction Surveys. However, after several years, sales were down and former owners were buying Mercedes and BMWs. Although several factors contributed to this reduction in Toyota's luxury car sales, one factor mentioned repeatedly was the lack of loyalty the owners felt for the cars and the company. This lack of loyalty made it easy for customers to switch to another brand of automobile. Toyota soon put together a corporate strategy that quickly turned the tide, gleaning a significant increase in repeat sales.

How does an organization ensure customer loyalty? Can the product or service alone guarantee repeat business? Or is it the organizational strategy, shown through both the product/service and the actions of its employees, that guarantees customer loyalty?

Customer and loyalty surveys are tools that relate strategy to budgeting and planning for activities and business processes. Example A-1 explores how customer satisfaction and loyalty surveys help set targets as part of activity-based budgeting (ABB).

Example A-1: Customer Satisfaction Surveys Help Set Targets

EZ Money Bank performed a survey of its external customers to measure customer satisfaction factors and customer loyalty factors. Former customers and people who had used other banks were also surveyed. They were asked to list factors that they believe lead to customer satisfaction and customer loyalty. Then they were asked to rank those factors by order of importance to them, personally. The top five factors listed by those surveyed were as follows:

Customer Satisfaction & Loyalty Factor	Ranking	Factor Type
Low interest rates and fees	1	Satisfaction
Quick evaluation period	2	Satisfaction
Knowledgeable staff	3	Loyalty
Extended hours for applying	4	Satisfaction
Extended hours for customer service	5	Loyalty

From this customer survey, EZ Money Bank could determine that the most important factor for customer satisfaction was "low interest rates and fees." Exhibit A.1 shows a copy of the customer perception of performance graph that management put together based on the completed customer satisfaction ratings (rankings are shown at the bottom of the chart starting from 0 and going to 100 percent). Below 80 percent would be considered unsatisfactory by the organization. This graph shows that the most important customer factor, "low interest rates and fees," is below 80 percent or unsatisfactory.

Based on this customer survey, EZ Money Bank decided that it must lower its fees in order to obtain the revenue goals that senior management has given to them. These surveys showed that EZ Money was doing great with their quick evaluation period for their customers. This also shows that they need to work on the knowledge level of their staff.

Based on this survey, EZ Money Bank believes that it needs to do a better job of converting inquiries into loans. This approach will help EZ Money to better use its capacity. This will increase its loan workload. As we will see, the loan application staff is spending a lot of time with miscellaneous activities. This time must be investigated. Then, action plans need to be developed to better use that time.

It may make sense to have the loan application people participate in some activities that are currently being handled by the loan officers. The loan application people might answer phone inquiries, sell mortgages (at least the document preparation portion), or take part or all of the application.

Cross-training the loan application staff might help when workload is very heavy. It might also help to use that capacity that is now being spent on miscellaneous activities. Since the loan application staff is in a lower salary grade, the bank would save money by having someone in a lower salary grade perform the activity. The bank would have to explore upgrading the position, additional training, and a number of other factors.

EZ Money would have to compare the cost to the current way of having loan officers answer phone inquiries, take loan applications, and prepare mortgages for resale. This approach might free up the loan officers to do more marketing in the community.

This is a good example of how using customer surveys as part of ABB helped show management some alternatives while addressing the customer satisfaction issue relating to low interest rates and low fees. Until EZ Money Bank looks at the actual cost of this activity under its present system and the alternate approaches, they will have no idea how much more cost effective it would be to better use these application processors.

In preparing the budget for any business process or activity, examine the financial implications of business processes or activities under different financial alternatives. In our example, the activity "answer phone inquiries" could be handled by the loan application processors or the loan officers.

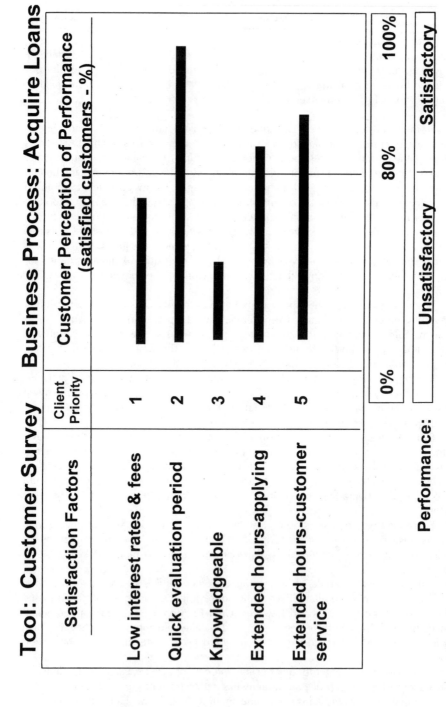

Exhibit A.1   Setting targets for business processes and activities.

- Handle loan phone inquiries—loan officers
- Handle loan phone inquiries—loan processors

First, set up the activity budget for the first alternative "handle loan phone inquiries—loan officers." Take the forecast of 1,000 loans. Look at the average time to answer a phone inquiry for a loan officer. Convert that into salary dollars for the activity. Perform the same calculation for the loan application processors.

Then, look at the conversion ratio for loan officers and application processors. Combine the analysis for the cost of loan officers versus application processors handling the activity with the analysis of the conversion ratio to derive an action plan.

The current loan officer conversion rate is one loan per three phone calls. The loan officers and application processors estimate that the conversion rate for application processors would be one loan per four phone calls. The loan officers believe that they need 15 minutes on average to answer a loan inquiry over the phone. The loan officers and application processors believe that loan processors would also need 15 minutes to answer phone inquiries. They produce the following activity analysis:

Loan Officers Handle Phone Inquiries

1,000 loans × 3 inquiries per loan for loan officers = 3,000 phone calls

3,000 phone calls × 15 minutes per inquiry (loan officers)
= 45,000 minutes/60 minutes per hour-workload of 750 hours

750 hours × $20 per hour = $15,000

Loan Processors Handle Phone Inquiries

1,000 loans × 4 inquiries per loan for loan officers = 4,000 phone calls

4,000 phone calls × 15 minutes per inquiry (application processors)
= 60,000 minutes/60 minutes per hour = workload of 1,000 hours

1,000 hours × $15 per hour = $15,000 (see Exhibit A.2)

We could expand this analysis to include space, rent, supplies, phone, etc. The reader saw how to perform that analysis in the EZ Money Bank case study in Chapter 8. However, what we see so far is that, from a cost standpoint, there is no difference in cost whether EZ Money handles the phone inquiries with loan officers or with application processors.

There are some other considerations. The bank is losing potential business because the application processors cannot convert as many phone calls into loans as the loan officers. This fact must be considered. Another factor is what happens when the loan officers are busy. Is it better to call back the inquiring party, or is it better to have the loan processor handle the phone inquiry? What about cost of the additional training required by the loan application processors? Obviously, cost is only one factor in deciding which alternative to choose.

Now the bank can compare the cost of having the loan officers and application processors answer phone inquiries. They can ask what could be done with the loan

Customer survey stimulates organization to consider whether to continue having the loan officers handle phone inquiries or should loan procesors handle inquiries so loan officers could do more marketing?

Activity	Salaries and Benefits	Space	Equipment	Travel	Other	Total
Handle phone inquiries						
By loan officers	$15,000					
By loan processors	$15,000					

Assumptions

By loan officers

Salaries: 1,000 loans x 3 inquiries/loan for loan officers = 3,000 phone inquiries
3,000 inquiries x 15 minutes per inquiry = 45,000 minutes/60 minutes per hour = workload of 750 loan officer hours
750 hours @ $20/hour of salary + benefits = $15,000

Space: $2,000/person * 750 loan officer hours/2,000 annual hours = $750
Equipment: $10,000/year in equipment * 750 loan officer hours/2000 hours = $3,750

By loan processors

Salaries: 1,000 loans x 4 inquiries/loan for loan processors = 4,000 phone inquiries
4,000 inquiries x 15 minutes per inquiry = 60,000 minutes/60 minutes per hour = workload of 1,000 loan processor hours
1,000 loan processor hours @ $15/hour of salary + benefits = $15,000

Space: $2,000/person * 750 loan officer hours/2,000 annual hours =
Equipment: $10,000/year in equipment * 750 loan officer hours/2000 hours =

Exhibit A.2 Set targets using customer survey.

officer's time if some of their time could be freed up. Management now has a clear view of the budgeted costs of each of these activities. Decisions based on an activity budget are much easier for both the department manager and the senior management. Activity budgets allow an organization to see specifically what it is getting and where it is spending its money. Senior management must decide what is the best use of the loan officers' time. Is it better to have the loan officers answering phone inquiries? Is it better for the loan processors to answer phone inquiries while the loan officers make goodwill calls to builders, car dealers, and other sources of mortgages and loans?

CORE COMPETENCY ANALYSIS

A second technique for cascading strategy to activities is core competency analysis. In core competency analysis, an organization should ask itself which business processes are critical to its industry. This gives the organization an **industry core competency**. Then the organization must ask which business processes it does well.

The organization should compare itself with **external benchmarks** of these business processes. Then it should perform a **competency gap analysis** to see how big the gap is between industry norms and its own performance. It should be determined which business processes need improvement. Finally, business process targets should be set for cost, time, and quality. (See Exhibit A.3 for examples of both industry and organizational core competency.)

Exhibit A.4 illustrates core competency analysis. Example A-2 will better illustrate these steps.

Example A-2: Budgeting for EZ Money Bank's Core Competency—A Well-Trained Staff

EZ Money Bank determines that a well-trained staff is one of its core competencies. It is willing to spend money and extra time to hold on to that competency. That means additional training for its staff, which will increase the workload of the training department. Therefore, EZ Money Bank must determine if the benefit justifies the cost for the activity "provide training for staff."

EZ Money Bank must first break down its costs. Then, it must develop a budget for such training in order to justify this core competency to have a knowledgeable staff.

EZ Money Bank determines that its staff requires three types of training in order to have this competency:

1. Provide initial training
2. Provide follow-up training
3. Provide cross-training

EZ Money Bank must first review the costs for these three types of training and then

INDUSTRY	CORE COMPETENCY
Banking	Customer relations
Insurance	Sales, Underwriting, Claims
Transportation	On-Time, Low Price, Safety
Oil	Exploration, Marketing

ORGANIZATION	
Fidelity	Performance, Variety
Southwest Airlines	Low Price, Quick Turnaround
Delta Dental Plans	Network of Dentists
FedEx	Customer Satisfaction, On Time
Nordstrom's	Customer Service

Exhibit A.3   Setting targets using core competencies: core competency examples.

Which business processes are critical to your industry?	►	Industry core competency

Which business processes does your organization do well?	►	Compare with external benchmarks	►	Perform competency gap analysis	►	Set activity/ business process targets (cost, time, quality)

Exhibit A.4   Setting targets using core competencies—tool: core competency analysis.

develop a budget for each of these activities. We will break down the three types of training and create a budget for each.

Provide Initial Training

A training person earns $50,000 per year. Based on the number of branches in the bank, the organization budgets for this training person to spend 50 weeks, providing initial follow-up and cross-training to the application processors. The average human resource person works 50 weeks per year because most take a two-week vacation. A person who earns $50,000 for 50 weeks costs the organization $1,000 per week of training. If EZ Money Bank budgets four weeks for the activity "initial training," the salary budget for this activity would become $20,000.

$50,000 annual salary / 50 weeks = $1,000 per week in salary for trainer

4 weeks of training × $1,000 per week = $4,000 total salary cost for initial training

Although the analysis should include other resources spent for the trainer, the only resource we will address is any specific supplies connected with the training. (See Exhibit A.5.)

Provide Follow-up Training

The same trainer who earns $50,000 per year will also provide follow-up training. Based on the number of branches that will need follow-up training, the organization budgets based on the fact that this training person will spend one week providing follow-up training. Remember, the human resource person earns $1,000 per week. If 20 weeks are budgeted for the activity "provide follow-up training," the salary budget for this activity would be $20,000.

$1,000 per week in salary × 1 week = $1,000 salary cost for follow-up training

However, the organization has set a **materiality limit**. This means that the cost of this activity is believed to be too small to charge out to the branches. EZ Money Bank believes that the amount does not justify the time and energy necessary to budget for it and then maintain a system to charge out this small amount. In addition, there is concern that some branches would not obtain this training if they had to pay for it. For analysis, therefore, they still look at it in total. They still determine it is worthwhile to perform this training. However, the branches are not charged for the training.

Provide Cross-Training

The same trainer who earns $50,000 per year can provide cross-training. The organization feels that it is important that staff are cross-trained in other activities throughout the organization. By understanding other business processes and activities within the organization, the staff members can work together more effectively and will be less likely to negatively impact the activities of other workers.

Based on the number of current people requiring cross-training in activities within

Organization decides a well-trained sales staff is a core competency. Additional training will increase the workload of the training department.

Current Activity	Salary	Space	Equipment	Supplies	Other	Total
Initial training	$20,000				$840	

Alternatives						
Follow-up	$20,000				$	$
Cross-train	$10,000	$			$	$

Assumptions

Initial training	Salaries:	1 trainer @ $50,000/year for 20 weeks = $20,000
	Space:	
	Other:	Training supplies $840
Follow-up training	Salaries:	1 trainer @ $50,000/year for 20 weeks @ 20 branches
	Space:	
	Other:	
Cross-training	Salaries:	1 trainer @ $50,000/year for 10 weeks @ 20 branches
	Space:	
	Other:	

Exhibit A.5 Set targets using core competencies.

the branch, as well as other departments, EZ Money Bank budgets 10 weeks to provide cross-training. EZ Money Bank estimates that cross-training will cost $10,000. (See Exhibit A.5.)

Considering the small dollars connected with these three activities, many organizations would choose not to charge out these activities to the departments carrying the workload for these activities.

However, other organizations may believe that they can charge out for these activities with minimal effort. They think that the departments creating the cost should be charged for as many activities as possible. Therefore, organizations with this philosophy would charge out for these training activities even though the dollar amounts are small.

BENCHMARKING

A third technique for cascading strategy to activities is benchmarking. Most business people are familiar with benchmarking. The original idea for benchmarking was copied from an old military process for aiming cannon fire. Before the age of electronics and modern weapons, soldiers or sailors would manually aim their cannons at a target. They could only approximate such variables as distance, velocity, wind conditions, and so forth. After they fired their first volley, they would have to manually readjust their cannons depending on whether they were short or long to their targets.

For years, organizations have performed financial benchmarking, taking aim at their financial goals or targets and then manually adjusting as needed. Benchmarking activities and business processes work in a similar fashion.

For example, say an organization determines that its accounting department expenses are average when compared to other organizations in its industry. It is assumed that this department is performing adequately. This could be a serious miscalculation. Departments, of course, do more than one task or activity. This particular accounting department could have two activities with two totally different performance ratings. One activity might be world class, whereas a second activity might be extremely inefficient. The organization is fooled into thinking that the department is performing adequately when, in fact, they are partially world class and partially very inefficient.

A second issue occurs with financial benchmarking when an organization calculates that its accounting department's expenses, as a percentage of revenue, are higher than other organizations in its industry. The organization now realizes that it has a problem. However, where is the source of that problem? Is the problem in preparing payroll? Is the problem in preparing financial statements? Financial benchmarking usually does not give the user that type of actionable information.

On the other hand, activity and business process benchmarking is much more useful. If an organization benchmarks the activity "prepare payroll" and discovers that it spends more money than other world-class preparers of payroll, it can begin focusing on how to improve this activity. It can communicate with outsourcing organizations such as Automated Data Processing (ADP) for help. It can ask suppliers of payroll systems for ideas. It can ask other organizations what they are doing to improve this activity. Now the organization has a way to zero in on improving their activities. It can now use specific ideas from others to facilitate improvement. (See Exhibit A.6.)

Benchmarking of activities and business processes can be used for the following:

- Time
- Quality
- New products or services
- Activity cost per unit of activity volume
- Business process cost per unit of volume
- Outcomes

Each of these items can be benchmarked separately.

Tool: Benchmarking activities and business processes to determine

Time

Quality

New products or services

Activity cost per unit of volume

Business process cost per unit of volume

Outcomes

Note: Expenses as percentage of revenue is usually not very useful.

Exhibit A.6   Setting business process and activity targets using benchmarking.

Time

There are several ways to benchmark time. An organization does not have to benchmark time using all of these methods for every activity or business process. Certain measures of time will be more meaningful in specific situations. They include queue time, touch time, waiting time, and elapsed time. Following are some of the ways to benchmark time.

Queue Time

Queue time is considered the span of time from when the activity input is received until the time the person performing the activity actually starts work. Think of a manager who orders supplies for his or her department. On Monday, the manager sends the order to purchasing. A day passes until purchasing receives the order. The queue time between when the manager sent the requisition to purchasing and when purchasing actually started to process the order was one day. Therefore, one day would be considered the queue time.

Touch Time

Touch time is considered the amount of time that the activity input is actually touched by the person or piece of equipment performing the activity. Think of the purchasing agent who may spend only 30 minutes reviewing a requisition, obtaining quotes from vendors, and actually ordering the items requested. The touch time in this situation would be only 30 minutes. It usually amazes people how little time is actually spent on touch time. (See Example A-3.)

Example A-3: Touch Time Can Be Minutes

Here are two examples of the small amount of time spent on touch time:

A manufacturer of leather briefcases did a survey of its manufacturing operations. It found that only 5 percent of the time in which a briefcase was manufactured was actually spent in touch time (time when a person or machine actually touched the product). The rest of the time was spent in storage, moving, and waiting.

A manufacturer of uniforms calculated that from the time the cloth was brought into the factory until the time the uniform was completed was approximately one week. Surprisingly, it was discovered that only three minutes during that week was touch time. For only three minutes during the week was someone or some machine actually cutting, sewing, folding, or stuffing that uniform.

As part of the budgeting process, it is important to begin to calculate touch time as a percentage of the total elapsed time and then explore ways to reduce elapsed time.

Waiting Time

Waiting time is considered the span of time from the moment the input has been initially acted on until the next task/step is performed or until the customer receives the output. For example, say someone from the purchasing department calls several vendors, asking for quotes. It may take the vendors two days to respond. Therefore, the waiting time until the vendors respond is two days. On Thursday, purchasing places the order. The order is delivered on the following Monday. There is the second instance of waiting time. This waiting time starts when the purchasing agent places the order and ends when the manager submitting the requisition actually receives the order. This second instance of waiting time might be counted as two working days (i.e., Thursday to Friday and Friday to Monday) or four total days (i.e., Thursday to Monday).

Some processes have several departments or groups performing activities or tasks. There can be several categories of waiting time in these instances. Our goal, as part of the budgeting process, is to identify these various categories and set the budget based on improving these various waiting times.

Elapsed Time

Elapsed time is considered the span of time from the moment the activity input is received until the time the customer receives the output. Think of a manager who orders supplies for their organization. On Monday, he or she sends the order to purchasing. A day passes until purchasing receives the order. Purchasing calls several vendors asking for quotes. It takes the vendors two days to respond. On Thursday, purchasing places the order. The order is delivered on the following Monday. Therefore, the elapsed time between when the manager sent the requisition to purchasing and when the manager actually received the order was seven days (i.e., Monday to Monday).

Quality

Benchmarking quality may consist of comparing the following:

- Error rates
- Customer satisfaction ratings
- Customer loyalty
- Achieving the outcome

Examples of error rates include errors made per financial statement closing, per tax return prepared, per work order, or per customer order. Customer satisfaction and customer loyalty ratings were discussed earlier in this chapter. A fourth measure deals with achieving the desired outcome. For example, a systems integration firm can follow all the specifications that the customer lays out for it, but the resulting system is not what the customer needs. Therefore, the desired outcome was not achieved even though the output created met all the specifications required by the customer. Some additional quality benchmarks might be measures of reliability, features, and ease of use.

NEW PRODUCTS OR SERVICES

When benchmarking new products or services, an organization may be interested in benchmarking the frequency and/or number of new product introductions. It may want to benchmark the average time from product/service conception until the product/service is in the marketplace. It might also benchmark the average time from product conception until a product is prototyped. It could benchmark the average amount of time it takes to obtain approval from regulatory agencies. It could benchmark new product/service sales as a percentage of total revenue. The number of different benchmarks an organization uses will often depend on the industry.

ACTIVITY COST PER UNIT OF ACTIVITY VOLUME

Many organizations have begun to collect activity unit costs. Some large organizations are beginning to benchmark activity unit costs across their offices and divisions. The following are some examples of this type of benchmarking:

- Cost to resolve a claim for insurance companies
- Cost to open a new account for banks and savings and loans
- Cost to clean an office floor for a cleaning service
- Cost for cutting a payroll check
- Cost to hire
- Cost per equipment repair

These are just some examples. The possibilities are limitless. Think about some business processes and activities that are performed in your office on a daily basis. Now try to think of them in terms of their actual cost. The list gets long pretty fast, doesn't it?

BUSINESS PROCESS COST PER UNIT OF VOLUME

As more and more organizations adopt activity-based management (ABM) strategy, there will be more readily available data on business process costs per unit. Already some benchmarking organizations, such as the International Benchmark Clearinghouse and Arthur Andersen, have defined some generic business processes. As more organizations begin to define and manage business processes, they will be able to benchmark these business processes. Some large organizations are beginning to benchmark their business process cost per unit across offices and divisions. The following are some examples of this type of benchmarking:

- Acquisition process cost per order or per customer
- Order fulfillment process cost per order
- Procurement process cost per item or per order
- Budgeting process cost per budget, per strategic plan, or per forecast
- Customer service process cost per customer call
- Operations process cost per unit produced
- New product creation process cost per new item produced
- Maintenance process cost per type of equipment

These are only a few possible process costs. Again, the list could get very long very quickly.

OUTCOMES

The term *outcomes* often applies to financial outcomes. Financial outcomes might consist of profit, revenue, economic value, and return on investment.

Outcomes tied to activities and business processes might be the same or different. For example, the Internal Revenue Service (IRS) has a desired outcome to collect a certain percentage of the income taxes due on a voluntary basis. This is a financial outcome. A city government has a desire to have safe neighborhoods without crime. These are examples of nonfinancial outcomes. Although it is important to benchmark activity and business process costs, it is also important to benchmark outcomes to see how your organization is performing.

Benchmarking has been around for quite some time; this book illustrates how to tie benchmarking into the budgeting process. It is the unification of benchmarking with budgeting that makes both more effective. Implemented together, they are more likely to produce better results than if they are implemented in a disjointed fashion, as shown in Example A-4.

Example A-4: EZ Money Bank Loan Processing Department—Benchmarking and Budgeting

EZ Money Bank's evaluation of the number of hours it is open for taking applications is benchmarked against the competition. The benchmark shows that the bank is open only 44 hours per week (5 weekdays times 8 hours per day plus 4 hours on Saturday). The most direct competitor is open 58 hours per week (5 weekdays times 10 hours per day plus 8 hours on Saturday). If EZ Money extended its hours to match that of the competition, it would have to be open 14 more hours. The bank believes that it could handle these extra hours by using a part-time person. This part-time person would cost the bank $20 per hour. Therefore, this would add $14,560 (52 weeks times 14 hours per week times $20 per hour).

The bank considers that a part-time person may not be as productive as a full-time person. Consequently, loans might be lost that might have otherwise been obtained. EZ Money could gain additional business from people who would otherwise not apply at the bank because they could not come to the branch during the day. (See Exhibit A.7.)

EZ Money's customer and loyalty survey is then reviewed, which indicates that extended hours are not a high-priority item for its customers. The bank's customers seem to rate it above 80 percent for this factor. Therefore, the bank decides that even though the benchmark indicates that it is performing poorly on this factor compared to its competitors, this is not an important item, so it will not extend its hours. It will use the savings to reduce its rates and fees.

One technique by itself may not be sufficient in budgeting and planning. It may be necessary to combine techniques to gain better insights into the proper decision. In this example, the organization combined benchmarking with customer surveys in order to give them the insight into the correct decision.

ACTIVITY AND BUSINESS PROCESS DEPLOYMENT, OR THE HOUSE OF ACTIVITIES

A fourth technique for setting targets during planning and budgeting is called activity and business process deployment, or the **house of activities.** We have modified a technique from quality, often used in designing a new product or service. This quality technique, called quality function deployment, relates different product features to customer requirements. It also gives the organization a one-sheet summary of how their features compare to the competition's.

Benchmarking shows competitors open 58 hours per week versus current 44 hours per week

Hours Open	Salaries and Benefits	Space	Equipment	Supplies	Phone	Total
Current hours	$	$	$	$	$	$
Extended hours	$14,560	$	$	$	$	$

Assumptions

Salaries:

Current

Space:
Equipment:
Supplies:

Salaries: 14 hours/week x 52 weeks/year x $20/hour = $14,560

Extended hours

Space:
Equipment:
Supplies:
Phone:

Exhibit A.7   Setting business process and activity targets using benchmarking of extended hours.

With some modifications, this technique can be used for planning budgeting. It can be used to:

- Relate activities and/or business processes to customer requirements
- Compare an organization with its competition for various customer requirements
- Compare an organization's performance of business processes with its competition
- Derive an importance weighting for budgeting business processes and/or activities
- Correlate various business processes and/or activities with each other

Refer to Exhibit A.8a for a discussion of this technique. Although the house of activity may appear complicated, it is simple if taken one section at a time. The left side of the house of activities consists of customer requirements. The organization surveys its customers to derive these requirements.

For example, in the case of Sony, the organization anticipates the customer's requirements before the customer knows that it has that requirement. For instance, the customer did not know that it had a requirement for Walkman radios or videos. Sony had to anticipate its needs and desires. World-class organizations think like Wayne Gretsky, the famous hockey player. When asked why he was so successful, Gretsky replied that he "goes where the puck is going to be." Sony goes where the customer's needs are going to be.

Once the customer's current or future requirements are determined, the customer is asked to rank these requirements in order of importance. The requirement that is most important to the customer is given the highest ranking. (See Example A-5.)

Example A-5: EZ Money Bank's House of Activity

As shown in Exhibit A.8a, EZ Money Bank has chosen to focus on the five requirements that are most important to the customer. Therefore, because there are five requirements, they gave the most important customer requirement a ranking of 5, the second most important requirement a ranking of 4, the third most important requirement a ranking of 3, the fourth most important requirement a ranking of 2, and the fifth most important requirement a ranking of 1. (*Note:* This example will illustrate the house of activity technique using business processes, but activities could also be used.)

EZ Money Bank decides that its key business processes are as follows:

BUSINESS PROCESS AND ACTIVITY DEPLOYMENT

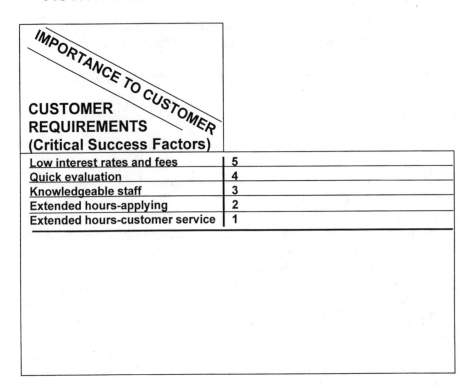

IMPORTANCE TO CUSTOMER CUSTOMER REQUIREMENTS (Critical Success Factors)		
Low interest rates and fees	5	
Quick evaluation	4	
Knowledgeable staff	3	
Extended hours-applying	2	
Extended hours-customer service	1	

Exhibit A.8a Set targets using house of activities.

- Train staff
- Develop loan programs
- Acquire loans
- Procure capital
- Provide customer service
- Process monthly loan payments

As can be seen from Exhibit A.8b, these business processes are placed into vertical columns near the top of the house of activities. The next step is to relate these key business processes to customer requirements. There are two basic weighting methods in general use today. The Japanese tend to weight relationships that are strong as having a weight of nine and relationships that are medium with a weight of five. In the United States, organizations are more likely to weigh strong relationships with a weight of five, medium relationships with a weight of three, and a small relationship with a weight of one (see Exhibit A.8c).

	Weighting	
Relationship	Japan	United States
Strong	9	5
Medium	5	3
Small	1	1

Once a weighting is selected, an organization then determines whether the relationship between the business process and a customer requirement is strong, medium, or small. In Exhibit A.8c, EZ Money Bank believes that the relationship between the business process "train employees" and the customer requirement "low interest rates and fees" is strong. A strong relationship is given a weight of 5. This weight of 5 is multiplied by the importance ranking for this activity of 5 to obtain a weighted importance of this business process of 25 as it relates to the customer requirement of "low interest rates and fees." (See Exhibit A.8d.)

EZ Money Bank weighs the next customer requirement, "quick evaluation period,"

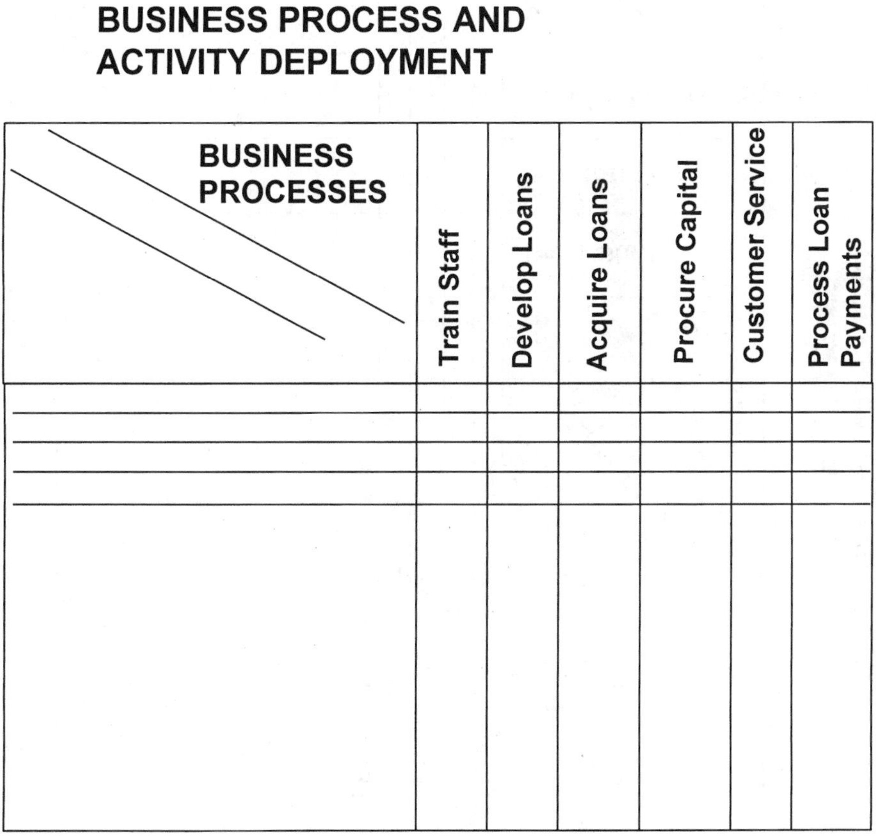

BUSINESS PROCESS AND ACTIVITY DEPLOYMENT

Exhibit A.8b Set targets using house of activities.

BUSINESS PROCESS AND ACTIVITY DEPLOYMENT

Relationships
Strong = 5
Medium = 3
Small = 1

CUSTOMER REQUIREMENTS (Critical Success Factors)	IMPORTANCE TO CUSTOMER	Train Staff	Develop Loans	Acquire Loans	Procure Capital	Customer Service	Process Loan Payments
Low interest rates and fees	5						
Quick evaluation	4						
Knowledgeable staff	3						
Extended hours-applying	2						
Extended hours-customer service	1						

BUSINESS PROCESSES

Exhibit A.8c Set targets using house of activities.

BUSINESS PROCESS AND ACTIVITY DEPLOYMENT

CUSTOMER REQUIREMENTS (Critical Success Factors)	IMPORTANCE TO CUSTOMER	Train Staff	Develop Loans	Acquire Loans	Procure Capital	Customer Service	Process Loan Payments
Low interest rates and fees	5	5=25		5=25			
Quick evaluation	4	5=20		5=20			
Knowledgeable staff	3	5=15		5=15			
Extended hours-applying	2			3=6			
Extended hours-customer service	1			1=1			
Importance Weighting		**60**		**67**			

Relationships
Strong = 5
Medium = 3
Small = 1

Exhibit A.8d Set targets using house of activities.

with a weight of 5 also. It multiplies the customer importance ranking of four times the relationship weighting of 5 to obtain a weighted importance ranking of 20. This process continues until the organization derives an importance weighting for each of the customer requirements of the first business process. Then, the individual weighted importance rankings are added for the first business process to obtain a total importance rating for that process. In this example, the total importance rating for the business process "train staff" equals 60.

Below is the total weighting process for the business process "acquire loans." It shows that the total importance weighting is 67.

Business Process: Acquire Loans

Customer Requirements	Ranking	Relationship	Importance
Low interest rates and fees	5	5	25
Quick evaluation	4	5	20
Knowledgeable staff	3	5	15
Extended hours—applying			6
Extended hours—customer service			1
Total			67

The following table shows the same process of calculating importance ranking for the other key business processes.

Relating the Importance of Business Processes to Customer Requirements

Business Processes	Train Staff	Develop Loans	Acquire Loans	Procure Capital	Cust. Serv.	Process Payments
Low rates and fees	25	25	25	25	25	25
Quick evaluation	20	20	20			
Knowledgeable staff	15	3	15		15	9
Extended hours —applying			6			
Extended hours —customer service			1			
Total	60	48	67	25	40	34

After calculating the total importance weightings for each key business process, EZ Money Bank easily can see which business processes should be emphasized in its budget and which should not. In this example, the greatest weighting has been given to "train staff" and "acquire loans." Yet, think about how many departments cut training when senior management asks them to reduce their budget by 10 percent. For this example, "develop new loans," "process loan payments," and "customer service" are also important to their customers. "Procuring capital" for this organization appears to be

BUSINESS PROCESS AND ACTIVITY DEPLOYMENT

IMPORTANCE TO CUSTOMER / CUSTOMER REQUIREMENTS (Critical Success Factors)	BUSINESS PROCESSES					
	Train Staff	Develop Loans	Acquire Loans	Procure Capital	Customer Service	Process Loan Payments
Low interest rates and fees — 5	5=25	5=25	5=25	5=25	5=25	5=25
Quick evaluation — 4	5=20	5=20	5=20			
Knowledgeable staff — 3	5=15	1=3	5=15		5=15	3=9
Extended hours-applying — 2			3=6			
Extended hours-customer service — 1			1=1			
Importance Weighting	60	48	67	25	40	34

Relationships
Strong = 5
Medium = 3
Small = 1

Exhibit A.8e Set targets using house of activities.

less important. For many manufacturing companies, especially in the food business, "procuring supplies" would be extremely important and would carry a very high weighting. Importance will vary by industry and company.

This example is not meant to represent generic correct weightings for organizations. Management must listen to their customers to determine the rankings of various customer requirements. They must then decide the relationship between their business processes and the customer requirements. Finally, if "train people" has the high importance weighting of 60 and procure capital has the lowest importance weighting of 25, they must translate this weighting information and other information into the appropriate budget dollars. The house of activities has given them a more practical way to make those budget allocation decisions. Organizations as diverse as Eastman Chemicals and United Methodist Church use this technique as part of their budgeting process.

COMPETITIVE EVALUATION

Refer to Exhibit A.8f for a moment. On the right side of the chart is a competitive evaluation. This competitive evaluation compares the organization with its competitors on various customer requirements. For example, the first customer requirement—low interest rates and fees—is compared with competing organizations A and B on a scale of 1 to 5, with 5 being the best. This information is obtained by a survey of:

- Current customers
- Lost customers
- Potential customers
- Some combination of the above

Exhibit A.8f illustrates that this organization ranks lower for this first customer requirement. Immediately, the organization must decide what it must do in terms of budgeting, business process redesign, training, and so forth in order to improve on this highest-ranking customer requirement. The example further illustrates that for three of the other customer requirements, this organization is in the middle of the rankings. However, for the customer requirement of "quick evaluation period," the organization is the best. Now it can decide what it must do as it relates to budgeting for these five key business processes.

BUSINESS PROCESS AND ACTIVITY DEPLOYMENT

CUSTOMER REQUIREMENTS (Critical Success Factors)

Low interest rates and fees	5
Quick evaluation	4
Knowledgeable staff	3
Extended hours-applying	2
Extended hours-customer service	1

Competitive Evaluation

(5 is best) 1 2 3 4 5

X = Our Organization
A = Competitor A
B = Competitor B

Exhibit A.8f   Set targets using house of activities.

TECHNICAL EVALUATION

The bottom of Exhibit A.8g incorporates a technical evaluation section. This section evaluates the organization as it compares to other organizations on their technical ability to perform a business process and/or activity. The organization obtains this information from a variety of sources such as independent assessment by an outside firm that does this type of evaluation. An example of this is "real decisions," which evaluates the productivity of data center operations. Technical evaluation is really benchmarking of various business processes and activities. These benchmarking results are then added to the house of activity.

RELATIONSHIP OF ACTIVITIES AND BUSINESS PROCESSES TO EACH OTHER

Finally, notice that there is a roof on Exhibit A.8h. The roof correlates various business processes with each other. This example shows a high correlation between the business processes "train employees" and "acquire loans." Therefore, when management evaluates budget dollars for these two highly correlated processes, they must consider them together and not in isolation with each other. Failure to redesign the "acquire loans" business process and train staff adequately will not give the organization the results they desire. We are not implying that training alone will improve acquiring business. Often, throwing training dollars at a poorly designed process will waste the organization's money. However, some organizations design a great process, but they do not spend the necessary training dollars.

One quickly sees that this type of information is much more useful than taking last year's budget and adding 5 percent. It does require additional time and a great deal more thought than simply adding some percentage to last year's numbers. However, this additional thought should pay off in deploying business process resources in a way that is more productive in meeting customer requirements. By deploying business process resources wisely in meeting customer requirements, the organization should also meet its own goals and objectives.

REVERSE ENGINEERING COMPETITOR'S PRODUCT/SERVICE

The last technique used to set targets is a simple one. It is called **reverse engineering a competitor's product or service.** Reverse engineering means

BUSINESS PROCESS AND ACTIVITY DEPLOYMENT

	Train Staff	Develop Loans	Acquire Loans	Procure Capital	Customer Service	Process Loan Payments
BUSINESS PROCESSES / IMPORTANCE TO CUSTOMER / **CUSTOMER REQUIREMENTS**						
TARGET WORKLOAD	40 hours/ year/FTE	new services per year = 2	1000 loans per year	14 times per year	calls/ year	payments/ year
TECHNICAL EVALUATION	A B X	B A X	X A B	A X B	A B X	B X A
(scale)	4 3 2 1					

Exhibit A.8g   Set targets using house of activities.

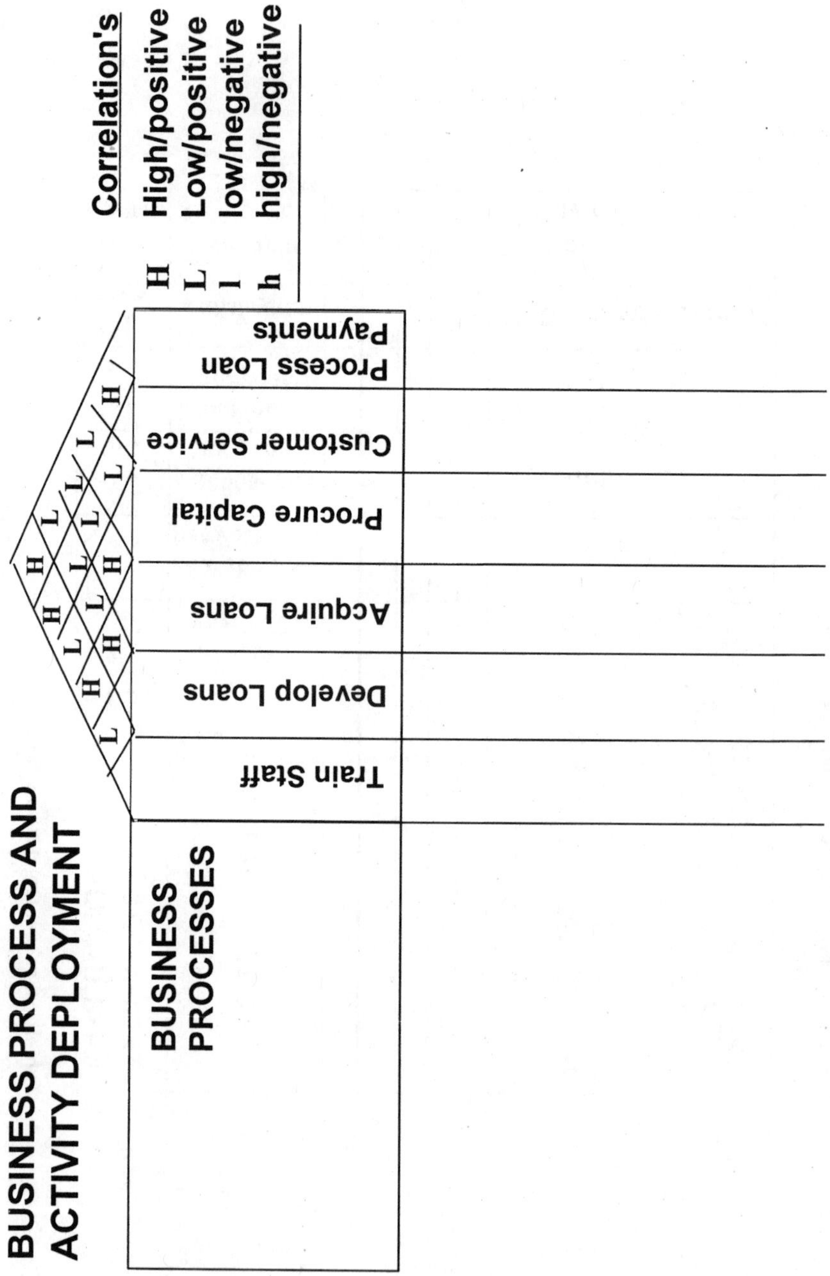

BUSINESS PROCESS AND ACTIVITY DEPLOYMENT

Correlation's

High/positive
Low/positive
low/negative
high/negative

H
L
l
h

BUSINESS PROCESSES

Train Staff
Develop Loans
Acquire Loans
Procure Capital
Customer Service
Process Loan Payments

Roof correlations: L H L H L L H L L H L L H

Exhibit A.8h   Set targets using house of activities.

BUSINESS PROCESS AND ACTIVITY DEPLOYMENT

Correlation's
H High/positive
L Low/positive
l low/negative
h high/negative

Competitive Evaluation
(5 is best) 1 2 3 4 5

X = Our Organization
A = Competitor A
B = Competitor B

Relationships
Strong = 5
Medium = 3
Small = 1

CUSTOMER REQUIREMENTS (Critical Success Factors)	IMPORTANCE TO CUSTOMER	Train Staff	Develop Loans	Acquire Loans	Procure Capital	Customer Service	Process Loan Payments
Low interest rates and fees	5	5=25	5=25	5=25	5=25	5=25	5=25
Quick evaluation	4	5=20	5=20	5=20			
Knowledgeable staff	3	5=15	1=3	5=15		5=15	3=9
Extended hours-applying	2			3=6			
Extended hours-customer service	1			1=1			
Importance Weighting		60	48	67	25	40	34
TARGET WORKLOAD		40 hours/ year/FTE	new services per year = 2	1000 loans per year	14 times per year	calls/ year	payments/ year

TECHNICAL EVALUATION (4 3 2 1)

	Train Staff	Develop Loans	Acquire Loans	Procure Capital	Customer Service	Process Loan Payments
	A	B	X	A	A	B
	B	A	A	X	B	X
	X	X	B	B	X	A

Correlation roof: L H L L H H L L L L (high/low correlations between business processes)

Competitive Evaluation diagrams:
A x —— x AB
        B
A B x
A   x B
B x A

Exhibit A.8i Set targets using house of activities.

dissecting a competitor's product or service to determine how they service their customers and produce their product or service in order to obtain ideas on how to redesign your product or service to better compete.

Example A-6: EZ Money Bank's Reverse Engineering

EZ Money's Bank management hires several shoppers to apply for loans at several competitors. It surveys how the competitors answer phone inquiries, take loan applications, and disperse funds. It decides to reverse engineer its loan application processes so that it can improve its own process.

EZ Money must then budget for a "redesigned loan process." This means that marketing, branch operations, training, and customer service will all have to contribute to the redesigned loan process. Therefore, the bank will have to budget for the additional workload in these areas. (See Exhibit A.9.)

Management must decide if reverse engineering the competition is worth the investment.

SUMMARY

Now that the five techniques to set targets have been discussed, it must be emphasized that these tools should be used to examine not only the costs of business processes and activities, but also the time taken to complete these activities as well as the final quality of the product or service.

Exhibit A.10 lays out just a sampling of what these tools can do for a few select activities in regards to cost, time, and quality. Think of ways these tools can improve your organization's activities. How can you use these tools to set targets and goals? Think how these tools can help you achieve your strategies.

EZ Money Bank hires shoppers to apply for loans at competitor's banks. They agree to redesign process based on what they learn.

Activity	Salaries and Benefits	Space	Equipment	Supplies	Other	Total
Redesign service	$18,000	$	$	$	$30,000	$
Marketing						
Sales						
Training						
Customer service						

PROPOSED

Salaries: 3 loan officers @ $20/hour for 200 hours = $12,000
2 loan processors @ $15/hour for 200 hours = $6,000

Space: 10% of 5 FTEs @ FTE
Equipment: 10% of 5 FTE equipment @ $
Supplies: $
Other $30,000 to shoppers

Exhibit A.9 Set targets using reverse engineering: reverse engineering competitor's service.

Tool	Activity	Cost	Time	Quality
Customer survey	Handle phone inquiries by loan processors	Now: $ Goal: $	TIMES Now: 15 minutes Goal: same	Now: convert 25% Goal: convert 33% of phone calls to loans
Core competency	Initial Follow-up Cross-train	Now: $ Goal: $	HOURS: Now: 20 Goal: 8	COMPLAINTS: Now: Goal:
Benchmarking	Process loans	Now: $ Goal: $	MINUTES: Now: Goal:	MISTAKES: Now: 3% Goal: 1%
Activity/business process deployment	Follow-up training	Now: $ Goal: $	Now: Goal:	REPEATS: Now: 4% Goal: 2%
Reverse engineering	Redesign service	Cost of Reverse Engineering Now: $ Goal: $	Reverse Engineering Now: 0 Goal: loan officer loan processor	Acquire Loans: Now: Goal:

Exhibit A.10 Set targets for business processes and activities.

___ Appendix B ___

COMPANY EXAMPLES

USING ACTIVITY-BASED BUDGETING FOR COMPETITIVE ADVANTAGE

Companies today are moving toward activity-based budgeting (ABB) because of the value in understanding the relationship of forecasted demand on activity workload, something traditional budgeting cannot provide. This appendix addresses key uses and highlights case examples of how companies are progressing through the stages of ABB.

While activity-based budgeting is used to support a multitude of business issues, the following five key areas provide a framework for the majority of implementations:

1. Supporting strategic decision making, such as product pricing, product mix, make versus buy, and investment decisions
2. Improving the concurrent engineering process, including cost awareness in the design decisions
3. Motivating continuous improvements and the understanding of competitive gaps
4. Enhancing the ability to benchmark cost information against best-in-class
5. Removing communication barriers by providing an understanding of activity workload, cost, and forecasted demand requirements.

The traditional budgeting process is painful for everyone involved—financial and operational; hence, the impetus for rapid improvement using ABB. A survey conducted by *CFO* magazine found that "while approaches to budgeting and forecasting may differ, most respondents are dissatisfied with their current processes and believe there is plenty of room for improvement."[1] In addressing methods to improve the process, ABB surfaced as a key approach for companies.

While only 23 percent of respondents were using ABB pervasively, 63 percent see ABB as significantly to extremely valuable as a methodology. These findings highlight the emerging transformation from traditional budgeting to ABB as well as the interest in understanding how companies with ABB are turning theory into practice.

The following cases will provide examples of companies using ABB in varies stages, from progression to full implementation. The selections are designed to document different uses and levels of ABB in practice.

RETAIL MANUFACTURER

This privately held company was focusing improvement efforts toward capacity planning, scheduling, and budgeting in its retail presentation and design department. This department is primarily responsible for developing retail designs (signs, fixtures, concepts, etc.) and strategies for in-store product displays. The department is subdivided into four main areas:

1. Strategy
2. Design development
3. Design implementation
4. Business services

The department vice-president stated that they needed to understand the different areas of capacity and to more effectively budget and schedule work within those areas in order to meet customer demands. Customers are internal, such as the business units and retail channels. In addition they wanted to understand the cost of their design cycle, referred to as a drive period along with the cost of producing differing products, such as a sign or fixture, within a drive period. Using this cost information together with product routings would enable them to budget future workload capacity.

Management within the retail presentation and design department was unable to determine work flow capacity; hence, they were outsourcing work and having purchasing compress vendor lead times, resulting in higher cost, in order to meet schedule dates. This is a creative department that had just gone though a major reorganization within the past two years and now the new vice-president was trying to instill the importance of product cost, managing workload within a budget, and meeting scheduled deadlines, rather than "all that matters is quality."

This department's in-house scheduling systems were not being used effectively, and, to make matters worse, their work flow information had not been updated in years. So even if they were to use the system, it would not reflect current capacity. Their work around was to use offline PC applications and manual handoff documentation.

A cross-functional team was formed to develop an activity-based cost management (ABCM) system to determine workload capacity and end-item product cost, so that management could budget forecasted drive period demand. The approach was to link their in-house scheduling system to an ABCM PC-based solution to provide current and past due drive period activity information, as well as an outlook to future drive period workload demand.

This activity budgeting process would be providing managers with valuable information, such as what the workload demand and cost would be for new, revamp, or lift product requests. This was important because these product types could be applied to different sign, banner, and display types, each consuming a unique or common activity cost, such as creating final art, setting up a photo shoot, or getting property approval rights.

Armed with this information, the retail presentation and design department would now be able to communicate their capacity to their internal customers, enabling strategic prioritization as to what products would be included in a drive period plan and what would be done in-house versus outsourced. (See Exhibit B.1.)

TRANSACTION PROCESSING AT SHARED SERVICE CENTERS[2]

A Fortune 1000 company had implemented three shared service financial centers for transaction processing worldwide. In doing so, the company had implemented an activity-based charge-out model for its shared services centers to bill its operating units. With the success of the project team's activity-based charge-out project, the team examined using ABB as a natural progression of the budget process.

The team aimed to determine whether improvements to the budget process could be made using activity-based management (ABM), reasoning that if cost center expense line items could be driven through the activity-based costing (ABC) model to products consumed by customers, a link backward through the model was also possible.

In other words, customers of each shared services center forecast their consumption of the center's products and services for the coming period. Department managers would then translate that volume of consumption back into cost center budgets for each department in the shared service centers.

Furthermore, given a forecasted level of internal customer consumption,

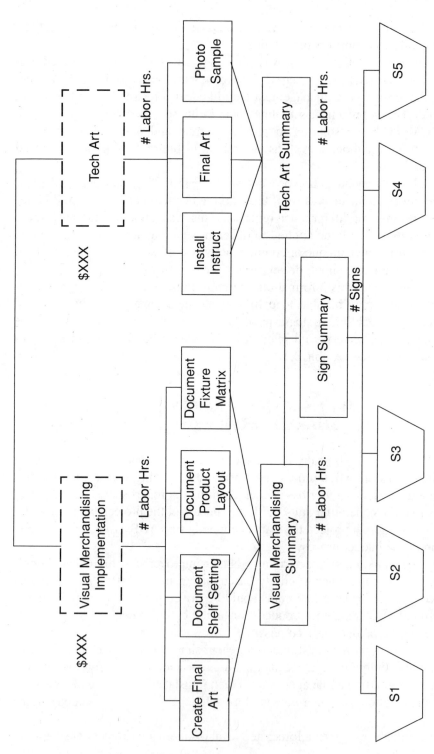

Exhibit B.1 Retail manufacturer model schematic. *Source:* Arthur Andersen.

an activity-by-activity analysis of each department allowed process improvement savings to be factored into the forecasted costs of each department.

The team then went one step further, using the cost management information to support a performance measurement and benchmarking system. Because the ABC model results in a unit cost for each product produced within each shared service center, it follows that each unit cost can be compared among different periods, internally to other similar departments at other service centers, or externally to other companies. Additionally, rewards or special compensation arrangements can also be set up based on achieving unit-cost targets (possibly set in comparison to some available world-class benchmark). (See Exhibit B.2.)

HEALTHCARE INSURANCE PROVIDER[3]

Rather than implement a full ABB system in one year, some companies have adopted a progression approach. This company, which is one of the Southeast's oldest and largest healthcare insurers, began by incorporating ABC into their budgeting process. Even though they were still functionally organized and produced a 12-month line item budget, as a first step to full implemen-

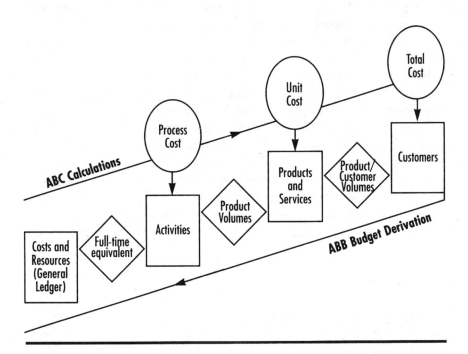

Exhibit B.2   Sherwood service center example.

tation, the company incorporated ABB concepts to secure a benchmark for full implementation. After each cost center produced a line item budget they projected how the budgeted resources would be traced to activities for the coming year. This process helped facilitate the annual planning process because the organization is moving toward planning by activities and processes.

They wanted to have a benchmark for projected activity costs in order to monitor their progress through the year. In addition, they needed to report on actual activity costs versus budgeted activity costs.

Furthermore, there were numerous strategic cross-functional projects going on throughout the year and they needed to be able to project what the costs of their projects would be for the year. It was determined that the best way to capture this information was through budgeting by activities.

Today, this insurer is in the process of migrating to full ABB. This process will entail determining their outputs and then reverse calculating which resources would be required to produce those outputs.

FINANCIAL SERVICES COMPANY[4]

This company, which is a holding company with business units providing risk management and retirement and asset management products and services, has used ABB for five to seven years depending on the business unit. The general ABB information, which was developed in 1992, integrates with actuals. Budget results are used as a planning tool, the basis for activity allocation tables, and values in ABC and general ledger, as well as key measurements and support for the high-level operating plan.

The preplanning process for ABB begins with a distributed budgeting package for users to complete. The comprehensive workbook includes a timetable, maintenance forms, cost center listings, cost object listings, budget system access listings, and electronic report distribution. The company provides users with an online, user-friendly system with the ability to view budget information in key forms for both strategic planning as well as operational needs. The budget system menu provides the following options for each cost center:

- Enter budget data
- Enter salary data
- Budget snapshot by activity
- Budget snapshot by account
- Budget data reports
- Budget volume change

Reports are available online, with summary as well as detail information for each cost center. Report options include cost center budget by activity, volume budget by driver, and missing volume by driver.

In addition, a range of cost centers can roll up to one summary report. For the strategic ABC budget reports, they provide company summaries by business units as well as reports for business unit costs assigned to inter-companies and costs assigned to others. To fully integrate and use ABB as a planning and measurement tool, the company is able to report actual versus budget results by business unit, division, services, cost center, and accounts.

TELECOM MANUFACTURER

The company designs and produces medium- and high-speed data communications equipment, which provide an interface between the telephone networks and computers.

Customers are divided into three groups: corporate end users, personal end users, and network service providers. The direct sales and service organizations support *corporate end user* business and government agencies, whereas value added resellers, distributors, and a direct marketing/response center are used to support the *personal end user*. To ensure integrated solutions meet the needs of *network service providers,* the company partners with other internal business units.

Because the company competes in a high tech, tight margin market, management recognized that if they were to secure a strong and defensible position in the network access market, they would need to change their cost accounting system and budgeting process to address the following factors:

- Product designs, which established upwards of 85 percent of product cost, were incorporating the latest in technology, which meant that products were becoming smaller, more customer specific, and far more expensive to manufacture.
- Manufacturing employed a "factory mall" concept where a number of different product lines are produced in one location. This resulted in shifting from labor-intensive operations to high tech, automated machine-assembly operations.
- Time to market was compressing, as was the window for realizing profits.
- Formation of multiple customer business units to better serve the customer meant differing profit and loss ownership. Gross allocating

of cost provided no line-of-sight understanding in establishing contracted service-level agreements.

The company's old manufacturing cost system assigned support and production overhead to products as a percentage of materials and direct labor cost. Clearly, with all the changes that were taking place, the old system could no longer provide an accurate means of determining the true cost of their products. An obvious example was the overcosting of older products, resulting in lower than expected margins. These products, because they required more direct labor assembly hours, were assigned a large amount of overhead or support cost, even though they were in the mature or declining stage of their life cycle. On the other hand, newer products designed with less direct labor hours received a much smaller amount of support cost. Allocating cost based on material cost caused just as many problems only in reverse. The more a product's material cost, the more overhead it received, even though in many instances the true cost had nothing to do with volume or the cost of material.

Having realized the limitations of their traditional costing and budgeting approach, the company implemented an ABC model and applied the ABB process. One of the biggest benefits of moving to ABC and ABB was seen as providing the company's design and production engineers the cost information needed, in the ever-so-important early stages of product development.

The critical nature of providing an ABB process, built off the ABC model, helped the design engineers get the information they needed to supplement quality and time constraints with manufacturing and purchasing considerations so they could make meaningful decisions. The engineers along with manufacturing accounting and production engineering were able to budget future product costs based on the activity driver unit cost, such as number of insertions, number of parts, and test hours. Support costs were now being assigned based on drivers such as the number of change orders, uniqueness by product family, and type of quality audit. Finally raw material support costs were segregated into various purchased part groupings for assigning material acquisition costs. The new model, which consisted of 4 cost elements (material, material acquisition, production, and support) 44 cost pools, and 13 activity drivers, is diagrammed on the next page. The accompanying pie chart illustrates the type of information the model provided. (See Exhibits B.3 and B.4.)

A target costing process using ABC and ABB information was established for all new and existing products to facilitate life cycle cost management. The target costing process begins with marketing managers estimating the price at which a new product with specified features and functionality can

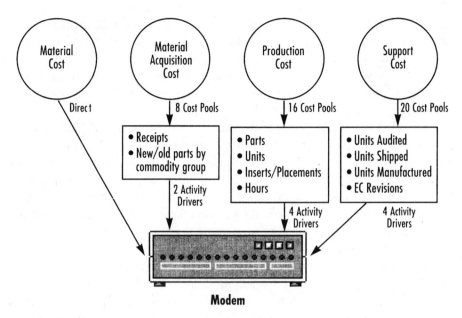

Modem

Exhibit B.3 Telecom Manufacturers cost model.

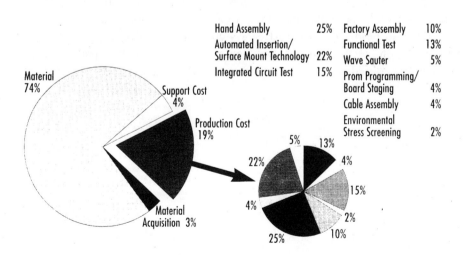

Exhibit B.4 Telecom Manufacturers example (pie chart).

be sold. From there, product and manufacturing teams interlock on a targeted product cost, which is a buildup of material and manufacturing activity cost. "Using ABB as the foundation for target costing becomes a very powerful tool for us," says a team member. "The company uses activity costs to support not only its projections of what incurred costs are going to be, but also, more importantly, what they should be."

The company is able to look at product volume forecasts, which in turn determines the activity level. With this information, an activity cost is set, allowing manufacturing the ability to predict spending. This information can be compared to the previous two years, highlighting what spending decisions have been influenced. The decisions that operational managers make relative to their departmental budgets can then be correlated to the impact they have on products and on gross margins, something that the traditional process was incapable of doing.

Team members, from product managers to design engineers to manufacturing managers, now all have ownership in understanding costs, which has resulted in better decisions in all areas. Here is how one senior manager sums up the impact of the process: "Our ABC, ABB, and target costing efforts have produced a new cost model and budgeting process with wide acceptance in the company. People are using it on an everyday basis for designing new products and improving existing products and processes. We are proud of the successes that we have been a part of, but most of all we recognize all the benefits that are coming about because we are using the information to make sound business decisions."

ABB provides critical information for strategic and operational success. These case study examples just begin to address the opportunities and benefits that can be derived with ABB. As companies evolve from traditional budgeting, the success stories and depth of research will expand. Those companies profiled serve as a lighthouse to guide others in ABB efforts.

_____Appendix C_____

REPORTS

FACILITIES REPORT

The facilities report shows information about the organization. The facilities represent each separate building, warehouse or other structure used by the organization. A unique cost rate can be set for each facility. The rate applies to all locations within the facility. A separate facilities should also be established for any area within a building that has a dramatically different facilities rate. The rate can be either a standard rate (predetermined rate) or actual (computed by the system from actual general ledger costs).

Exhibit C.1 also shows the pyramidal reporting relationships of a series of functions. Each reporting unit is shown as the next lower level. Finally the report shows the space occupied by the group. The sum of the individual groups should equal the total building space occupied.

The traditional hierarchical structure is an extremely valuable tool in bringing clarity to everyone's role in the organization. In a typical organization, the manager of Information Technology (IT) is responsible for producing software products and the accounts payable manager is responsible for paying for purchased material and services. In a well-organized entity there is little confusion over who is responsible for each of these decisions.

It also facilitates maintaining specialized knowledge. Each group is expert in a functional area—the sales in selling products; the human resources people in training, compensation, and interviewing techniques; the accountants in how to collect and present cost; the marketing and sales in advertising and playing golf.

MASTER GENERAL LEDGER ACCOUNTS REPORT

The master general ledger accounts report (Exhibit C.2) shows information about the organization's chart of accounts. The first step in entering general ledger data is to set up the chart of accounts format. This step is critical to making an ABB system such as PlanIt, an on-going management system. You must identify the natural account number and its description. The natural account number describes the expense category but not the location of the cost.

You can optionally associate an account to a business process. This feature is useful if you wanted to roll up costs directly to a business process. Advertising, for example, may roll directly up to the sales and marketing process rather than taking it to an activity.

Each master general ledger account should be assigned an account type. An account type identifies the type of cost and represents a cost pool.

The report also summarizes all the locations that use the account code.

ACCOUNTING TYPE MASTER LISTING REPORT

The account type master listing report shows information about the types of general ledger accounts and how cost should be collected into cost pools. See Exhibit C.3.

DEPARTMENT COST REPORT

The department cost report (Exhibit C.4) shows departmental cost. The cost includes actual, budget, and variance for both the period of analysis and year-to-date. For this case study, the current period is one full year.

ACTIVITY REPORT

An activity is a combination of people, technology, raw materials, methods, and facilities that produce an output. It describes what an organization does, the way time is spent, and the outputs of the process. Ultimately, an enterprise can manage only what it does—its activities.

The activity report has two major sections—Resources and Activities. See Exhibit C.5. The resource section summarizes all the resources assigned to the department. The resources are summarized by type of resource: people, equipment, material, information system, other resources and facilities. The number of resources assigned to the department and their corresponding cost are shown.

The activity section shows the activities and the activity cost. The activity cost is broken down by resources traced to the activity and the prorated resource cost. The report also shows the activity output, number of outputs, and cost per output.

RESOURCE BY ACTIVITY REPORT

The Resource by Activity Report (Exhibit C.6) is a summary of all the resources assigned to the department and the activities that consume the resources. The information includes the resource base data, resource quantity, and the number of resources assigned to each location.

The activity section shows all the activities that consume the resources.

Facility Code	Level	Locations using facility code	Space Occ	Actual rate	Standard rate
(0) Invalid facilities code	1		0		
(AA000007) Downtown	1	(01) Company	0		
	2	(100) Loan Department	0		
	3	(LP) Loan Processor	400	$14.46	$20.00
	3	(LO) Loan Officer	600	$14.46	$20.00
	2	(200) Leasing Department	800	$14.46	$20.00
	2	(300) IT	750	$14.46	$20.00
	2	(400) HR	400	$14.46	$20.00
	2	(500) Finance	0	$14.46	$20.00
	3	(501) Accounts payable	300	$14.46	$20.00

Exhibit C.1 Facilities report.

General Ledger Description	Account Process Description	Account Type Description	Location Description
(0) Invalid Master GL description			
(1000) Travel	(100000003) Process & Sell Loans	(PL000024) Travel & entertainment	(300) IT
			(501) Accounts payable
			(200) Leasing Department
			(LO) Loan Officer
			(400) HR
			(300) IT
			(LP) Loan Processor
(400) Salary & Wages		(AB000027) Salary & Wages	(501) Accounts payable
			(200) Leasing Department
			(LP) Loan Processor
			(LO) Loan Officer
			(400) HR
			(300) IT
(410) Benefits		(PL000167) Employee benefits	(501) Accounts payable
			(200) Leasing Department
			(300) IT
			(400) HR
(500) IS systems		(PL000009) Software purchases	(501) Accounts Payable
			(200) Leasing Department
			(LP) Loan Processor
			(LO) Loan Officer
(600) Rent		(PL000197) Facilities rent	(501) Accounts payable
			(200) Leasing Department
			(LP) Loan Processor
			(LO) Loan Officer
			(300) IT
			(400) HR
(700) Equipment depreciation		(PL000013) Depreciation-Equipment	(501) Accounts payable
			(200) Leasing Department
			(LP) Loan Processor
			(LO) Loan Officer
(800) Office supplies		(PL000080) Office supplies	(501) Accounts payable
			(200) Leasing Department
			(LP) Loan Processor
			(LO) Loan Officer
			(400) HR
(900) Phone		(PL000210) Telephone/Fax Dept	(501) Accounts payable
			(200) Leasing Department
			(LP) Loan Processor
			(LO) Loan Officer
			(400) HR
(901) Long distance			(501) Accounts payable
			(200) Leasing Department
			(LO) Loan Officer
			(300) IT

Exhibit C.2 Master general ledger accounts.

Account Type Description	Resource Type	Resource Description	Trace/ Allocation Basis

Balance Sheet—Current Assets
(PLS00001) Balance Sheet
    (PLS00003) Cash
        (PLS00004) Petty cash
        (PLS00005) Cash in bank
   (PLS00002) Current assets
    (PLS00006) Receivables
        (PLS00007) Accounts receivable
        (PLS00008) Allowance for doubtful accounts
        (PLS00009) Notes receivable
        (PLS00010) Other receivables
        (PLS00011) Interest receivable
        (PLS00012) Dividends receivable
    (PLS00013) Prepaid expenses
    (PLS00014) Government securities
    (PLS00015) Inventories
    (PLS00020) Common Stock Subscript Receivable

Balance Sheet—Current Liabilities
   (PLS00031) Current liabilities
    (PLS00032) Accounts payable
    (PLS00033) Accrued expenses
    (PLS00034) Short term notes payable
    (PLS00035) Taxes payable
    (PLS00036) Cash Dividends Payable

Balance Sheet—Long Term Assets
   (PLS00021) Long term assets
    (PLS00022) Equipment
        (PLS00025) Office equipment
        (PLS00026) Accumulated depreciation—office eq
    (PLS00027) Buildings
        (PLS00028) Accumulated depreciation—buildings
    (PLS00029) Land
    (PLS00030) Other assets

Balance Sheet—Long Term Liabilities
   (PLS00037) Long term liabilities
    (PLS00038) Bonds payable
    (PLS00039) Discounts on bonds payable
    (PLS00040) Premium on bonds payable

Exhibit C.3   Account type master listing.

Account Type Description	Resource Type	Resource Description	Trace/ Allocation Basis

(PLS00041) Notes payable—Long term
(PLS00042) Deferred Income Tax

Balance Sheet—Equity
(PLS00043) Equity
    (PLS00044) Capital Stock
        (PLS00045) Common Stock
        (PLS00046) Paid-in capital in excess of par
        (PLS00047) Cash Stock Subscribed
    (PLS00048) Retained earnings
    (PLS00049) Cash Dividends
    (PLS00050) Appropriations

Income Statement—Revenue
(PL000150) Revenue
    (PL000072) Sales
    (PL000073) Sales discounts
    (PL000074) Sales returns and allowances
    (PL000117) Other income

Exhibit C.3   *Continued.*

Beginning period: January/1/1998
Ending period: December/31/1998

Account Code & Description	Actual	Current Period Budget	Variance	Actual	Year to Date Budget	Variance
400—Salary & Wages	$45,000.00	$0.00	($45,000.00)	$0.00	$0.00	$0.00
410—Benefits	$15,000.00	$0.00	($15,000.00)	$0.00	$0.00	$0.00
500—IS systems	$2,000.00	$0.00	($2,000.00)	$0.00	$0.00	$0.00
600—Rent	$15,000.00	$0.00	($15,000.00)	$0.00	$0.00	$0.00
700—Equipment depreciation	$25,000.00	$0.00	($25,000.00)	$0.00	$0.00	$0.00
800—Office supplies	$1,200.00	$0.00	($1,200.00)	$0.00	$0.00	$0.00
900—Phone	$1,500.00	$0.00	($1,500.00)	$0.00	$0.00	$0.00
901—Long distance	$1,500.00	$0.00	($1,500.00)	$0.00	$0.00	$0.00
Process total $106,200.00		$0.00	($106,200.00)	$0.00	$0.00	$0.00
(100000003) Process & Sell Loans						
1000—Travel	$12,000.00	$0.00	($12,000.00)	$0.00	$0.00	$0.00
Proces total $12,000.00		$0.00	($12,000.00)	$0.00	$0.00	$0.00
Location Total: 118,200.00			($118,200.00)	$0.00	$0.00	$0.00
LO—Loan Officer						
(0) Invalid process code						
400—Salary & Wages	$104,000.00	$104,000.00	$0.00	($104,000.00)	$0.00	$0.00
$0.00						
410—Benefits	$26,000.00	$0.00	($26,000.00)	$0.00	$0.00	$0.00
600—Rent	$12,000.00	$0.00	($12,000.00)	$0.00	$0.00	$0.00

Exhibit C.4 Department cost report—EZ Bank.

Account Code & Description	Actual	Current Period Budget	Variance	Actual	Year to Date Budget	Variance
700—Equipment depreciation	$30,000.00	$0.00	($30,000.00)	$0.00	$0.00	$0.00
800—Office supplies	$1,100.00	$0.00	($1,100.00)	$0.00	$0.00	$0.00
900—Phone	$1,800.00	$0.00	($1,800.00)	$0.00	$0.00	$0.00
901—Long distance	$2,900.00	$0.00	($2,900.00)	$0.00	$0.00	$0.00
Process total	$177,800.00	$0.00	($177,800.00)	$0.00	$0.00	$0.00
Location total	$177,800.00		($177,800.00)	$0.00	$0.00	$0.00
LP—Loan Processor						
(0) Invalid process code						
400—Salary & Wages	$48,000.00	$0.00	($48,000.00)	$0.00	$0.00	$0.00
410—Benefits	$12,000.00	$0.00	($12,000.00)	$0.00	$0.00	$0.00
600—Rent	$8,000.00	$0.00	($8,000.00)	$0.00	$0.00	$0.00
700—Equipment depreciation	$20,000.00	$0.00	($20,000.00)	$0.00	$0.00	$0.00
800—Office supplies	$5,000.00	$0.00	($5,000.00)	$0.00	$0.00	$0.00
900—Phone	$1,200.00	$0.00	($1,200.00)	$0.00	$0.00	$0.00
Process total	$94,200.00	$0.00	($94,200.00)	$0.00	$0.00	$0.00
Location total	$94,200.00		($94,200.00)	$0.00	$0.00	$0.00
Grand Total	$841,750.00	$0.00	$841,750.00	$0.00	$0.00	$0.00

Exhibit C.4 *Continued.*

Location: **(LO) Loan Officer**

Resources		#	$	
Job classification	(AA000006) Branch Manager salary	1.00	$40,000.00	
	(AA000006) Branch Manager benefits			$10,000.00
	(AA000007) Loan Officer	2.00	$64,000.00	
	(AA000007) Loan Officer overtime			$16,000..00
	(AA000007) Loan Officer benefits			
Equipment	(PCs) PC	1.00	$30,000.00	
	(Telephone) Telephone	3.00	$1,800.00	
Material	(PL000001) Office supplies	1.00	$1,100.00	
Other resources	(AA000053) Long distance	1.00	$2,900.00	
Facilities	(AA000007) Downtown	600.00		$8,676.90
			$139,800.00	$34,676.90
				$174,476.90

Activities

	Activity:	**Manage loan officers**		45
		(AA000006) Branch Manager	$4,761.90	
		(PCs) PC	$1,016.95	
		(AA000053) Long distance	$2,407.00	
		(AA000007) Downtown	$284.49	
		Allocated location equipment cost	$59.02	
			$8,529.36	$188.23
	Activity:	**(Transfer—LP) Manage loan processor**		45
		(AA000006) Branch Manager	$4,761.90	
		(AA000007) Downtown	$284.49	
		Allocated location equipment cost	$59.02	
			$5,105.41	$112.14

Exhibit C.5 Rsource and activities report.

Activities

Process/Activity:Process loans

    Activity: **Answer phone inquiries**   # of phone inquiries   3,000

            (AA000007) Loan Officer $15,000.00

            (PCs) PC $3,813.56

            (AA000007) Downtown $1,066.83

            Allocated location equipment cost $221.31

                                $20,101.70 $6.63

    Activity: **Take loan applications**   # of loan applications   1,100

            (AA000006) Branch Manager $10,714.29

            (AA000007) Loan Officer $35,000.00

            (PCs) PC $11,186.44

            (PL000001) Office supplies $1,100.00

            (AA000007) Downtown $3,129.37

            Allocated location equipment cost $649.18

                                $61,779.28 $55.57

    Activity: **Evaluate auto loans**   # of auto loan applications   540

            (AA000006) Branch Manager $5,952.38

            (AA000007) Loan Officer $10,000.00

            (PCs) PC $3,813.56

            (AA000007) Downtown $1,066.83

            Allocated location equipment cost $221.31

                                $21,054.08 $38.58

Exhibit C.5   *Continued.*

Activities

Process/Activity: *Process loans*

Activity: **Evaluate mortgages**   # of mortgages evaluated   560

(AA000006) Branch Manager	$11,904.76
(AA000007) Loan Officer	$20,000.00
(PCs) PC	$7,627.12
(AA000007) Downtown	$2,133.66
Allocated location equipment cost	$442.62
	$42,108.17 $74.40

Process/Activity: *Sell loans*

Activity: **Sell standard mortgages**   # of standard batches   4

(AA000006) Branch Manager	$4,761.90
(PCs) PC	$1,016.95
(AA000053) Long distance	$406.00
(AA000007) Downtown	$284.49
Allocated location equipment cost	$59.02
	$6,528.36 $1,617.34

Activity: **Sell jumbo mortgages**   # of jumbo batches   10

(AA000006) Branch Manager	$7,142.86
(PCs) PC	$1,525.42
(AA000053) Long distance	$87.00
(AA000007) Downtown	$426.73
Allocated location equipment cost	$88.52
	$9,270.54 $918.20
	$174,476.90

Exhibit C.5 *Continued.*

Unit/Department Code: LO—Loan Officer

1.00 (AA000006) Branch Manager

Overtime	8.58			$50,000
Shift Premium				
Total available work hours:		2,088	196	
		2,284		**50,000.00**
Holiday	2.80	64		$1,401.05
Vacation	3.50	80		$1,751.31
Absentee	1.75	40		$875.66
Net available work hours:		**2,100**		

(100000042) Take loan applications	19.70	450	$10,714.29	0.4091	# of loan applications
(100000043) Evaluate auto loans	10.95	250	$5,952.38	0.4630	# of auto loan applications
(100000044) Sell standard mortgages	8.76	200	$4,761.90	50.0000	# of standard batches
(100000050) Manage loan officers	8.76	200	$4,761.90	4.4444	Invalid Output Code
(100000051) Evaluate mortgages	21.89	500	$11,904.76	0.8929	# of mortgages evaluated
(100000053) Sell jumbo mortgages	13.13	300	$7,142.86	30.0000	# of jumbo batches
(100000061) Manage loan processor	8.76	200	$4,761.90	4.4444	Invalid Output Code
Total activity usage of resource:	100.00	2,100	$54,028.02		

2.00 (AA000007) Loan Officer

Overtime	3.69			**$80,000.00**
Total available work hours:		4,176	160	
		4,336		**80,000.00**
Holiday	2.95	128		$2,361.62
Vacation	3.69	160		$2,952.03
Absentee	1.11	48		$885.61
Net available work hours:		**4,000**		

(100000041) Answer phone inquiries	17.30	750	$15,000.00	0.2500	# of phone inquiries
(100000042) Take loan applications	40.36	1,750	$35,000.00	1.5909	# of loan applications
(100000043) Evaluate auto loans	11.53	500	$10,000.00	0.9259	# of auto loan applications
(100000051) Evaluate mortgages	23.06	1,000	$20,000.00	1.7857	# of mortgages evaluated
Total activity usage of resource:	100.00	4,000	$86,199.26		

Exhibit C.6 Resource by activity report.

1.00

(PCs) PC
Holiday

	3.16	**2,088**	**$30,000.00**	
Net available work hours:		64		
		2,024		
(100000041) Answer phone inquiries	37.06	750	$3,813.56	0.2500 # of phone inquiries
(100000042) Take loan applications	108.70	2,200	$11,186.44	2.0000 # of loan applications
(100000043) Evaluate auto loans	37.06	750	$3,813.56	1.3889 # of auto loan applications
(100000044) Sell standard mortgages	9.88	200	$1,016.95	50.0000 # of standard batches
(100000050) Manage loan officers	9.88	200	$1,016.95	4.4444 Invalid Output Code
(100000051) Evaluate mortgages	74.11	1,500	$7,627.12	2.6786 # of mortgages evaluated
(100000053) Sell jumbo mortgages	14.82	300	$1,525.42	30.0000 # of jumbo batches
Total activity usage of resource:	291.50	5,900	**$30,000.00**	

3.00

(Telephone) Telephone
Holiday

	3.16	**6,264**	**$1,800.00**
Net available work hours:		192	
		6,072	
(100000041) Answer phone inquiries—Loan Officer			$221.31
(100000042) Take loan applications—Branch Manager			$132.79
(100000042) Take loan applications—Loan Officer			$516.39
(100000043) Evaluate auto loans—Branch Manger			$73.77
(100000043) Evaluate auto loans—Loan Officer			$147.54
(100000044) Sell standard mortgages—Branch Manager			$59.02
(100000050) Manage loan officers—Branch Manager			$59.02
(100000051) Evaluate mortgages—Branch Manager			$147.54
(100000051) Evaluate mortgages—Loan Officer			$295.08
(100000053) Sell jumbo mortgages—Branch Manager			$88.52
(100000061) Manage loan processor—Branch Manager			$59.02
			$1,800.00

Exhibit C.6 *Continued.*

(PL000001) Office supplies

Net available resources		**1**	**$1,100.00**	
(100000042) Take loan applications	0.04	1	$1,100.00	0.0009 # of loan applications
Total activity usage of resource:		**1**	**$1,100.00**	

(AA000053) Long distance

Net available resources		**1**	**$2,900.00**	
(100000044) Sell standard mortgages	0.01	0	$406.00	0.0350 # of standard batches
(100000050) Manage loan officers	0.04	1	$2,407.00	0.0184 Invalid Output Code
(100000053) Sell jumbo mortgages	0.00	0	$87.00	0.0030 # of jumbo batches
Total activity usage of resource:		**1**	**$2,900.00**	

(AA000007) Downtown

	600	**$8,676.90**
(100000041) Answer phone inquiries—Loan Officer		$1,066.83
(100000042) Take loan applications—Branch Manager		$640.10
(100000042) Take loan applications—Loan Officer		$2,489.27
(100000043) Evaluate auto loans—Branch Manger		$355.61
(100000043) Evaluate auto loans—Loan Officer		$711.22
(100000044) Sell standard mortgages—Branch Manager		$284.49
(100000050) Manage loan officers—Branch Manager		$284.49
(100000051) Evaluate mortgages—Branch Manager		$711.22
(100000051) Evaluate mortgages—Loan Officer		$1,422.44
(100000053) Sell jumbo mortgages—Branch Manager		$426.73
(100000061) Manage loan processor—Branch Manager		$284.49
Total activity usage of resource:	**600**	**$8,676.90**

Exhibit C.6 *Continued.*

NOTES

Chapter 3

1. Anthony J. Rucci, Steven P. Kirn, and Richard T. Quinn, "The Employee-Customer-Profit Chain at Sears," *Harvard Business Review*, January/February 1998, p. 82.

Chapter 4

1. *Davenport, Tom, Process Innovation: Reengineering Work Through Information Technology*, Boston, HBS Press, 1993.

Appendix B

1. *CFO*, "Budgeting and Forecasting," (March 1998).
2. Player, Steve and Roberto Lacerda, *Activity-Based Management: Arthur Andersen's Global Lessons from the ABM Battlefield*, John Wiley & Sons, Inc., 1999.
3. Player, Steve and Carol Cobble, *Cornerstones of Decision-Making: Profiles of Enterprise ABM*, Oakhill Press, 1999.
4. IIR Conference, "Implementing Activity-Based Budgeting," Orlando, December 9–10, 1996, presentation on "Mastering the ABB Process at Allmerica Financial," by Stan Casillo, Allmerica Financial.

GLOSSARY

ABM implementation: (1) Develop understanding of ABM. (2) Develop awareness of need for ABM by choosing/quantifying significant problems, publishing ABM objectives. (3) Prepare pilot site by initialing data analysis, planning pilot, selecting implementation team, selecting pilot site. (4) Implement pilot. (5) Expand ABM throughout organization by target costing, benchmarking, budgeting, reporting. (6) Integrate ABM into routine operations.

Activity: A structured set of work steps that consume resources and information to convert inputs into an output. Typically, an activity is performed within a single group. Activities and tasks can be classified into control, process, move, decision, store/file, input, report, and get information types.

Activity-based costing (ABC): Determining the cost of cost objects with activities and business processes. Activities consume costs and cost objectives consume activities and business processes.

Activity analysis: Quantifies an organization's work; shows the work that is done today.

Activity-based management (ABM): Structuring an organization's activities and business processes to meet customer and external needs with the least resources to produce a consistent output. ABM is the planning and control of an organization through its activities and business processes.

Activity dictionary: A listing of organization activities and attributes (input, output, output measure, customers, suppliers, performance measures, cost drivers, functions, business processes, outcomes, value/nonvalue, primary/secondary, strategic, discretionary, required, and life cycle).

Activity unit: A group of related activities. Also known as a cost center, department, or work cell.

Allocating: Costs based on mutual agreement because no cause-and-effect relationship exists or the effort to establish a cause-and-effect relationship is of insufficient value.

Appropriated cost: Budgeted cost as distinguished from expended/spent (actual) or committed cost.

Attributes: Activity characteristics, including primary/secondary; strategic, discretionary, required (non–valued-added), cycle time, quality, and capacity.

Baseline for cost and resources: Define organizational processes, resources (including job classifications), and chart accounts, and trace costs to resources.

Benchmarking/Best practices: Comparing activities and business processes internally or externally with other locations, other similar organizations, or the best in the world.

Bill of activities: A listing of activities, business processes, and direct costs related to a service, customer, or other cost object where the cause-and-effect relationship can be cost-effectively established.

Business process: A significant business output that requires work to be performed by several different groups as a sequence of related and interdependent activities or performed at multiple locations (e.g., provide services, provide resources, market and sell service, procure supplies, create service, distribute products/services, provide customer service, infrastructure support).

Committed cost: Amount contracted out from appropriations, as distinguished from expended/spent (actual) or appropriated costs.

Cost center: Responsibility center that is accountable for costs (e.g., department, responsibility center).

Cost driver: Any condition or factor that results in the increase of activity workload and cost. The root cause of cost as it relates to non–value-adding activities.

Cost object: Reason for collecting cost. Typical cost objects include services, current and new; customers; channels; and projects.

Expenditure/Spent cost: The actual cash cost incurred as distinguished from appropriated (budgeted) or committed costs.

Fixed cost: (1) Operating costs that do not vary with changes in the level of activity over a relevant range of such activity. (2) Those costs not affected by variation in activity level in a given period.

Function: A group of activities having a common objective, using common processes, and requiring similar skills and experience.

Indirect costs: (1) Costs common to a multiple set of cost objectives and not directly assignable to such objectives in a specific time period. Such costs are traditionally allocated, by systematic and consistent techniques, to services, processes, and time period. (2) Costs that are not directly assignable or traceable to a service or process, but are traceable to an activity. (3) Expenses that do not have a close causal relation with the items being produced (e.g., accounting, human resource, and senior mangement departments).

Input: The event (such as physical or electronic documents) that triggers an activity. An activity may have more than one input but only one ouput.

Life-cycle activity: An activity that should be amortized over the life cycle of a service (e.g., design new service).

Life-cycle costing: Accumulation of costs for activities that occur over the entire life cycle of a service, from inception to abandonment.

Management accounting: Identification, measurement, accumulation, analysis, preparation, interpretation, and communication of information that assists in fulfilling organizational objectives. Also called internal as opposed to financial accounting.

Noncash cost: Generally, an amortized or depreciated cost.

Non–value-added activity: Activities that do not contribute to meeting customer requirements, and could be eliminated without degrading the service or ongoing stability of the organization (e.g., consequence of not doing it right the first time, unsynchronized work flow—bottlenecks, waiting, storing, moving). Even though an activity is value-added, some of the tasks may be non–value-added.

Non–value-added cost: An activity cost other than the minimum amount of equipment, supplies, space, and workers' time that is absolutely essential to meet customer requirements or organizational stability.

Non-traceable activities: Activities, business processes, and direct costs in which a cause-and-effect relationship cannot be cost-effectively established with the item being costed.

Organizational structure: The arrangement of lines of responsibility.

Outcome: Fundamental purpose of the group. They should be quantifiable and clearly understood.

Output: What your customer gets from you. Types of outputs include: repetitive—standard work; repetitive—nonstandard work; cognitive work; time-based work; project work; diverse work.

Output measure: Quantifies workload or the amount of work completed. It provides a useful indicator and measurement on the overall performance of the activity.

Overhead cost: Costs other than direct costs.

Performance improvement questions: Questions such as: Unnecessary checks and balances? Inspect or approve someone else's work? Multiple signature? Multiple copies? Storing without reason? Copies to people who don't need them? People or positions that impede efficiency? Unnecessary written correspondence? Poor training?

Performance driver: Prime factor influencing the performance of an activity.

Performance measures: Measures and goals for cost, time, and quality of activities, business processes, and cost objects.

Performance reporting: System of reporting and planning based on data collected from performance drivers and performance measures.

Period cost: Costs always expensed in the same period in which they are incurred; they are not deferred or amortized/depreciated.

Planned cost: Derived from reviewing workload, activities, and business processes.

Planning: Delineation of goals, predictions of potential results of various ways of achieving goals, and a decision of how to attain the desired results.

Primary activities: Produces an output that is consumed outside the group that performs the work (e.g., pay vendor, issue license).

Process: (1) Proceeding or moving forward; progressive course; tendency; progress; procedure. (2) A continuing development involving many changes. (3) A particular method of doing something, generally involving a number of steps or operations.

Process controls: Monitor the process as it executes in order to detect process variations: (1) Detail process steps. (2) Assess which steps are most likely to have variation. (3) Determine the factors that cause process variation. (4) Determine how to monitor high variation steps. Review process controls when: the process changes; there is significant change to input; and significant process variation remains in process. Stabilize and then monitor the process.

Process improvement tools: (1) Bureaucracy elimination. (2) Duplication elimination. (3) Value-added analysis. (4) Cost driver/root cause analysis. (5) Simplification.

Process management: Continuously improve (change) the processes and activities of an organization to effectively and efficiently meet or exceed changing customer requirements. It is achieved by progressively implementing many changes to ensure that the process is made better than its previous performance. Activities and processes have process controls in place to monitor the process as it is being performed. The process controls ensure that the process is in control and consistently produce good outputs. Costs must be viewed in terms of used and unused capacity costs rather than the traditional fixed and variable distinction. Separating the used and unused component enables management to understand the root cause of the problem rather than burying the variance in the wrong place.

Process maps: Graphic or pictorial representation of the activities that make up a business process.

Quality: (1) Conformance to specifications. (2) Satisfaction of customer needs.

Resources: Factors of service creation and production consumed by an activity (e.g., people, facilities, technology, travel, and supplies).

Secondary activities: Make the primary activities more effective or are administrative in nature (i.e., manage employee, train employee).

Service: The result of activities provided to internal or external customers.

Service costs: Costs of activities and business processes that are directly or indirectly involved in the production of services to internal or external customers.

Service development: All activities required to define, design, develop, test, and maintain a service.

Service lead time: Time from the first stage of operations to when the service, activity, or business process is finished (i.e., queue time).

Setup: Process of preparing people, equipment, or a work center for the production of a service.

Standard cost: Normally, the anticipated cost of an activity, business process, or specific service at a given level of volume and under an assumed set of circumstances.

Strategic activity: Critical to success; key in a chain of activities; center of innovation and creativity; source of differentiation by customers; a proprietary process.

Strategic planning: Planning that is long range in nature and concentrates on customers and markets to be served.

Target cost: A cost that is market based and equals what customers are willing to pay.

Task: Specific steps describing how an activity is done. Tasks are detailed steps in producing an output. They should sufficiently describe how the output is produced. Include only tasks of significant time/importance.

Technology cost: The purchase price, start-up cost, interest, current market value adjustment, operating costs, and risk premium of acquiring technology.

Throughput: Total time of service production through a facility (e.g., work center, department, office).

Total quality management (TQM): A management strategy in which functions work together to create a quality product or service as defined by the customer.

Tracing: Cost based on a cause-and-effect relationship.

Value-added activities: Activities that contribute to meeting customer requirements and could not be eliminated without degrading the service, or are essential to the ongoing stability of the organization.

Value-added cost: Cost of those activities that contribute to customer requirements and could not be eliminated without degrading the service, or are essential to the ongoing stability of the organization.

Variable cost: (1) Traditionally, a cost that increases as the volume of activity increases and decreases as the volume of activity decreases. (2) Those costs that are affected by the level of workload in a period.

Workload: The amount of input volume that a particular activity or business process must convert into output.

Work center: A specific area of the organization consisting of one or more people or equipment that perform essentially the same function. A work center may consist of work cells or work stations.

Work in progress: A service that is partially completed.

INDEX